Reconnected
Kids

Reconnected Kids

Help Your Child Achieve Physical,
Mental, and Emotional Balance

Dr. Robert Melillo

A PERIGEE BOOK

A PERIGEE BOOK
Published by the Penguin Group
Penguin Group (USA) Inc.
375 Hudson Street, New York, New York 10014, USA
Penguin Group (Canada), 90 Eglinton Avenue East, Suite 700, Toronto, Ontario M4P 2Y3, Canada
(a division of Pearson Penguin Canada Inc.)
Penguin Books Ltd., 80 Strand, London WC2R 0RL, England
Penguin Group Ireland, 25 St. Stephen's Green, Dublin 2, Ireland (a division of Penguin Books Ltd.)
Penguin Group (Australia), 250 Camberwell Road, Camberwell, Victoria 3124, Australia
(a division of Pearson Australia Group Pty. Ltd.)
Penguin Books India Pvt. Ltd., 11 Community Centre, Panchsheel Park, New Delhi—110 017, India
Penguin Group (NZ), 67 Apollo Drive, Rosedale, North Shore 0632, New Zealand
(a division of Pearson New Zealand Ltd.)
Penguin Books (South Africa) (Pty.) Ltd., 24 Sturdee Avenue, Rosebank, Johannesburg 2196,
South Africa
Penguin Books Ltd., Registered Offices: 80 Strand, London WC2R 0RL, England

While the author has made every effort to provide accurate telephone numbers and Internet addresses at the time of publication, neither the publisher nor the author assumes any responsibility for errors or for changes that occur after publication. Further, the publisher does not have any control over and does not assume any responsibility for author or third-party websites or their content.

First edition: April 2011

Library of Congress Cataloging-in-Publication Data

Melillo, Robert.
    Reconnected kids : help your child achieve physical, mental, and emotional balance / Robert Melillo.
        p. cm.
    "A Perigee book."
    Includes index.
    ISBN 978-0-399-53648-9
    1. Behavior disorders in children.   2. Problem children—Behavior modification.   3. Parenting.
4. Brain-damaged children—Treatment.   I. Title.
    RJ506.B44M454 2011
    618.92'89—dc22   2010049481

PRINTED IN THE UNITED STATES OF AMERICA

10 9 8 7 6 5 4 3 2 1

Neither the publisher nor the author is engaged in rendering professional advice or services to the individual reader. The ideas, procedures, and suggestions contained in this book are not intended as a substitute for consulting with your physician. All matters regarding your health require medical supervision. Neither the author nor the publisher shall be liable or responsible for any loss or damage allegedly arising from any information or suggestion in this book.

Most Perigee books are available at special quantity discounts for bulk purchases for sales promotions, premiums, fund-raising, or educational use. Special books, or book excerpts, can also be created to fit specific needs. For details, write: Special Markets, Penguin Group (USA) Inc., 375 Hudson Street, New York, New York 10014.

To my parents, Catherine and Joseph Melillo

ACKNOWLEDGMENTS

To my parents, Catherine and Joseph Melillo, who taught me the most about parenting and unconditional love. Thank you for all your support and love for me and my family. To my wife, Carolyn Melillo, the most beautiful woman and best mother I have ever known. Nothing is possible without you, and with you nothing is impossible. Thank you for your love, support, and strength. To my children, Robby, Ellie, and Ty. You constantly challenge and inspire me. I love you all more than life itself. Everything I do is ultimately for you. To my business partner and nephew, Bill Fowler. None of this would have happened without your dedication, love, and inspiration. To my sister, Susan, and her husband, Bill; my brother, Domenic, and his wife, Susan; and all my nieces and nephews, Jeff, Carolyn, Katie, Colleen, Keith, Joey, Alexandra, Olivia, and Nick. I love you and thank you all. Also to my Brain Balance Family who are on the front lines every day helping children and their families. It is an honor to work side by side with you every day. To my agent, Carol Mann, and her staff. Thank you for making my books a reality. A special thank-you to my editors at Perigee, Marian Lizzi and Christina Lundy, who worked so diligently on this manuscript, and Candace Levy, for her wonderful attention to detail. Lastly, to Debora Yost. You are such a pleasure to work with and your insight is so valuable to me. Thank you.

CONTENTS

FOREWORD

It was becoming increasingly clear that, by the age of three, my son was not reaching developmental milestones as expected. His pediatrician confirmed that standing, walking, first words, and sentences were all late. His delayed development qualified him to receive early intervention from a local community clinic. It was at that point that my wife and I began to realize we needed more than just a vague diagnosis with very few answers.

As a child and family psychologist for more than thirty years, I have worked with children in various Boston hospitals, psychiatric clinics, and universities. My early training was in neuropsychology at New England Medical Center, followed by a fellowship at Harvard Medical School in couples/family therapy, which led to a busy clinical practice and research. One would think that with this background I was well prepared to manage and understand exactly what needed to be done, but that was not the case. The researcher in me searched professional journals and articles looking for answers. The clinician in me consulted my professional colleagues. The father in me talked to other parents and scoured books for clarity. The only acceptable solution for our family was to find a clear understanding of our son's problem that was linked with an acceptable therapeutic intervention. Thus, as parent, researcher, and clinician, I began a journey that would eventually and serendipitously bring Robert Melillo and me together.

One day, while browsing in my local bookstore, I noticed on the top shelf, in the childhood disabilities section, a title that really caught my attention, *Disconnected Kids*. I opened Robert Melillo's book to page twenty-eight and just started reading. One particular section caught my eye regarding developmental milestones. "One new skill leads to another new skill and it is supposed to happen at an expected point in time. When it doesn't, it is a warning flag." He goes on to say, "Milestones are the obvious checkpoints that brain development is not going according to nature's schedule. This happens when the electrical activity that generates brain growth gets out of timing." As I continued to read, I found a wonderful, refreshing, and hopeful way of thinking about my research, my patients, and my son's difficulties.

Both Dr. Melillo and I have chosen careers treating children and families with various neurological deficits for more than three decades. Both of us are involved in childhood neurodevelopmental disorders research and strive to be on the cutting edge of new medical and psychological therapies. Not only are we concerned with the abundant use of psychopharmacological remedies for children with behavioral problems, but also we have taken it upon ourselves to bring new, creative clarity to the myths and misunderstandings of how the brain works.

As kids and parents work through Melillo's Brain Balance Program, new challenges emerge. A major challenge for parents is readjusting the family system to behavioral changes in the child— the primary focus of this book. In *Reconnected Kids*, Melillo likens the child's brain with functional disconnect to a symphony orchestra where the conductor (brain) allows the two sides (left and right hemispheres) to become out of sync with each other. To fix the problem all the instruments need to be brought back to the correct rhythm, harmony, and key. Simply correcting the violins isn't enough; the rest of the orchestra needs adjustment as well. Similarly most neurological systems in disharmony require more than one solution to correct imbalances. To address only an auditory or visual processing problem, a nutritional problem, a reading problem, or a dysfunctional family problem alone is not enough. Melillo's emphasis on correcting the entire orchestra is right on target.

Melillo's Family Empowerment Program not only offers another way of thinking about these childhood neurological disorders but also adds specific treatment recommendations. His program takes the next step in providing parents and practitioners with a clinically innovative and academically grounded approach to treating children with neurological deficits, as well as an intervention process that has widespread potential. In *Reconnected Kids*, Melillo has reached beyond psychopharmacological solutions and conventional, maybe outdated, therapies and brings a refreshing, hopeful, and scientifically responsible approach to the field of childhood neurological disorders.

All the best to you and your children.

Leslie Philipp Weiser, MPh, PhD
McLean Hospital, Harvard Medical School,
Belmont, Massachusetts

INTRODUCTION

Reconnecting with Your Kids

In my first book, *Disconnected Kids*, I presented parents of children with some of the most distressing neurological challenges with proven, practical solutions to their children's most perplexing behavior problems. As with many groundbreaking books, the book raised a few questions. It even raised a few eyebrows.

Disconnected Kids was groundbreaking because, unlike most experts who confront children with problems such as autism and Asperger's syndrome, I was confident enough to tell parents that there *is* hope their child can get better—*significantly* better. I said it is not out of the realm of possibility that they could even be cured. I gave hope to parents of kids with attention deficit/hyperactivity disorder (ADHD), dyslexia, and other learning disabilities that, absolutely, their children have a chance of succeeding in school and life just like every other "normal" child. And I was armed with the proof: more than a decade's worth of research and study and more than a thousand children who have successfully gone through my Brain Balance Program.

Disconnected Kids was also groundbreaking because it was the first (and still the only) book to view all behavior and learning disorders from a neurological perspective—that is, as *one* condition with different sets of symptoms caused by an imbalance in either the left or the right hemisphere of the brain. We call the condition functional disconnection syndrome, or FDS.

And *Disconnected Kids* was revolutionary because it was the first (and still the only) book to show parents how to detect a brain imbalance in their children and offer an at-home program to help fix it. The at-home program is based on the same principles, practices, and exercises used at my Brain Balance Achievement Centers.

When *Disconnected Kids* was published more than two years ago, there were only three Brain Balance centers in the United States. Today we have close to sixty centers in cities from coast to coast, and more are in the planning here and in Europe. Nevertheless, Brain Balance is seldom the first program parents turn to when they've been told their child has a neurological problem such as autism, Asperger's syndrome, ADHD, obsessive-compulsive disorder, oppositional disorder, or any of the myriad conditions that affect a child's ability to learn and/or behave normally.

I have spoken about Brain Balance before thousands of parents and teachers who have tried every program and intervention in existence to help a child with a learning or behavior problem. When I question them about their experience, I hear that many programs were helpful but mostly just minimally. In some cases, the programs didn't produce any change at all.

I can say that this is almost never the case with the Brain Balance Program. Parents see a dramatic and often rapid change in their children in multiple areas of brain function and behavior. What I've found, however, is that parents often don't know how to interpret these changes. Are they good or bad? Especially confusing are the changes they witness in their children's behavior and emotional regulation. A child might come to the program well behaved and compliant but display very little emotion. Then, after going through the program, the child becomes oppositional, disruptive, and very emotional. At first glance, these emotions and behaviors are obviously confusing and, to some parents, even alarming. If we are supposed to be helping a child's brain develop properly, then why has the child's behavior gotten so negative?

ANSWERS—AND MORE QUESTIONS

Almost every day, my email inbox contains questions from parents who have read and are using the program detailed in *Disconnected Kids* and from parents who had or have children enrolled in one of our Brain Balance Achievement Centers. "My child's behavior is changing but he seems to be getting more obstinate," write many parents. Another common observation is, "My child is finally exhibiting emotion but it seems so negative."

I tell them that this isn't necessarily bad, and it most likely will be short-lived. I explain that every stage of child development has positive and negative behaviors that coincide with the maturation of the right and the left hemispheres of the brain. Parents, however, need to know how to interpret and anticipate these changes so they understand that the actions are a good sign, even when they manifest in not-so-good behavior.

Other parents are finding the cause of their child's problem is not as black or white as they had hoped it would be. "I did all the checklists in the book, and it seems my child has both a left and a right brain imbalance" is another comment I hear. I reply that this, in fact, may be the case because the child's *entire* brain may be developing too slowly, what I call the Peter Pan Problem—the brain (for reasons I'll get to later) doesn't want to grow up! I assure parents that this, too, is a brain imbalance and that the Brain Balance Program can help fix it.

Other parents get ambiguous results after going through the program's checklists. The reason, I tell them, is that a child's difficult behavior does not always stem from a neurological problem at all. Some kids just behave badly! In fact, this is the case for most bad behavior you witness in children today. (I'll get into the reasons for this and will give you the opportunity to use the Master Hemispheric Checklist, which helps ascertain a left or right brain deficit.)

Behavior is the key concern we hear from parents time and time again. Parents who typically come to our centers are quite knowledgeable and more educated than the average parent about childhood neurological disorders. They can grasp the neurology of their child's problem and the logic of how Brain Balance exercises can help solve the problem, but they end up perplexed when their child suddenly starts acting out or displaying a behavior that they've never seen before.

Even parents who understand that bad behavior can actually reflect a positive change feel discomfort because they aren't sure how to respond to it.

This is the reason I wrote *Reconnected Kids*. In many ways it picks up where *Disconnected Kids* left off. A child may no longer have the issues he or she had before going through the Brain Balance Program, but new behaviors make some parents question if there could be a new neurological problem. I can assure you right now that the answer to that question is *no*.

A FAMILY APPROACH

Listening to parents describe their struggles and concerns made me realize that it isn't enough to just help mentally challenged children. Their parents and siblings need assistance, too. It's not because they are less capable as parents but they simply need guidance managing new and/or challenging behaviors.

I am amazed at how much I learn from parents. Just when I think I have all the answers, a parent comes up with something totally unexpected that makes me wonder, *How did I miss that?*

This is a change of attitude on my part. In the past I told parents that as the brain changes, behavior will change, and they'll see bad along with good. Once the brain gets back in balance, so will the behavior. I counseled parents to be patient. The Brain Balance Program didn't get too involved with managing the behavior of reconnected kids. For parents who found a child too hard to handle, we recommended taking them to a behavioral specialist.

As it turns out, this is not always the best resolution. Many behavioral specialists don't really understand the neurology of behavior or learning disabilities. They particularly don't have the knowledge of what is happening in the brain as a child goes through the Brain Balance Program, and they haven't seen the dramatic changes that can be accomplished. Instead, they're used to achieving small changes over a longer period of time.

I realized there was a real need to develop behavioral strategies that adhere to the basic principles of Brain Balance. To help the children, I saw the need to develop a program that helps their parents cope with their behavioral changes in a positive way. Oftentimes, unfortunately, the parents' own behavior impedes a child's full behavior recovery. Parents become disillusioned, sullen, angry, and even depressed that this problem is happening to their family. It creates a negative environment that is impossible for any child to overcome, let alone a child with a neurological problem. We can correct the neurology, but the bad behavior will not change if the child is living in a negative environment and being raised by parents with poor parenting skills.

To come up with a solution, I researched and examined every home behavioral program and approach currently available. I found that most of the programs generally are very similar and are set up as a positive and negative reinforcement system aimed only at the child. I found that none of the approaches out there today takes into consideration the underlying neurology of a brain imbalance. Available programs also ignore critical factors, particularly the child's environment.

Poorly behaved children, especially those suffering from a brain imbalance, over time adopt certain secondary behaviors as protective mechanisms to deal with the way others react to their behavior. Children with a brain imbalance don't have a good sense of their bodies, so they have no idea why they behave in inappropriate ways, but they do understand that others around them react negatively toward them and may treat them differently. Often this is in mean, hurtful, or dismissive ways. Other children may think they are weird; they may tease, poke fun at, or avoid them. So children with a brain imbalance adopt behaviors to protect themselves and their emotions. These behaviors often make the problem worse and cause even more negative behaviors directed toward them.

The same thing happens with their interaction with teachers, coaches, relatives, siblings, and even their own parents. Even when we improve the underlying neurology and get the brain back into sync, these secondary behaviors can persist in some children because people with whom they interact haven't changed *their* behaviors.

I recognized the greatest challenge I was facing in coming up with a solution: How do you motivate parents, who are already living with so many negatives in life, to promote a positive family environment with positive family values?

Then it hit me. Many years ago, before I got involved in working with childhood mental disorders, I worked with patients in some of the worst kinds of pain you could ever imagine. For many of them it was painful just to walk. Because of their disability, their muscles grew weak and many became overweight. It's no surprise that they didn't do much else except sit around all day and watch television. Many became depressed. They were some of the least motivated people I've ever encountered.

The problem I faced was that they needed to do physical rehabilitation, which was going to cause more pain and discomfort before they started to feel better. With each patient, I faced the same dilemma: How do you motivate people who are so depressed and unmotivated to help themselves? I knew they could only succeed in rehab if they possessed the inner desire to truly want to make it work. So, I did a lot of research and developed a program that encompassed the universal law of attraction, which is based on the belief that everyone has within himself the power to transform any weakness into strength and perfection. I used this principle to design a program that would get them motivated to go to rehab, work through the pain, and get to the point at which they realized they would get better as long as they kept working at it. The program worked wonders for both their health and self-esteem.

For the last fifteen years, I have been perfecting and using the same techniques to guide my own life, and I am now teaching it to parents as the Brain Balance Family Empowerment Program. I don't call it a behavior program because it is much more than that. It is a plan for the whole family that will benefit every aspect of family life.

Many families are finding that the Brain Balance Family Empowerment Program is a life-altering experience, and I believe you will, too. It's not a program just for families who have been involved in Brain Balance. In fact, *all* parents and children can benefit from its positive message and results, whether a child has or has had a neurological disorder or not. It is designed to:

- Resolve all negative behaviors in children, for whatever reason, and bring peace and harmony to family life.
- Empower every member of the family to practice positive living.
- Empower every member of the family to reach for and attain what's most important to him or her in life.
- Show parents how to give their children the best opportunity to rise to their ultimate potential.

To me, the parent–child relationship is the most sacred of all relationships. It is a relationship that needs to be encouraged, supported, and protected.

My personal experience as a parent is one of the reasons I have focused most of my career on working with children with learning disabilities and behavioral disorders. I can empathize with other parents because I, too, have experienced developmental issues and behavioral struggles with my children, as all parents do.

Everything I do—writing books and scientific papers, lecturing, conducting research, and continuing my own education—is all for one collective purpose: to help children reach their potential and improve the quality of their lives and the lives of their families and others around them.

In *Disconnected Kids*, I offer parents a program that can help correct the brain imbalance that causes behavior and learning problems in children. It has shown thousands of parents that, yes, despite the discouraging words from other therapists, there *is* hope that these kids can get better. My goal in *Reconnected Kids* is to help all parents become a positive influence so their kids can live in a positive, safe, and loving environment and go on to achieve their full potential in life.

Disconnected Kids, *Reconnected Kids*, and the sixty (and counting) Brain Balance Achievement Centers are just the beginning. My work will not be done until we can find answers that will help *all* children with behavior and learning problems, no matter how severe those problems may be.

Dr. Robert Melillo
April 2011

Part 1

IS THIS BEHAVIOR GOOD OR BAD?

· 1 ·

Parents, Kids, and Behavior Today

The state of your life is no more than a reflection of your state of mind.

—DR. WAYNE DYER, MOTIVATIONAL SPEAKER

Parenting is tough. In fact, I'd venture to say that this is the hardest time in history to be a parent. I speak from experience, both as a professional specializing in childhood behavior and learning disorders and as a dad. I've looked at this objectively from a neurological point of view, and I am convinced that previous generations can't even imagine what it is like to be a parent today.

These are unprecedented times, and parents today are dealing with unprecedented issues. Depression, anxiety, obesity, diabetes, and suicide among children and teens were practically unheard of in past generations but are getting uncomfortably too common today.

During the last two decades we have witnessed an alarming and dramatic rise in childhood behavioral disorders, not only in this country but throughout the world. Autism, which was considered a rare disorder only twenty years ago, is rapidly on the rise and showing no signs of abating. It is now estimated that 1 out of every 91 children born today in the United States will be diagnosed with autism. Just a few years ago, it was 1 in 150. These are staggering statistics by any stretch of the imagination. The statistics for attention deficient/hyperactivity disorder (ADHD) are even more shocking. It is now the leading childhood disorder in the United States and throughout the world, affecting 10 percent of all U.S. children.

A recent study conducted by researchers in Denmark found that other behavioral disorders, including obsessive-compulsive disorder and Tourette's syndrome, are rising at approximately the same rate as autism.

Learning disorders are also mounting. An estimated 15 percent of school-age kids have dyslexia, which was once considered rare. Another 7 percent struggle so hard to do math there's an official name for it (*dyscalculia*), and it's considered a neurological disorder. Put it all together, and we can conservatively say that 20 to 25 percent of all children—approximately 14 to 17.5 million kids in the United States—are affected by some form of behavior or learning problem. Most experts agree that it is only expected to get worse.

Boys, it appears, are being hit the hardest: 3 out of every 4 children with autism is a boy, and 1 out of every 38 boys born today will have autism, according to the Centers for Disease Control and Prevention (CDC). And ADHD affects an estimated four to six times as many boys as girls. While girls are excelling in sports, school, and making friends, boys are lagging behind. For the first time in history, there are more girls graduating from college and getting athletic scholarships than boys.

These facts and statistics are creating a new source of anxiety for parents.

WHAT'S THE MATTER WITH KIDS TODAY

Poor and inappropriate behavior is not isolated to kids with neurological disorders. Most of the bad behavior you witness in kids today has

Are These Autism Numbers for Real?

Some experts argue that the dramatic rise in the rate of autism isn't real, that other factors are in play rather than something in the brain.

One faction claims that we have more autism because we have better ways of diagnosing it, so we are discovering it more often and sooner. Another says that a redefinition of autism is resulting in other conditions, such as Asperger's syndrome, pervasive developmental disorders, and mental retardation, being categorized under the umbrella term *autism spectrum disorders.*

Critics also claim that California, which has one of the highest rates of autism in the country, and other states with high rates are only skewing high because they offer better medical services, and people with problem children migrate to those areas to get care. California has seen a 600 to 700 percent increase in autism in the last ten years.

To help resolve this argument, researchers at the MIND Research Institute of the University of California at Davis, reporting in the *Journal of Epidemiology,* concluded that, at best, 200 percent of the reported increase in autism in California could be attributed to improved diagnosis, earlier recognition, diagnostic substitution, and/or migration. This means that 400 to 500 percent—roughly two thirds—of the increase represents new cases.

I am among a growing number of experts who don't doubt the MIND Research Institute's explanation. I am also among the growing number of professionals who believe that the growth rate in autism needs to be taken seriously. In fact, most experts agree that only about 25 percent of the increase in diagnosis of autism and other related disorders that we have witnessed over the past two decades can be attributed to improved diagnosis, early recognition, or diagnostic substitution. By anyone's standard this would meet the criteria of an epidemic, and what many believe to be the largest childhood epidemic of our time.

nothing to do with an organic problem, either mental or physical. They are just badly behaved kids. At least kids with neurological conditions have a reason for their behavior problems: They can't help it! The rest are created by circumstances within parental control. Yet statistics show that 80 percent of today's parents complain about their kids' behavior and lack of motivation. And they aren't the only ones complaining.

> Most of the bad behavior you see in kids today
> has nothing to do with a mental disorder.

Teachers who have been working in the school system for twenty years or more say that today's children and adolescents are harder to control, show less respect for authority figures, are less physically active, have shorter attention spans, get poorer grades, and overall are generally unmotivated. They eat poorly, they don't exercise, and they are addicted to their computers, cell phones, and iPods. Teachers say kids today feel entitled; they expect everything to be handed to them.

The impact of all this is having a boomerang effect on parents. In previous generations, when you graduated from high school you went to college, joined the military, or got a job; you left home to start out on your own and didn't come back to live with Mom and Dad. Census figures today show that kids are returning home after college, and many of them settle in indefinitely.

Sure, the economy plays a role, but the economy has nothing to do with the bigger issue: the general malaise and lack of motivation and maturity we are seeing in so many children today. It's as though they want to stay kids forever, like Peter Pan. (I call it the Peter Pan Problem, and I'll explain more about this later.)

Then there's the growing problem of our "growing" kids. Statistics show that 32 percent of kids in the United States are overweight, including 16.3 percent who are obese. In the last thirty years, obesity among kids age six to eleven jumped from 4 to 17 percent, and it is taking its toll on children's health.

Studies indicate one in four overweight children are showing early signs of type 2 diabetes (impaired glucose tolerance), what used to be called adult-onset diabetes, and 60 percent already have one major risk factor for heart disease. Just two decades ago type 2 diabetes was completely unheard of in children, and many experts believed it was impossible.

WHAT'S THE MATTER WITH PARENTS TODAY

During the last twenty years, there has been a dramatic change in the typical family lifestyle, and from a neurological point of view, it is not for the better. It has affected children's physical and mental health and social, emotional, and cognitive development. And what an odd caricature it makes: young bodies with older people's health problems and with minds that are immature and undeveloped in many areas.

When I was growing up, parents believed it was necessary for children to struggle a little, that it built character. Today's parents hate to see their children struggle at all. They want to give them everything. Parents get upset if their child is cut from a sport's team. In some communities, they don't keep score so that there are no losers and kids won't feel bad. From a neurological perspective, this produces children who don't learn and understand the value of hard work. They don't know that life doesn't just hand you things—that you have to get out there and make things happen.

When kids are given everything they want, they don't learn to provide for themselves.

Children need to experience winning and losing because life consists of winners and losers. They need to figure out how to be a winner, how to be a success. Being a winner requires motivation and self-reliance, yet today's kids are more unmotivated than any time in history.

When kids are given everything they want, they don't learn to provide for themselves. It breeds insecurity and immaturity. As they grow up, these children start to feel as if they could never provide for themselves the life their parents have given them, so they'd rather move back in with Mom and Dad than struggle and do without until they can make it on their own. They're not grown up because they didn't learn how to grow up—and now they don't want to grow up. They've become classic Peter Pans.

Ask any teacher what's wrong with kids today and most likely you'll get the same answer I hear from teachers all the time: the parents!

Many parents today blindly believe their children can do no wrong.

When I speak with older people and grandparents, I often hear them describe how different parenting is today. I observe it myself almost daily in our Brain Balance centers. This is not the "wait till your father gets home" generation, where kids faced being in trouble at home if they created trouble in school. Not these days. Too many parents today blindly believe that their kids can do no wrong. Rather, it is the teacher, the coach, the system, or somebody else's fault.

It is incongruous that today's parents are more involved in their children's lives than were previous generations, yet so many—especially the most well-meaning and best-intentioned parents—are oblivious to their children's poor behavior, bad habits, and lack of motivation. I find they choose not to see it because they are just too busy. After all, they rationalize, they can't do everything! Besides, all kids are like that, they say. They see the current status quo as normal. In fact, it is only the perception of what's normal that has become skewed.

A study reported in the medical journal *Canadian Family Physician* in September 2007 is a case in point. For the study, researchers asked the parents of a group of schoolchildren what they considered their kids' weight to be for their age: normal, underweight, overweight, or obese. Sixty-three percent of parents of overweight children said their kids were normal weight; 15 percent of parents of obese children classified them as being overweight; and 22 percent of parents of normal-weight children incorrectly stated they were underweight.

Some parents aren't exactly good role models either. Today's adults are the most overweight, unhealthy, stressed-out, depressed, and unmotivated group of adults in history. Statistics show that an estimated 66 percent of American adults are overweight, and the majority are parents with children at home. Also, 59 percent of adults report that they get no physical exercise. Since 1990, there has been a 76 percent increase in the incidence of type 2 diabetes in adults between the ages of thirty and forty.

Additionally, the incidence of ADHD, depression, anxiety, diabetes, cardiovascular disease, autoimmune diseases, and a number of serious mental illnesses (like psychosis) are all increasing at epidemic levels in the United States. Here's the kicker and the undeniable reality: Whatever affects the parents impacts the children. This is why it comes as no surprise that we see these or similar disorders rising in our children. As the saying goes, the apple doesn't fall far from the tree.

You are your children's role model. If you're overweight, unhealthy, sedentary, and unhappy, chances are your children will be, too. You're setting your children up in a negative environment, which, you'll learn as you read more of this book, is detrimental to the health of growing young minds.

Parents can't be blamed for the poor behavior displayed by a child with a neurological problem. Neither can the child. The bad behavior is caused by a brain imbalance. However, if you have a child who is physically and mentally healthy but acts badly, you have to examine your parenting skills and how your own behavior and actions are affecting your child. If you don't change, you can't expect your child to change.

A SHIFT IN PRIORITIES

Kids aren't behaving badly because all of a sudden we are having an epidemic of terrible parents. In fact, quite the opposite is true. I believe the current generation of parents cares more about their kids and works harder on their parenting skills than any previous generation. I also believe they are more informed, concerned, intelligent, and well intentioned than any other generation of parents. However, somehow, somewhere along the line they got misguided.

A mix of both economic hard times and the desire to have it all and lavish their children with everything advertisers say is necessary for them to keep up with their peers is impacting the amount of time parents are spending with their kids.

Today, in more families than ever before, both parents are working full time. Statistics show 75 percent of families with dependent children have two wage earners, some out of necessity and others out of desire. This also means that 75 percent of children are spending their early years, and even their infancy, in some type of daycare.

Absentee parenting can have a negative impact on a child's brain development.

This is a concern to me, and it has nothing to do with the societal debates, either pro or con. It has to do with the negative impact absentee parenting has on the development of kids' brains. Studies show that kids in daycare aren't touched or held as much as they would be if they were at home with a parent. Kids in daycare are not allowed to randomly explore their environment. Yet touch, especially from a parent, and spatial exploration are intrinsic requirements for brain growth.

As I'll explain in more detail in Chapter 2, the brain depends on outside stimuli to facilitate the processes involved in growth. Movement is crucial. Without it, the brain and the behaviors it controls won't grow! This isn't something that parents consciously think about a lot because you can't see a brain growing the way you can see your kids getting taller and their feet getting bigger. Parents outwardly make sure that the body is physically growing as it is supposed to, but how much thought is given to the stimuli needed to ensure the brain grows?

Quantity of time is as important as quality of time.

There is no more powerful stimulus to healthy brain development than a parent. There is no equal substitute for a parent's smell, touch, voice, and warmth. When both parents work, it not only limits their time with their child, but quality of time becomes limited as well.

Many parents will argue, "I may spend less time with my child, but my time with my child is quality time." Excuse the expression, but this is a bunch of bunk. Quality over quantity simply doesn't cut it from a neurologic perspective. That's how important parental stimulation is! It is the single most important factor in getting a baby's brain on the correct path, meaning quantity of time *is* important, crucially important.

Parents who work full-time typically come home tired and spent. They just don't have the same amount of energy and vitality they used on the job all day to spend on their child. I am not being judgmental. Working parents tell me all the time, "The last thing I feel like doing is . . .": helping my kids with their homework, answering a million questions, and fighting with them to eat right, turn off the TV, or stop playing on the computer. Tired parents want to relax in front of the TV, too, or spend some time alone.

Behavior Disorders in Children

Bad behavior and other emotional issues in children can be a sign of a neurological disorder caused by an imbalance in either the right or the left hemisphere of the brain. If your child has a behavior problem, it could be due to one of these conditions. Keep in mind, however, that the majority of kids with bad behavior do not have a mental disorder.

The most common neurological conditions that can cause behavior problems in a child are:

- **Attachment disorder:** A problem with mood and behavior and lack of socialization as a result of a failure to bond with primary caregivers in early childhood.
- **Attention deficit/hyperactivity disorder (ADHD):** The inability to pay attention to the point that it disrupts relationships and situations.
- **Autism:** An extreme inability to communicate normally and interact socially, which is often accompanied by strange behavior issues.
- **Asperger's syndrome:** Often referred to as little professor syndrome because of high intelligence. Behavior problems include obsessive fixation on things or topics of knowledge.
- **Oppositional defiant disorder:** Characterized by openly hostile and defiant behavior, usually aimed at authority figures.

- **Conduct disorder:** Characterized by aggressive and destructive behavior.
- **Obsessive-compulsive disorder:** An anxiety disorder characterized by a fixation on unusual patterns of behavior.

If your child has one of these conditions or is diagnosed with one, it does not mean that the brain is damaged or ill in any way. In Brain Balance we see all these disorders as different symptoms of one underlying problem called functional disconnection syndrome (FDS). The condition can generally be improved by bringing the brain back in balance through the Brain Balance Program. To learn more about the program, see Part 3.

THE PROBLEM WITH TECHNOLOGY

This is an area where parenting is really tough. The TV, computer, Internet, cell phone, iPod, DVD, and other electronic gizmos are stiff competition for parental attention because they are generally a lot more interesting to our kids than we are! The digital age has made it harder than ever for a parent to get and keep their kids' attention. And we see the fallout from it all the time.

I believe the home computer and the lifestyle changes it has created are the largest contributors to the meteoric rise in childhood developmental disorders. It is also the reason kids have shorter attention spans and why they expect instant gratification. A recent study of thirteen hundred kids from grades three through five found that kids who spent an average of four hours a day watching television, playing videos, or using the computer were more than twice as likely to have attention span problems than kids who spent two hours or less in the same activities.

When kids are in front of the computer, their bodies are inert. Kids spend too much time being idle, and we have an obesity epidemic to prove it. Every minute a kid sits at the computer (and in front of the TV, for that matter) reduces the amount of time the body moves.

How does a four-year-old child become obese? I can tell you it is not from eating too much. Ask your parents, or think back to your own childhood. How many overweight four-year-olds can you and they recall? The answer, I bet, is none.

Today's kids aren't active like kids were in other generations, and it's all to their detriment.

The problem with kids and their weight today isn't nearly as much about eating as it is about moving. Today's kids aren't active like kids were in previous generations, and it's all to their detriment. They are not playing outside after school, they're not climbing trees, playing ball, or riding bikes. They are sitting inside in front of a TV or computer screen. Babies are in bouncy chairs.

Parents rationalize that children learn more by using the computer—that it will make them more intelligent and better prepared for the future. Unfortunately, they are wrong, and study after study proves it. Intelligence is contingent on the proper development of the brain's frontal lobes, which depend on movement. Brain scans show that when kids are playing computer games or watching TV there isn't much activity happening in the brain. The worst thing you can do developmentally is park a young child in front of a TV or computer for hours on end.

Parents also rationalize that this is what all kids do and the way all kids act, so it has to be okay.

Only it's not. What's getting shortchanged is the child's brain growth and the intellectual and behavior development that goes with it.

When brain development gets compromised, many parents don't know about it until after there are behavior or learning issues and some doctor or specialist hands them a diagnosis of ADHD, obsessive-compulsive disorder, oppositional defiant disorder, processing disorder, autism, or some other kind of disorder.

WHAT PARENTS CAN DO NOW

We can't turn a blind eye. We must see these trends as problems that are detrimental to the development of healthy minds, and we must attack them head-on. In the short term, here are some of the things you can do.

- **Understand the needs of the growing brain.** Awareness of how the brain grows and what is required to make it grow properly and to its full potential is the first thing we can do to help turn these trends around. That is what the rest of Part 1 is about. Read it. It is essential in helping you determine if your child's behavior issues are being caused by a neurological problem, a psychological problem, or your parenting skills and/or home environment.
- **Get back to basics.** Limit kids' TV and computer time to no more than an hour or two a day, and never, ever permit either in a child's bedroom. Like the television, a computer should be centrally located so you can keep an eye on how often it is being used and what it is being used for.
- **Get your kids on the move.** Make them go outside and use their bodies. Interact with your kids in active fun and games.
- **Spend as much time as possible with your kids.** Talk to them, play games, read to them, or get them to read to you.
- **Set boundaries.** Kids need to live by a set of rules. Set them and stick with them. I show you exactly how you can do this in Chapter 7.

THE LONG-TERM PLAN

Regulating your child's behavior is important, but it is not enough. A great deal rides on the example you set as a role model. Certain environmental influences are important to healthy brain development, and the most important environmental influence—and the most controllable—is parents themselves. If you are depressed, stressed-out, unhealthy, overweight, and unhappy with your job or life, chances are this is where your kids are headed, too.

Are you the best role model you can possibly be? I think there is room for improvement in all of us. A bad role model can become a good role model. A good role model can become a great role model. A great role model can become a near-perfect role model.

Changing negative behavior in an individual child and helping him or her achieve the best opportunity in life won't be successful if you focus on that child to the exclusion of the rest of the family. That's what the Family Empowerment Program is all about. It is your long-term plan for the best life for every member of your family. It starts by addressing the primary issue—the parents—before it tackles issues parents are having with their kids.

This is also what makes the program unique and truly empowering. The Family Empowerment Program is designed to help you reconnect with your kids and bring about significant, lasting, and positive change that will benefit every member of the family. It's a powerful tool that shows parents how to help kids of all ages find motivation and purpose in life and reach their full potential. It directs your kids to grow up and mature into healthy, productive, and motivated adults. And it is the tool that will help you recapture your lost dreams and fulfill them.

That's right, *your* dreams. When I present this prospect to parents, it always takes them by surprise. I can tell you, however, that there is nothing selfish about this goal. I have seen enough misbehaved kids and unhappy and resentful parents to know that self-directed, content, and happy parents are the key to family harmony.

In the end, what children desire the most is their parents' pride and love. For children to have that drive means having parents who deserve respect, admiration, and love.

I believe we can all do a little better as parents. Some of us could do a lot better. We can all start *now*.

· 2 ·

How a Child's Brain Grows

The best thing about dreams is that fleeting moment
when you are asleep and awake, when you don't know the
difference between reality and fantasy, when for just that one
moment you feel with your entire soul that the dream is
reality and it really happened.

—UNKNOWN

Parents generally don't give it a lot of thought, but babies aren't born with much of a brain. A child is born with little more than a brainstem and just enough brain power to keep the heart beating, the lungs breathing, the bowels moving, and other less obvious necessities of life functioning.

A baby enters the world mostly to sound and very little vision, just shades of gray and shadowy movement. For the most part, the world is out of focus. A newborn recognizes Mom mostly through her voice, her touch, the way she smells, and how she moves her body to caress and care for her infant.

Even though baby can't move very well—head, eyes, fingers, and toes are not yet flexible—she can feel everything. Genes are already interacting with stimuli to build the neural network that will process the information that builds the brain.

AS THE BRAIN BUILDS

As you might expect, the brain is built from the bottom up—from the brainstem, the least complex area, to the cerebral cortex, the most complex area—and from side to side—the left hemisphere and the right hemisphere. What you may not realize is that the two different sides of the brain don't grown in unison.

The human brain is so sophisticated and equipped to do so many things that specific duties reside either on the right or on the left. This means that each side does half the job of the whole. And to function as a whole, the neural networks in the left and right must be in continual communication.

> **Brain-building genes are particularly vulnerable at birth.**

Brain-building genes are particularly vulnerable at birth because they need to click into action at precisely the right time to build the neural pathways the way Mother Nature intended. Neurons must interact between left and right at lightening speed to create even the simplest movement or the tinniest thought. It is what makes the human brain one of the most complex structures in the universe.

While in the womb and right after birth, the right side of the brain—the part commonly thought of as the intuitive side—starts to grow first. It pretty much keeps this emphasis for the first few years of life, helping baby interpret the world around her and take her first steps. When she cries and says no to everything, even when she means yes, it is her right brain talking. This forms the foundation of skills that the right hemisphere will control for life.

Later, around age three, emphasis switches to the left brain, the side often referred to as the logical side. The left brain will now use the skills learned from the right brain to help your toddler explore the details of the world around her, wrap her little fingers around a crayon, hear detailed sounds, and see with great clarity the faces of those who love her. She is fascinated and curious about her world. Her mind is wondering, *Who is that? Why do they do that? How does that happen?* This is the left hemisphere growing, and it will continue this way for the next few years.

Growth will then move back to the right brain, and development of the hemispheres will continue to flip-flop back and forth in perfect rhythm and perfect timing, building new neurons and pathways and strengthening others as the brain regulates each new behavior and fine-tunes another until baby grows into a young adult. Understanding behavior—and helping identify if a neurological problem is causing your child's behavior problem—means understanding how the left and right brains behave.

> Understanding behavior means understanding
> how the left and right brains behave.

THE POSITIVE AND NEGATIVE BRAIN

According to top researchers like Richard Davidson from the University of Wisconsin and Rodolfo Llinas from New York University, behavior and emotions are bound together as if in concrete. They are based in the primitive human instinct for survival we know as fight or flight. Or, as behaviorists prefer to say, approach and avoidance.

Each behavior is driven by the motivation to reach a specified goal, whether it be the desire for love, warmth, friendship, crayons, or a piece of candy.

There are lots of words to describe our emotions and the way we feel, but there are only six specific emotions: three fall under the category of approach and three fall under the category of avoidance. These can also be broken down into good (positive) emotions and bad (negative) emotions.

Left Brain Positive (Approach) Behavior	Right Brain Negative (Avoidance) Behavior
Happy	Sad
Anger	Fear
Surprise	Disgust

Ideal behavior is an appropriate balance
of positive and negative behaviors.

Approach, or positive, emotions reside in the left brain, and avoidance, or negative emotions, reside in the right brain. Ideal behavior is an appropriate balance of positive and negative behaviors that are responsive, flexible, and constantly changing to the current situation.

Left Brain Behavior

The left hemisphere sees the world in small pictures, like the stills that make up a movie. It ignores the whole and zeroes in on the details. The left brain can be described as follows:

The small muscle brain. The left hemisphere controls fine motor skills. Everything done with the hands and fingers and feet and toes, such as tying shoes and playing the piano, are left brain skills. The left brain moves the small muscles of the throat and mouth in rapid sequence so we can speak. It processes the rapidly differing sounds of letters and syllables and translates them into language.

Positive behavior is found in the left brain.

The literal brain. Everything that has to do with language—reading, writing, speaking, and interpretation—reside in the left brain. This is where letters turn into syllables, syllables into words, and words into sentences. This hemisphere reads individual words in a sentence and translates their meaning, letter by letter, and syllable by syllable.

The conscious brain. The left brain is involved in every conscious move the body makes. It enables you use it to read a book, solve a math problem, or memorize a poem. It is also involved in conscious thoughts, such as talking to yourself.

The logical brain. The left brain is about systemizing; it's linear and logical in its thinking. It likes to examine things one at a time and in order. It likes basic science and math and other logical pursuits. It figures out what comes next in a sequence and how to form a pattern. Language develops because of pattern-recognition skills. Learning a new language or how to play a musical instrument is a pattern skill. Computer games and video games are all about pattern-recognition skills. The left brain loves computer games.

The routine brain. The left brain hates change. It loves to do the same routine over and over. When you eat the same breakfast every day or stay in the same job even though you hate it, your left brain is doing your thinking for you.

The impulsive brain. When you run a yellow light at an eight-way intersection at rush hour, it is your left brain that's making you do it. The left brain is ready to take risks.

The thinking brain. If other kids in school call your kid "The Brain," you can be pretty sure he doesn't have a left brain deficiency.

This side of the brain is responsible for intelligence, especially verbal intelligence. Traditional IQ tests measure this side more than it does the right brain.

The curious brain. Behaviorally, the left brain controls approach behavior, the fight part of our fight-or-flight instinct, and helps us determine whether to outsmart the lion in the jungle or run like crazy. It wants to approach a situation, study all the details, figure it out, and remember it.

The positive brain. Emotionally, the left side is in charge of positive emotions and motivations—happiness, having fun, and personal energy.

The processing brain. The left brain is responsible for processing high-frequency sounds and the details of visual images, but these don't travel at the same speed. Perfect timing is essential so we can watch, listen, and understand.

The immune-driving brain. When a child is sick and has an infection, the left hemisphere mobilizes immune system antibodies to fight it off. This side of the brain stimulates the growth and development of immune tissue, called lymphoid tissue, that houses white blood cells and other chemicals. When kids have a left brain deficiency, they get sick a lot.

Right Brain Behavior

The right brain holds the big-picture view of the world. It is great at seeing the whole, but not the parts. It sees the forest, so to speak, but can't see the trees. The right brain can be described as follows:

The big muscle brain. It is in charge of moving the major muscles. When you climb the stairs or shake someone's hand, it is the right brain at work. It controls posture and gait.

The spatial brain. It allows you to feel yourself in space. It controls balance and what is known as proprioception, the ability to know where the body is in relationship to gravity and in relationship to self and others.

The social brain. It is the nonverbal communicator. Without it, social cues are missed. It reads and interprets body posture, facial expression, and tone of voice and helps you interpret what another person is thinking or feeling. Nonverbal communication is the foundation of socialization. It lays the foundation for verbal communication that will develop later on the left side. Without nonverbal proficiency, verbal expression is next to impossible.

Negative behavior resides in the right brain.

The subliminal brain. Because the right brain is nonverbal, it learns subconsciously or subliminally. You may not always recognize it as such, but meeting a new person is learning a new face. This new image is stored in the right brain. This type of learning is called procedural or implicit memory.

The curious brain. The right brain likes new or novel situations or locations. It hates to do the same thing over and over. Routine bores it easily.

The cautious brain. When you slam on your brakes at a yellow light, it is your right brain telling your left brain to cool it. The right brain is governed by avoidance and wants to flee instead of fight. It is the part of the brain that keeps a child safe. Before the curious left brain wants to approach, the right brain sends the signal of whether it is safe or dangerous.

The safe brain. The right brain can sense right from wrong. It controls impulses and will stop a child from doing something, especially when it is socially inappropriate.

The emotional and empathetic brain. If we don't learn to feel and read our own emotions, it is impossible to understand the emotions in other people. It's what we call emotional intelligence, or EQ.

Once we can intuit, we know what another person is feeling and thinking because we know why we are feeling and thinking the same way. We possess empathy.

The sensory brain. The right brain holds the sensory controls, so it senses and feels the whole body. It regulates the emotions that are internalized as a churning gut, pounding heart, and fast breathing. It is attuned to smell and taste. Therefore, if a smell is good, the right brain tells us that the person or object is good; if the smell is bad, then it tells us the person or object should be avoided. It is also responsible for receiving information from the auditory system.

The negative brain. The right brain is charged with negative emotions, such as fear and anger.

The immune-inhibiting brain. The right brain prevents the immune system from overreacting, so it doesn't inadvertently turn on its own protective antibodies and create autoimmune diseases.

Left Versus Right

Here is an easy way to remember the activities that reside in each side of the brain. Think of the body as a car and the brain as the engine. The left brain is like the gas pedal and the right brain is like the brake.

Left Brain	Right Brain
Small picture	Big picture
Serial processing	Parallel processing
Verbal communication	Nonverbal communication
Small (fine) muscle control	Large (gross) muscle control
IQ	EQ
Reading words (phonemic awareness, decoding)	Reading comprehension (main idea, inference, pramatics)
Math calculations (basic arithmetic operations)	Math reasoning (word problems, geometry)
Planning (theoretical)	Doing (practical)

Conscious actions, memory, learning	Unconscious actions, memory, learning
Explicit memory (declarative)	Implicit memory (procedural)
Positive emotions (approach)	Negative emotions (withdraw)
High-frequency sound	Low-frequency sound
Low-frequency vision	High-frequency vision
Light touch	Deep touch
Pleasant smell processing, left nostril	Unpleasant smell processing, right nostril
Receiving auditory input	Interpreting auditory input
Linear and logical thinking	Abstract thinking
Curious, impulsive actions	Cautious, safe actions
Likes routine, sameness	Likes newness, novelty
Activates immunity, increases antibody sensitivity	Suppresses immunity, decreases antibody sensitivity
Literal meaning	Metaphorical (alternative) meaning
Local spatial awareness	Global spatial awareness
Pleasant sense of taste and smell	Unpleasant sense of taste and smell
Social display (emotional motivation)	Social skills (emotional skills, empathy)
Intention	Attention
Motor	Sensory
Top down	Bottom up
Biographical narrative	Biographical memory
Cause and effect	Present is in the now
Explaining	Describing
Practical, deliberate	Intuitive, gut feeling
Teleceptive	Interoceptive
Unconnected to body, digestion, and automonic regulation	Connected to body, digestion, and autonomic regulation
Reduces stress, primarily on left side	Reduces whole body stress

HOW GENES GROW THE BRAIN

At one time, scientists believed that mental and physical growth were mutually exclusive, but this is not the case. One cannot exist without the other. Every biologically important event, from recognizing a mother's touch or a father's smile to sitting, crawling, walking, and talking, depends on electrical communication in the brain.

Though genes are responsible for building the brain, they, for the most part, depend on environmental influences to stimulate them into action.

Balanced brain development depends on outside influences.

At precise times during development, various environmental factors must interact with the senses to turn on the genes to signal a new brain-building process to begin. The more a brain cell is stimulated, the more it will increase in size and processing speed, strengthen its connections, and form new synapses.

Although the brain is able to provide a certain amount of stimulation on its own—dreaming is the best example—it mostly depends on outside sources to spark neural growth. The two most powerful sources of stimulation, as I emphasized in Chapter 1, are movement and a parent's touch. Others are light, sound, odor, taste, temperature, and gravity.

We know that muscle movement is important motor stimulation for the brain. If kids don't move, their brains don't grow. It's why it is so important for kids to get off the computer and away from the television and go outside and play!

As powerful as these positive environmental forces are, there are negative forces in the environment that turn off these genes. There is plenty of evidence showing that certain lifestyle choices and environmental influences can interfere with healthy brain development (and they are discussed in depth in *Disconnected Kids*). They include:

- Lack of physical exercise
- Overweight and obesity
- Environmental toxins
- Poor nutrition and food choices
- Absentee parenting
- Television and computers
- Stressful pregnancy and birth
- A stressful lifestyle

In the brains of children with neurological disorders, such as autism, ADHD, and oppositional disorders, we can see that certain genes are not being expressed. It's as if they were stuck in the off position.

This is why paying attention to developmental milestones is so important. They are the best tools parents have to help evaluate if the brain is growing properly or if it is growing out of balance.

Out-of-control, peculiar, or unexplainable behaviors are often the first clue that the brain is not developing properly, that some environmental influence at some stage of either left or right brain development turned off a brain-building gene or genes.

When the brain is out of balance—when genes are unable to respond to the environmental and sensory cues to properly build the approach and avoidance centers of the brain on time—emotions become suppressed in one side and exaggerated in the other side. This is why a child with a left brain deficiency, such as processing disorder, can be described as the glum and moody type, and a child with a right brain deficiency, such as ADHD, can be wild and disruptive.

I explain how this happens in the next chapter.

· 3 ·

When Things Go Wrong

A BRAIN OUT OF BALANCE

To learn to succeed you must first learn to fail.

—MICHAEL JORDAN

Why do certain children end up with a mental disability and others don't? It has nothing to do with being mentally challenged in an intellectual way. In fact, I believe it's quite the opposite.

I believe the children we see with attention deficit/hyperactivity disorder (ADHD), autism, and the myriad other neurological handicaps started out in life genetically more gifted than the average child. I believe they are actually brilliant in their own special way because they were born with one side of the brain already a little out of balance—with one hemisphere *ahead* of itself.

Many of the children we see with ADHD, autism, and the myriad other neurological handicaps started out in life genetically more gifted than the average child.

When something hostile in the environment intrudes and interferes with the stimulation that signals brain growth, it causes the brain to miss a step in the brain-building process. When, as is usually the case, one miss is followed by another and another—when one side keeps shooting ahead and the other side can't keep up—growth gets out of balance. This means the whole brain gets out of balance. So, what started out as a gift becomes a disability. A child ends up with an unevenness of skills—too much of the behavior governed by one side of the brain and not enough of the behavior controlled by the other.

Depending on the side of the brain affected and the severity, the child could be labeled as having autism, Asperger's syndrome, or any variety of mental disabilities, but there is really only one cause—a brain imbalance called functional disconnection syndrome (FDS).

It's been shown that some children with FDS are unusually gifted because their unevenness of skills is accentuated in certain areas in one side of the brain, which can result in specific talents. The most obvious example is savant syndrome, in which a child appears to be severely mentally handicapped but is brilliant at one thing, such as music or memory skills, or has enhanced fine motor drawing ability (incredible artistry) or perfect pitch. Children with ADHD and Asperger's syndrome generally have high verbal IQ and are very gifted academically, but have poor nonverbal IQ scores and social emotional impairment. The difference between ADHD and autism and Asperger's syndrome is really only a matter of degree.

THE AMAZING POTENTIAL OF THE BRAIN

What is a thought, an idea, a memory? What do they look like? Where are they found in the brain? These questions have baffled philosophers and scientists alike for generations.

For many years the best scientists believed that each memory was kept in a single cell so sophisticated that it could house all the details of a person's face. They called it the grandmother cell. Only they never found such a cell. It was just a theory.

At a certain point it became obvious that if we had cells that could house each and every memory of a lifetime, we would easily run out of cells. Even with a hundred billion neurons making tens of thousands of connections resulting in trillions of signals, there are still not enough cells in the brain to house all the information we need to function even at the most basic level.

The brain is much more sophisticated and complex than originally thought.

It became clear that the brain is much more sophisticated and complex than originally thought. Each cell in the brain does not perform a single job. It performs multiple jobs—hundreds, thousands, millions. Each brain cell has the capacity to perform an unlimited number of tasks because cells in different parts of the brain and on both sides of the brain work together by interrelating and forming unique patterns to create a task, such as making a memory or crying over a cup of spilled milk.

Recalling a memory, say somebody's name and phone number, involves calling multiple layers of cells into a specific pattern that sends the message such as: "Mary Ann Jones, 555-2020." Some cells, or even all of the same cells, may come into play *but in a different pattern* when your child runs into the street and you bolt to protect him. This gives the brain an unlimited amount of storage capacity. Such is the amazing potential of each and every brain.

Each new learning, each new behavior, each new memory is created by a team recruited from the billions of neurons present in every healthy brain. When they are in sync, and you want to call Mary Ann, no problem. The number flashes into your consciousness in an instant. When the circuits get scrambled, you may not even be able to remember a person's name, let alone her phone number. Once in a while, this is no problem, but in a child with a brain imbalance, circuits in the left and right brains literally can't find each other and get tripped up, sending out the wrong words and action. Like an out-of-melody orchestra, the circuits on both sides of the brain are whistling a different tune. That's why it's called a functional disconnect.

THE SYMPHONY OF THE BRAIN

Think of the brain as if it were an orchestra, with thoughts and actions as the notes that change moment to moment to create a musical composition. When the conductor (the brain) directs the musicians (neurons) to use their instruments (synapses) to create music (thoughts and actions), the music begins to play.

Sitting in the audience, you see the conductor lead the orchestra, floating from one side to the next. Each musician is a unique individual controlling different instruments—violin, viola, clarinet. You see these same instruments on both sides, but they all don't play at the same time and not always at the same tempo. Sometimes the conductor signals the right to play louder while he tones down the left. On the cue from the conductor's baton, certain instruments come into play, then others join in. Generally, there is never a time in most concerts when all the instruments are put into play at the same time. The brain works in the same way.

A brain out of balance is like a
symphony out of tune.

The key to both sides playing beautiful music together is that each musician must not only play the right notes but must play them at precisely the right time. The notes are constantly changing from moment to moment—the strings join in, go out, crescendo, pause. Same with the horns. All the time, this ebb and flow must be perfectly timed.

On occasion a musician might miss a beat without notice, but if the conductor focuses on the right and doesn't pay attention to the left, the players on the left can get confused, slow down, or even stop. The two sides get out of harmony. Suddenly, the music they were playing doesn't sound familiar at all. The exact same thing happens in the brain of a child with FDS.

In an orchestra, the conductor doesn't correct this disharmony by getting the stronger musicians to play faster and drown out the others. It may make the disharmony less noticeable, but it doesn't fix the problem. This is essentially what medications do. They make the problem in the brain less noticeable, but they don't fix the problem.

To correct the problem, the conductor has to identify which musicians are playing off-key and teach them how to get into rhythm. Helping just a few isn't going to make the entire orchestra better. All the faults must be identified and brought back into harmony. Even if just one instrument is off tempo, it can ruin the piece.

A lot of therapies or programs are like this. They focus on only one particular problem, such as visual processing, auditory processing, nutrition, or academic skills. Improving one problem alone does not make for sweet music. In some instances, it can even make it worse. We must identify each instrument that's off-key and correct it.

We know the instruments aren't broken, so they don't need to be repaired. The musicians just need more practice and encouragement. This, in essence, is what we do in Brain Balance. We find the malfunction in the brain and stimulate it so it gets back in rhythm with the rest of the brain.

For example, a child with mild ADHD could be analogous to an orchestra with three or four musicians out of tempo on the right side of the orchestra, but a child with severe autism would be like having fifty musicians off beat on the right side. Both involve a problem on the right side, but they each require an individual approach to correct the problem. The underlying problem, however, is still the same: One side of the brain can't keep up with the other side. It will throw the whole brain out of balance just like an inexperienced musician can spoil a concert.

THE MATTER OF BEHAVIOR

This book is not about how to correct the brain imbalance of a child with FDS. My book *Disconnected Kids* contains a complete program that parents can use to help correct a brain imbalance. (You can read about how the program works and the results we are getting in Part 3.) This book is about behavior and what influences it, whether or not your child has or had a diagnosed neurological condition.

There are only a few reasons for bad behavior in kids: a neurological problem, a psychological problem, or poor parenting skills. When behavior becomes an issue with any child, however, the likelihood of a neurological problem frequently comes up.

If your child has a behavior-based neurological problem, the only way to bring behavior to normal is to correct the problem. But first, you have to identify the problem. That's what the next two chapters are about. The rest of this book is your blueprint to help tame the behavior and bring harmony into your household—no matter what the cause of the problem.

· 4 ·

Why Is My Child Acting This Way?

Love me when I least deserve it, because that's
when I really need it.

—SWEDISH PROVERB

It's likely you picked up this book because there are behavior issues in your family. You may be seeing a problem in one child or all of your children. You may have a child who has a behavior problem or learning disability, or you suspect your child has one. Or maybe your child is behaving badly and you just can't figure out why.

It is likely that the concept of functional disconnection syndrome (FDS) is new to you. You never heard of it before and no doctor ever mentioned it to you. And now you're wondering if a brain imbalance could be causing the behavior issues you can't seem to control or if it could explain why your child is struggling so much in school. Could it be FDS?

**Inappropriate behavior and acting
out are hallmarks of FDS.**

The answer is maybe. Inappropriate behavior and acting out are hallmarks of FDS, as are learning difficulties in school, especially if they are centered on reading and math. The problem also could be psychological, stemming from emotional issues, such as abuse or attachment disorder. Most behavior issues, however, are neither neurological nor psychological. You just may have a badly behaved child who needs motivation, a better aim in life, and a concrete set of goals.

How are you to know? It's important that you find out.

If your child does have a neurological imbalance, you don't want to wait to take corrective action. The longer the problem is ignored, the worse it will likely get and the harder it will be to produce positive results. No matter how good a parent you are, you'll still question yourself and it may have an affect on the other children in your family.

To help you figure out where your child stands from a neurological point of view, take this easy-to-follow test. I call it the Master Hemispheric Checklist, and we use it all the time in our Brain Balance Achievement Centers to help us ascertain if a child:

- Has a right brain deficiency (the most common type)
- Has a left brain deficiency
- Has no brain imbalance at all

I first introduced this checklist in *Disconnected Kids* as a way to help parents pinpoint the source of their child's issues on their own. Most parents have found the checklist helpful in identifying their child's particular problem and planning corrective action. It is also useful in ruling out a neurological problem.

If, after completing the checklist, you suspect your child has a problem, then it would be useful for you to follow the corrective program detailed in *Disconnected Kids* or to enroll your child in a Brain Balance Achievement Center near you. (You can find a list of centers on page 303.) The Melillo At-Home Brain Balance Program is similar to the Brain Balance Program we use clinically in our centers. It's proven to produce results similar to what we accomplish in a professional setting. It's in your best interest to follow up by following the program in *Disconnected Kids*.

If your child doesn't have a problem, it will become obvious after you complete the checklist. It may mean that you have a child with a behavioral problem that could benefit from some psychological intervention. Or, most likely, it means that both you and your child need a new focus and redirection to get the behavior under control. The Family Empowerment Program featured in this book is designed to get you there.

The Family Empowerment Program will also help formerly disconnected kids going through the growing pains of trying to catch up with their brain, a short period of time that can cause peculiar behavior in children and create angst and uncertainty in their parents. (You'll learn more about this in Chapter 6.) It is the next step after the Brain Balance Program for children diagnosed with FDS and their parents.

Before you get started on the Family Empowerment Program, complete the Master Hemispheric Checklist. Even if you did it when you read *Disconnected Kids*, do it again to see how well your child has progressed. After you complete the checklist, I'll explain how to interpret the results and what it means if you find that your child has a brain imbalance.

THE MASTER HEMISPHERIC CHECKLIST

The Master Hemispheric Checklist consists of characteristics that are common to children with FDS—half signify a right brain imbalance or deficit and half signify a left brain deficit—divided into these seven aspects of brain growth:

- **Motor:** Muscle tone, coordination. and strength.
- **Sensory:** Correlating to the five senses of touch, smell, taste, vision, and hearing.
- **Emotional:** Ability to control and display emotions at the proper times.
- **Behavior:** Acting appropriately and social interactions.
- **Academic:** Abilities required for learning and retention.
- **Immune:** Tendencies toward allergies and chronic illnesses.
- **Autonomic:** Self-regulating body functions.

If the trait fits your child, put a check in the box next to the characteristic, then add up the number of checks you made and enter it at the bottom of each category list. Consider the description carefully. One reason parents come up with ambiguous or skewed results is because they don't accurately identify their child's traits.

► Characteristics of a Right Brain Delay

MOTOR CHARACTERISTICS

- ☐ Clumsiness; odd posture.
- ☐ Poor coordination.
- ☐ Not athletically inclined; has no interest in popular childhood participation sports.
- ☐ Low muscle tone—muscles seem kind of floppy.
- ☐ Poor gross motor skills, such as difficulty learning to ride a bike and/or runs and/or walks oddly.
- ☐ Repetitive/stereotyped motor mannerisms (spins in circles, flaps arms).
- ☐ Fidgets excessively.
- ☐ Poor eye contact.
- ☐ Tends to walk on toes or walked on toes when younger.

Total _____

SENSORY CHARACTERISTICS

☐ Poor spatial orientation—bumps into things often.

☐ Sensitivity to sound.

☐ Confusion when asked to point to different body parts.

☐ Poor sense of balance.

☐ High threshold for pain—for example, doesn't cry when gets a cut.

☑ Likes motion—spinning, swinging, going on rides.

☐ Touches things compulsively.

☐ Disinterested in makeup or jewelry (girl only).

☐ Does not like the feel of clothing on arms or legs; pulls off clothes.

☐ Does not like touching things or being touched.

☐ Incessantly smells everything.

☐ Prefers bland foods.

☐ Does not notice strong smells, such as burning wood, popcorn, or freshly baked cookies.

☐ Avoids food because of the way it looks.

☐ Hates to eat and is not even interested in sweets.

☐ Extremely picky eater.

Total _____2_____

EMOTIONAL CHARACTERISTICS

☑ Spontaneously cries and/or laughs and has sudden outbursts of anger or fear.

☐ Worries a lot and has several phobias.

☑ Holds on to past hurts.

☐ Has sudden emotional outbursts that appear overreactive and inappropriate to a situation.

☐ Experiences panic and/or anxiety attacks.

☐ Sometimes displays dark or violent thoughts.
☐ Doesn't exhibit much body language, such as lack of facial expression.
☐ Too uptight; cannot seem to loosen up.
☐ Lacks empathy and feelings for others.
☐ Lacks emotional reciprocity.
☐ Often seems fearless and is a risk taker.

Total _____

BEHAVIORAL CHARACTERISTICS

☐ Thinks logically.
☐ Often misses the gist of a story.
☐ Usually the last to get a joke.
☐ Gets stuck in set behavior; can't let it go.
☐ Lacks social tact and/or is antisocial and/or socially isolated.
☐ Poor time management skills; is always late.
☐ Disorganized.
☐ Has a problem paying attention.
☐ Is hyperactive and/or impulsive.
☐ Has obsessive thoughts or behaviors.
☐ Argues all the time and is generally uncooperative.
☐ Exhibits signs of an eating disorder.
☐ Failed to thrive as an infant, such as low birth weight or struggling to breast-feed.
☐ Mimics sounds or words repeatedly without really understanding the meaning, a disorder called echolalia.
☐ Appears bored, aloof, and abrupt.
☐ Considered strange by other children.
☐ Inability to form friendships.
☐ Has difficulty sharing enjoyment, interests, or achievements with other people.

- ☐ Acts inappropriately giddy or silly.
- ☐ Acts inappropriately in social situations.
- ☐ Talks incessantly and asks repetitive questions.
- ☐ Has no or little joint attention, such as the need to point to an object to get your attention.
- ☐ Avoids looking in the mirror/didn't recognize self in the mirror or in pictures as a toddler.

Total _____

ACADEMIC CHARACTERISTICS

- ☐ Understands math operations but has poor math reasoning skills.
- ☐ Poor reading comprehension and logic skills.
- ☐ Misses the big picture—only sees the parts instead of the big picture.
- ☐ Very analytical.
- ☐ Has poor pragmatic skills.
- ☐ Very good at finding mistakes, especially spelling errors.
- ☐ Takes things literally.
- ☐ Doesn't always reach a conclusion when speaking.
- ☐ Started speaking early.
- ☐ Has tested for a high IQ but scores run the whole spectrum or IQ is above normal in verbal ability and below average in performance abilities.
- ☐ Was an early word reader.
- ☐ Is interested in unusual topics.
- ☐ Learns in a rote (memorizing) manner.
- ☐ Learns extraordinary amounts of specific facts about a subject.
- ☐ Is impatient.
- ☐ Speaks in a monotone; has little voice inflection.

☐ Is a poor nonverbal communicator; doesn't use expression when speaking.

☐ Doesn't like loud noises, such as fireworks.

☐ Speaks out regarding what he or she is thinking.

☐ Talks in your face—is a space invader.

☐ Good reader but does not enjoy reading.

☐ Thinks analytically—is led by logic.

☐ Follows rules without questioning them.

☐ Is good at keeping track of time.

☐ Easily memorizes spelling and facts and figures.

☐ Enjoys observing rather than participating.

☐ Can't figure out something new without being shown how to do it or reading an instruction manual.

☐ Math was the first academic subject that became a problem.

Total _____

COMMON IMMUNE SYSTEM CHARACTERISTICS

☐ Has lots of allergies.

☐ Rarely gets colds and infections.

☐ Has had or has eczema or asthma.

☐ Skin has little white bumps, especially on the back of the arms.

☐ Displays erratic behavior—good one day, bad the next.

☐ Craves certain foods, especially dairy and wheat products.

Total _____

COMMON AUTONOMIC NERVOUS SYSTEM CHARACTERISTICS

☐ Has bowel problems, such as chronic constipation or diarrhea.

☐ Has a rapid heart rate and/or high blood pressure for age.

☐ Appears bloated, especially after meals, and often complains of stomach pains.

☐ Has body odor.

☐ Sweats a lot.

☐ Hands are always moist and clammy.

Total _____

SCORE:

Add the seven scores together and enter the total here: _____

▶ Characteristics of a Left Brain Delay

MOTOR CHARACTERISTICS

☐ Good muscle tone.

☐ Poor or slow handwriting (fine motor functions).

☐ Difficulty with fine motor skills (called *dyspraxia*), such as buttoning a shirt.

☐ Poor or immature hand grip when writing.

☐ Tends to write very large for age or grade level.

☐ Stumbles over words when fatigued.

☐ Exhibits delay in crawling, standing, and/or walking.

☐ Loves sports and is good at them.

☐ Poor drawing skills.

☐ Difficulty learning to play music.

☐ Likes to fix things with the hands and is interested in anything mechanical.

☐ Difficulty planning and coordinating body movements.

Total _____

SENSORY CHARACTERISTICS

- ☐ Does not seem to have many sensory sensitivities, such as to sound, touch, or smell.
- ☐ Good sense of own body and awareness of body in space.
- ☐ Good sense of balance.
- ☐ Eats just about anything.
- ☐ Is not a picky eater.
- ☐ Likes to be hugged and held.
- ☐ Does not have any oddities concerning clothes.
- ☐ Has auditory processing problems (such as problems with phonics).
- ☐ Seems not to hear well, although hearing tests are normal.
- ☐ Had ear infections and was delayed in speaking.
- ☐ Has a tendency toward motion sickness.
- ☐ Is not undersensitive or oversensitive to pain.

Total _____

EMOTIONAL CHARACTERISTICS

- ☐ Overly happy and affectionate; loves to hug and kiss.
- ☐ Frequently moody and irritable.
- ☐ Loves doing new or different things but gets bored easily.
- ☐ Lacks motivation.
- ☐ Withdrawn and shy.
- ☐ Excessively cautious, pessimistic, or negative.
- ☐ Doesn't seem to get any pleasure out of life.
- ☐ Doesn't like to socialize.
- ☐ Cries easily; feelings get hurt easily.
- ☐ Seems to be in touch with own feelings.
- ☐ Empathetic to other people's feelings; reads people's emotions well.

☐ Gets embarrassed easily.
☐ Very sensitive to what others think about him or her.

Total _____

BEHAVIOR CHARACTERISTICS

☐ Procrastinates.
☐ Is extremely shy, especially around strangers.
☐ Is very good at nonverbal communication—expresses body language and reads body language well.
☐ Is well liked by other children and teachers.
☐ Is well behaved in school.
☐ Understands social rules.
☐ Poor self-esteem.
☐ Hates doing homework.
☐ Is very good at social interaction.
☐ Makes good eye contact.
☐ Likes to be around people and enjoys social activities, such as going to parties.
☐ Doesn't like to go to sleep-overs.
☐ Is not good at following routine.
☐ Cannot follow multiple-step directions or answer multiple-step questions.
☐ Is in touch with own feelings.
☐ Jumps to conclusions.

Total _____

ACADEMIC CHARACTERISTICS

☐ Very good at big-picture skills.
☐ Is an intuitive thinker led by feelings.

☐ Good at abstract thought-free association.

☐ Has poor analytical (logic) skills.

☐ Is very visual; loves images and patterns.

☐ Constantly questions why you're doing something or why rules exist.

☐ Has poor sense of time.

☐ Enjoys touching and feeling objects.

☐ Has trouble prioritizing.

☐ Is unlikely to read instruction manual before trying something new.

☐ Is naturally creative, but needs to work hard to develop full potential.

☐ Would rather do things instead of observe.

☐ Uses good voice inflection when speaking.

☐ Misreads or omits common small words.

☐ Has difficulty reading long words.

☐ Reads laboriously and too slow.

☐ Had difficulty naming colors, objects, and letters as a toddler.

☐ Needs to hear or see concepts many times to learn them.

☐ Has shown a downward trend in achievement test scores or school performance.

☐ Schoolwork is inconsistent.

☐ Was a late talker.

☐ Has difficulty pronouncing words—poor with phonics.

☐ Had difficulty learning the alphabet, nursery rhymes, or songs when young.

☐ Has difficulty finishing homework or finishing a conversation.

☐ Acts before thinking and makes careless mistakes.

☐ Daydreams a lot.

☐ Has difficulty sequencing events in the proper order.

☐ Often writes letters backward.

- ☐ Is poor at basic math skills.
- ☐ Has poor memorization skills.
- ☐ Overall, has poor academic ability.
- ☐ Has an IQ lower than expected and verbal scores are lower than nonverbal scores.
- ☐ Performs poorly on verbal tests.
- ☐ Needs to be told things several times before they understand.
- ☐ Stutters or stuttered when younger.
- ☐ Is a poor speller.
- ☐ Doesn't read directions well.

Total _____

COMMON IMMUNE SYSTEM CHARACTERISTICS

- ☐ Gets chronic ear infections.
- ☐ Prone to benign tumors or cysts.
- ☑ Had taken antibiotics more than ten or fifteen times before the age of ten.
- ☐ Has had tubes put in ears or the doctor recommended them.
- ☐ Catches colds frequently.
- ☐ Has no allergies.

Total _____

COMMON AUTONOMIC NERVOUS SYSTEM CHARACTERISTICS

- ☐ Has a bed-wetting problem.
- ☐ Has or had an irregular heartbeat, such as an arrhythmia or heart murmur.

Total _____

SCORE:
Add the seven scores together and enter the total here: _____

▶ **Reading the Results**

Your child has an imbalance in the left hemisphere of the brain
if the left brain score is higher than the right brain score. Your
child has an imbalance in the right hemisphere of the brain if
the right brain score is higher than the left brain score. This is
the classic unevenness of skills that is the hallmark of FDS.

The difference in the scores does not have to be significant to indicate
FDS. Even a difference of one or two points may still indicate an
imbalance. However, if the score is this close, it is best to go through
the checklist a second time and consider each response carefully.

To determine the severity of the imbalance, tabulate the number of positive responses from the entire checklist (both left and
right). The higher the number, the greater the imbalance. If
the total is under 50, the imbalance is mild; from 50 to 99, the
imbalance is moderate; the imbalance is severe if over 100.

If you have a lot of checks in both the left and right brain checklists, your child still has FDS, but it most likely means that the
whole brain is maturing too slowly. I'll explain what this means
and give you more guidance to figure this out in the next chapter.

PROFILE OF A RIGHT BRAIN DEFICIENCY

A right brain deficiency is the most common of the two and shows
up first as a behavior problem. These are kids who usually tried
their moms right from the get-go. They probably kicked and moved

around in the womb so much they kept their mothers awake at night. Most likely, giving birth to them wasn't easy either. As toddlers, these kids run their mothers ragged, as their incessant curiosity has them moving all over the place.

The most glaring trait of children with right hemisphere deficits is they don't have a good sense of their bodies in space—they don't have a feel for their own bodies, a function we call *proprioception*, or the ability to use muscle control and balance to resist gravity.

> These children are usually a behavior problem
> from the get-go.

The reason for this is that kids with a right brain imbalance have poor muscle tone, especially of the large postural muscles near the spine. The most obvious symptom is an odd gait.

This comes from a delay in acquiring gross motor skills—the ability to stand up, walk, run, etc.—during infancy and early childhood. Gross motor skills are coordinated by the body's large muscles and depend on good whole body movement. Children with a right brain delay have poor balance, are uncoordinated, appear clumsy, and don't have a good sense of rhythm. They'll trip and fall a lot for no good reason.

This oddness can also be detected in their social skills. They are space invaders and may say inappropriate things without understanding why they are wrong. Like all kids, they crave friendships, but have a hard time making them.

These children generally are very smart, but their first words come late. In fact, as toddlers they might not speak much at all. However, what they lack in expression they make up in learning. These children often start school with impressive reading and spelling skills. Unfortunately, it isn't too long before the world starts caving in. Feedback from teachers usually arrives early. Acting out; meltdowns; and obstinate, impulsive, disruptive, and oppositional behavior are all part of the package.

Suddenly, these smart kids start to struggle in school. They read, but it soon becomes apparent that they don't get the gist of the story. They struggle with math. They start loosing ground academically because of all they've missed when they weren't paying attention. Their foundational skills become so weak that their precocious knowledge starts to look like Swiss cheese—it's full of holes they can't feel.

This leads to frustration and fear, which makes them become more and more oppositional. They usually take it out on Mom first, then they go up and down the ladder of authority figures.

These children also have sensory issues—they are either over-sensitive or undersensitive to the world around them. Also, they are usually very fussy eaters. Because they don't have a good sense of smell or taste, they avoid certain foods. They don't eat foods that kids normally like, especially sweets.

Autoimmune disorders, such as allergies and asthma, often go hand in hand with a right brain imbalance. These children are often very sensitive to the environment and may have a number of contact allergies. They also have immune problems because the right brain cannot properly do its job of suppressing the immune system. As a result, internal inflammation in the body and brain is common and can become chronic. These children generally have poor digestion. A rapid heartbeat is also common.

Mothers of kids with a right brain deficiency often tell me that they had a sense early on that their child was kind of different from other kids. In retrospect, they sensed a disconnect right from the start.

Right brain deficiencies are often diagnosed as:

■ Attention deficit disorder (ADD)
■ Attention deficit/hyperactivity disorder (ADHD)
■ Asperger's syndrome
■ Autism
■ Conduct disorder (CD)
■ Developmental coordination disorder (DCD)

- Nonverbal learning disability (NLD)
- Obsessive-compulsive disorder (OCD)
- Oppositional defiant disorder (ODD)
- Pervasive developmental disorder (PDD)
- Tourette's syndrome

Traits of a Right Brain Deficiency

- Thinks analytically all the time.
- Has difficulty modeling someone else's behavior but can do as told.
- Often misses the gist of a story and is the last to get a joke.
- Gets stuck in set behavior; can't let it go.
- Tends to be a risk taker.
- Lacks social tact and may be antisocial and socially isolated.
- Has inappropriate social interaction (one-sided social interaction).
- Has a hard time making friends.
- Is considered strange by other children.
- Acts inappropriately giddy or silly.
- Talks incessantly and asks repetitive questions or repeats words.
- Has poor time management skills and is always late.
- Is poorly organized and room is always a mess.
- Has a problem paying attention.
- Can't sit still—is hyperactive and/or impulsive.
- Has obsessive thoughts or behaviors.
- Argues all the time and is generally uncooperative.
- Appears bored, aloof, and abrupt.
- Acts immature for age.
- Inability to share enjoyment, interests, or achievements with other people.
- Had difficulty as a child getting your attention (didn't point to get you to look at or get something).
- Didn't look at self in mirror as a toddler.

PROFILE OF A LEFT BRAIN DEFICIENCY

The signs of a left brain deficiency are usually subtler than those of a right brain problem and can often go undetected until a child is in school.

These children generally start out easy. They don't get in trouble in school, pick fights, or drive their parents ragged with their hyperactive behavior and fussy eating patterns—at least not early on. Rather, these kids appear kind of shy and even withdrawn. Some may even be sullen and sad. They may not be motivated to do the things kids typically like to do. They'd rather hang out around the house with their parents than go out to play with friends.

Their biggest problem early on is illness. These children are prone to chronic infections, like colds and ear infections. They may also have an abnormal or irregular heartbeat, called *arrhythmia*.

These kids are fun to watch. They are well coordinated and may even show some early athletic ability. Nevertheless, they are a bit clumsy when it comes to working with their hands, which is most often detected in their dreadful handwriting.

These are very spatial kids. They love the outdoors and physical activity. They prefer solo activities—climbing, riding a bike, skating, and skateboarding—but shy away from team sports, such as soccer and baseball, because they have a hard time understanding and sticking to the rules.

These are the kids who were usually slow to start speaking. They may not be good verbally and may not like to talk a lot. Or they may mess up their sentences when speaking, making it hard to understand them.

———

These are kids who are not living
up to their potential.

———

Preschool and elementary teachers love these kids because they are not a discipline problem (this generally shows up a little later). Their apparent disinterest in academic pursuits, however, concerns their teachers. These are the kids teachers lament are not living up to their potential. They don't seem to have much motivation as far as school is concerned and they can appear to be lazy.

Poor language skills are a hallmark of a left brain imbalance, especially as a child gets older. These children have trouble learning and remembering almost everything. What they learn and retain one day is often gone the next. They have problems with reading and spelling because they can't identify the sound of letters. This can show up in their speaking ability as well. All this can be the result of a problem with visually processing words and sounds. Not only does this affect reading and speaking skills, these children can be bad at music and may not be able to carry a tune.

Children with left brain imbalances may have unique abilities to read people and situations and are afraid other kids think of them as stupid. They are very concerned about how they look and are acutely aware of how other kids are looking at them. They'll make a big deal over what they are wearing, acting out if they don't like an outfit you have chosen for them to wear.

If these kids overcome their shyness and insecurities, they can be very social. They are popular outside of the classroom and can take on the role as leader.

Left brain deficiencies are often diagnosed as:

- Acalculia (poor calculating skill)
- Central auditory processing disorder
- Dyslexia
- Dyspraxia (movement and coordination problems)
- Dysgraphia (poor handwriting)
- Learning disorder
- Language disorder

■ Processing disorders, such as auditory, visual, tactile, and smell
■ Reading disorder
■ Selective mutism

Traits of a Left Brain Deficiency

■ Procrastinates.
■ Is extremely shy, especially around strangers.
■ Is very good at body language (nonverbal communication).
■ Is well liked by other children and teachers.
■ Does not have any behavioral problems in school.
■ Understands social rules.
■ Has poor self-esteem, especially when it comes to academics.
■ Hates doing homework.
■ Is very good at social interaction.
■ Makes good eye contact.
■ Likes to be around people and enjoys going to parties.
■ Doesn't like to go to sleep-overs.
■ Not good at following routines.
■ Can't follow multiple-step directions.
■ Seems to be very in touch with feelings.
■ Jumps to conclusions.
■ Very aware of personal appearance.
■ Likes to look in the mirror.
■ Is self-conscious and feels being made fun of by others.
■ Generally is very easygoing.
■ Is difficult to motivate at times.

WHAT FDS IS NOT

It is important to keep in mind that if your child has any of the brain deficits profiled in this book, it does not mean the brain is damaged or ill in any way. What it means is that your child has a healthy brain that, for the various reasons already described, is not developing normally.

Completing the Master Hemispheric Checklist should help you ascertain what that problem is. The next step is taking the corrective action that is detailed in *Disconnected Kids* or enrolling your child in a Brain Balance Achievement Center.

If you haven't been able to identify a left or right brain deficit as a result of using the Master Hemispheric Checklist, your child still may have FDS. The next chapter should help you better figure this out.

· 5 ·

The Peter Pan Problem and the Immature Brain

I don't know whether you have ever seen a map of a person's mind. Doctors sometimes draw maps of other parts of you, and your own map can become intensely interesting, but catch them trying to draw a map of a child's mind, which is not only confused, but keeps going round all the time.

—J. M. BARRIE, *PETER PAN*

Were you surprised by the results you got from the Master Hemispheric Checklist? If so, it's not that unusual. It's likely you found the results were not favorable to only one side of the brain—you checked off just about as many right brain traits as left brain traits.

Is it possible your child has both a left brain *and* a right brain deficiency? Yes, it's possible. In fact, it's becoming more and more common.

So, what does it mean?

Assuming there is no unknown neurological or metabolic disease and you can rule out a psychological problem, mostly likely it means that the whole brain is maturing too slowly. It still means the child has FDS and that one side is probably lagging behind the other. However, both sides are not maturing at a speed that corresponds to the child's chronological age. This is what I call the Peter Pan Problem, which I first introduced in Chapter 1.

When I lecture to parents and describe the symptoms of right brain and left brain deficits, I point out the unevenness of skills that many parents notice when filling out the checklist. However, at times a parent will come up to me afterward and say that their child seems to have both a left and right brain deficiency. They can't detect any exceptional skills, only delayed ones. This may be what you're finding, too.

> More kids these days have brains that
> are too immature for their age.

We are seeing kids like this at our Brain Balance Achievement Centers more and more these days with the following telltale signs: They are not particularly motivated and seem to be somewhat lazy. They act as though they are entitled and expect to get everything just handed to them. They have poor diets and would be happy eating nothing but junk food. They're captivated by the television and video games. As they get older, they settle in with the status quo. They don't think much about the future and are content under the comfortable wings of their parents. Their parents remark about their immaturity and are concerned how they'll ever make it on their own.

And they should be concerned. These kids are refusing to grow up and take on responsibility, just like Peter Pan. Or, more precisely, their brains are refusing to grow up and express the genes that will build the skills required for kids to take on responsibility later in life.

Just as with a right or left brain deficiency, this type of whole brain immaturity does not mean the brain is damaged. It just means the brain and its neural networks are not getting proper and adequate stimulation for the brain to grow in timed sequence. In young low-functioning children, we sometimes find the brain is so immature that all skills are deficient for their age. Brain growth is out of sync. Like an out-of-tune orchestra, it is playing out of harmony. And we're finding this much more often in boys than in girls.

THE IMMATURE BRAIN

Remember the story of Peter Pan? He was a naughty child who could fly and refused to grow up because he wanted to stay a little boy forever. He recruited a bunch of boys and took them to the island of Neverland, where they could play with fairies and act childish all day. Only boys were allowed in Neverland, and they called themselves the Lost Boys. Peter Pan felt rejected by the adult world and, as a defense, he rejected what he perceived to be rejecting him. He would hide from adults, so he didn't have to interact with them. In truth, Peter was just fearful and insecure. He took avoidance behavior to the extreme—not unlike what we are seeing today in children with immature brains.

Peter Pan's personality has often been likened to autism spectrum disorder, which is characterized by a severe abnormality in social interaction and communication and severely limited interests. Autism spectrum disorder includes autism, Asperger's syndrome, and unspecified pervasive developmental disorder, which is also called atypical autism. Truth be told, Peter Pan and his Lost Boys all had signs of ADHD.

CHECKING FOR MILESTONES

One way to detect for FDS involving immaturity of the whole brain is by a close analysis of a child's developmental milestones. For example, did your child crawl, walk, and talk on schedule? Did he have the natural movements expected in infancy and early child-hood and that you've seen in other children?

Many pediatricians tell parents that every child is different and to not be concerned if a child is late reaching milestones. This is true, but only to a small degree. Missed milestones often indicate something is not happening in the brain when it should.

> Missed milestones often indicate something
> is not happening in the brain.

Osnat Teitelbaum and Philip Teitelbaum, PhD, of the University of Florida, demonstrated this more than ten years ago in a study in which they observed videos of babies interacting with their environment. The Teitelbaums found that they could predict a later diagnosis of an autism spectrum disorder in children as young as six months who had trouble rolling over and sitting up unassisted. (Brain disorders are rarely diagnosed before age three and usually when a child is older.)

The reason for this, the Teitelbaums found, was that these children hadn't yet let go of their primitive reflexes (also called infantile reflexes), so their more mature postural reflexes could take over. The areas of the brain that control motor skills were not maturing and taking over the responsibility. They were refusing to grow up.

PRIMITIVE REFLEXES AND WHY THEY'RE IMPORTANT

There are two things that make the human brain truly unique among all species, and it has nothing to do with the size of our brains. In fact, in proportion to body size, rodents have larger brains than humans do.

One is that the human brain can coordinate a large number of cells in both hemispheres to simultaneously fire in networks. This ability increases our processing capacity exponentially and is responsible for the unique intellectual abilities and self-consciousness we enjoy.

The second thing that makes the human brain unique is our ability to stand and walk upright on two feet. Walking is the most complex function performed by the brain.

There is a general rule in science: simple movements, simple brains; complex movements, complex brains. Simple and complex movements are directly connected to each other. In fact, you can't have one without the other.

To walk upright requires synchronization of both sides of the brain at precisely the same moment. It requires coordination of large groups of muscles on both sides of the body to work together in perfect timing. It sounds simple and easy enough because we do it without any thought. However, what we don't see is the mastery of the circuitry in the brain that makes it happen. Once we develop this ability on or near age one, we can lift ourselves up and walk. As the body continues to mature, the body develops more coordination and can complete more complex movements. We talk and start to develop social skills.

Because the brain is in early development, these abilities are driven by primitive reflexes—automated movements that require no thought. Primitive reflexes are the basic necessities of survival and are housed in the brainstem of the central nervous system. The development of the central nervous system begins at conception and continues in a regular sequence. Parts of this sequence are identified by the movement patterns, or reflexes, that occur as a child grows. Each reflex plays a part in the necessary growth of the fetus and infant. Each reflex also prepares the way for the next stage of development.

Primitive reflexes are important even before birth. They develop while in the womb to assist the birthing process. If they are faulty, a child may have a difficult birth. Breech is a sign that these reflexes may not be fully activated and symmetrical. In this case, a brain imbalance may be suspected or even noticed at birth.

When a baby is born, primitive reflexes allow for basic movement. These are the automated reflexes you see, such as curling of the legs and moving the head to suckle a mother's breast. They don't require any thought. They are instinctive. When a child is born by caesarean section, the baby isn't using these reflexes, which could affect the timing for inhibiting them.

At three to five months of age, primitive reflexes herald one of the first and most important milestones: rolling over. Movement of primitive reflexes activates the senses and organizes them in relationship to the rest of the body and surrounding world. This is the type of stimulation I discussed in Chapter 2 that is so essential to healthy brain development.

Muscle movement and sensory stimulation prompt genes to build the brain and grow the neurons and connections that advance a newborn from one milestone to the next. As the brain gets larger and more connections form, higher levels of brain function are ready to come into play. At this point, primitive reflexes, for the most part, are no longer necessary, so the brain inhibits them, allowing more complex motor reflexes, known as postural reflexes, to emerge. Primitive reflexes never completely disappear, but come under control of the brain. The brain breaks them up into bits and pieces and reassembles them to create smooth coordination of complex movements. And here's where trouble can begin.

If a child does not move enough to stimulate
the genes to build the brain, the brain
cannot develop properly.

If a child does not move enough to stimulate the genes to build the brain, the reflexes will not become inhibited. Because many of the primitive reflexes are bilateral, meaning they reside on both sides of the brain, it can create a delay in the maturity of the whole brain and lead to an imbalance characteristic of FDS.

When this happens, there is usually some other interference in play, such as environmental toxins, stress hormones excreted by the mother during pregnancy, or any of the other influences discussed in Chapter 3.

ON THE LOOKOUT FOR PETER PAN

If you took the Master Hemispheric Checklist and suspect your child has immaturity in both sides of the brain, there are a two other check-points that can help you pinpoint the problem. One is to go back and review the milestones during your child's first two years of life. You may have recorded them in a baby book or you may have to use your memory. (You can find a list of these milestones in Chapter 6.)

The other clue you can go after is your child's dominance profile—the side of the body your child favors to do such things as write, throw a ball, or look through a peephole.

Ideally, children should have a dominant side when it comes to using their hands, feet, eyes, and ears. This means that if a child is right handed, she should naturally use her right foot to kick a ball, favor her right eye to peak through a peephole, and cup her right ear when trying to overhear something.

Ideally, children should have a dominant physical side that is consistent from head to toe.

This does not mean all children who are left handed should be right handed, but it does mean all children who are left handed should naturally favor the left side from head to toe.

If your child has mixed dominance, meaning she may favor her right hand, ear, and eye but left foot, it is a sign of a brain imbalance, but it is also a big clue to an immature whole brain.

This mostly likely is a result of infantile reflexes that are still active in the brain. In Brain Balance, we must inhibit these reflexes before we can accurately assess the level and extent of the functional disconnect.

In addition to reviewing your child's milestones, taking the Mixed Dominance Test will help you ascertain if your child's brain has not completely inhibited its primitive reflexes. If the answers are not all right or all left, it is a sign of mixed dominance.

▶ Mixed Dominance Test

HAND

You likely already know if your child is left or right handed, but take this test anyway. Do this test outdoors.

1. Find a ball, such as a baseball, that is small enough for your child to catch with one hand. Stand a few feet away from your child and start tossing the ball back and forth. Little kids have a tendency to play catch with two hands, so you'll have to instruct your child to try to catch the ball with only one hand. Which hand did your child use?
2. Which hand does your child use to draw, hold a crayon, or write?
3. Which hand does your child use to brush his teeth?

FOOT

Foot preference is not something that is taught, such as being encouraged to use the right hand when learning to write. This exercise will tell you which foot is dominant.

1. Find a small, light-weight ball and roll it across the floor. Ask your child to kick it back to you. Repeat this three times.
2. Ask your child to take off her shoes and, while standing, to write her name on the floor with her toes. She doesn't have to actually finish this task. You want to find out which foot she uses. Do this on three different occasions, not in sequence.

EYE

1. To test your child's near vision, hand him a kaleidoscope or magnifying glass and ask him to look through it. Which eye does he use?
2. To test far vision, take a tube, such as one from a roll of paper towels, and ask your child to look through it at a small stationary object, such as a doorknob or light switch, using one eye. Hand the tube to your child by pointing at the center of the body and ask him to take it with both hands. Then, instruct him to hold it at arm's length, and slowly bring it toward the eye. Note which eye he uses to focus on the object. Go through the entire exercise three times with three different objects.

EAR

Ideally you should use a tuning fork for this test. A type called c128 is preferable. Demonstrate this task for your child before asking her to do it. Make sure you turn your head and put one ear to the tuning fork when demonstrating. If you don't have a tuning fork you can use a cell phone.

1. Hit the tuning fork and aim it about twelve inches in front of the middle of your child's face. Ask your child to turn her head without touching the tuning fork and listen to the sound.

   If you're using a cell phone, pick an appropriate time when you're on the phone and tell your child that someone (grandparent or friend) is speaking to her. Hold it out in front of her, again at the center of the body, instead of handing it to her, so she has to turn her head to listen.
2. Another way to do the ear test is to get in a room with your child with the door closed. Say you think someone is calling her name. Tell her to put her ear up against the door and listen. Hold the door shut, so she doesn't choose to open it instead.

Do one or all of these exercises three times, one right after the other, and note which ear the child uses.

FINDING PETER PAN

If these tests in addition to the Master Hemispheric Checklist point to a brain imbalance, you should use the program detailed in *Disconnected Kids* or enroll your child in a program at one of the Brain Balance Achievement Centers. (A list of centers can be found on page 303.)

You will also benefit immensely from setting family values and rules, as discussed in Chapter 7, and from following the Brain Balance Family Empowerment Program.

I have found that as you balance the brain, these primitive

reflexes will disappear, and children naturally adapt to a right or left side dominance. The behavior issues associated with a brain imbalance also disappear.

However, the behavior issues associated with a brain deficit—whether it be left, right, or the whole brain—can sometimes confuse parents. They see new behaviors in their kids that can hit them by surprise, mostly because they aren't what a parent expects to see. As the brain gets back in balance, good and bad behaviors are part of the program. This means that there are times when bad behavior is actually a good thing. I explain why in the next chapter.

· 6 ·

Behavior

WHEN BAD IS GOOD (AND VICE VERSA)

Only those who risk going too far can possibly
find out how far one can go.

—T. S. ELIOT

Behavior, like everything else involved with the brain, has two sides: good and bad. But, of course, every parent knows this. What most parents don't realize, though, is that there is left brain behavior and there is right brain behavior, and some good and some bad reside in both. So it only makes sense that you're going to see both good and bad in your child as the brain goes through its natural growth cycles.

So, bad can sometimes be good. The terrible twos is the most obvious example. A two-and-a-half-year-old who is a perfect little angel might make you think that you're the luckiest parents in the world, but it really isn't a good sign.

Problem is, in most situations, it isn't always easy for a parent to know when acting badly is actually a good thing and vice versa. This is especially true for parents of children with FDS.

THE MEANING OF BALANCED BEHAVIOR

Balanced behavior—that is, the stellar behavior every parent expects and would love to see—is the ability to respond and act appropriately in any given situation. It means a child's brain must have the flexibility—that is, the proper electrical signals—to jump back and forth between negative and positive emotions and behaviors. A child must be able to comprehend what behavior is appropriate in order to behave properly.

Unfortunately, this is a tall order for children with FDS. When a child has a brain imbalance, it means behavior is out of balance, too. Behaviors get stuck because one hemisphere is electrically underpowered. Your child isn't acting out to get back at you; she's acting out because this is what her brain is telling her to do.

Out-of-balance behavior can be displayed as temper tantrums, meltdowns, obstinacy, and disobedience, as is often the case in a right brain deficiency. Or it can be seen as withdrawal, shyness, compulsivity, and oppressiveness, as is usually seen in a left brain deficiency.

Displaying positive and negative behaviors is critical to normal brain development.

Actually, there is nothing abnormal about any of these behaviors—*if* they are occurring at the appropriate time in brain development. At each stage of development there are positive and negative emotions and behaviors that are not only normal but are critical to normal emotional and behavioral development. They become abnormal only when they hang around too long and occur at the wrong age, as is the case for kids with FDS. Even stereotypy, or what is referred to as stims, in which children flap their arms, rock back and forth, or run around in circles, is typical for a four- to five-year-old but not in an older child. Other things, such as stuttering, tics, obsessiveness, compulsivity, and oppositional behavior are all normal at a certain age. When new behaviors come into play, they go away. So, it's not the behavior that's out of sync, it's the timing!

Reward or Punishment?

Left brain deficiency calls for positive reinforcement.
Right brain deficiency calls for negative reinforcement.

Since all behaviors are built on approach and avoidance, the strategy you must use to contain them is through their motivational equivalent—reward and punishment.

A child acts out in one of two ways: approach or avoidance. If the child makes the correct choice, the behavior should be rewarded so that he repeats the behavior. It reinforces the behavior.

If the child makes the wrong choice, then the behavior should be punished in some way so the child doesn't repeat the behavior.

A child internalizes reward and punishment with different emotions. Reward produces happy, even euphoric emotions, which come from the brain's release of the chemical dopamine. This feeling can be addictive, so it can drive a child to act a certain way just so he can get the reward.

Punishment comes from the brain and the gut. It causes contractions in the gut muscles that produce a sick-to-the-stomach or pit-in-the-stomach feeling.

Reward is felt in the left hemisphere, and punishment is felt in the right hemisphere. This is the key to the strategies you will use to try to maintain discipline and control your child's behavior.

A child with a slower left brain is deficient in reward responsiveness and is overresponsive to punishment. The child with a weak or slower right brain is withdrawal deficient and overresponsive to reward. So to help motivate a left brain deficient child you must use reward activities. This means positive reinforcement. For the right brain deficient child, you use punishment, or negative reinforcement. Here's how it works.

THE LEFT BRAIN CHALLENGE
*Use the positive "If you do [behavior],
you will be rewarded" approach.*

To motivate the left brain deficient child, use positive reinforcement. Give your child a goal that he can achieve and reward him when he meets it. For example, make your child earn privileges like watching television or playing computer games or getting a new pair of sneakers. Punishment and negative reinforcement does not work on a child with a left brain deficiency. Rather, keep it positive: "If you do [behavior], you'll get [reward]." You stimulate with hope.

THE RIGHT BRAIN CHALLENGE
*Use the negative "If you don't [behavior],
you will get punished" approach.*

To motivate a child with a right brain deficit, you must use negative reinforcement. This does not mean that you take away something that she has earned; this is not a good tactic. Rather, you use punishment as reinforcement. For example, the punishment might be no TV or no computer time. It's really all about the emphasis. Your focus is: "If you don't do [behavior], you will not get [reward]." You stimulate with fear.

IT'S ALL ABOUT TIMING

A healthy brain develops like clockwork, flipping back and forth between left and right as genes respond on cue to environmental and sensory stimuli at a specific time in a child's growth.

Think of the brain as the atomic clock that governs three developmental clocks:

- **Physical:** Includes fine and major muscle (motor) development, so we can stand, walk, write, wave, knit, and physically get around; also governs sensory development, such as vision, hearing, and smell.
- **Emotional/social:** Drives behavior and our ability to interact socially and form relationships.
- **Cognitive:** Governs everything involved in learning skills, language, and intelligence.

These areas of development must be in exact rhythm with the brain's timing. If one or more of the clocks doesn't get wound properly by environmental and sensory stimuli, it will slow down and won't show up on time for its developmental rendezvous—the milestones you read about in baby books and your pediatrician looks for during well-baby visits. Suddenly, everything goes out of kilter, and it's hard to tell which clock or clocks are accurate and which ones aren't running on time.

The earliest sign of a potential developmental disability is when a child is late reaching or never reaches a certain milestone. The sooner a potential problem is identified, the sooner corrective action can be taken and the better the long-term outcome will be.

Most developmental problems could be identified a year or two sooner if closer attention were paid to milestones.

This is why I disagree with pediatricians who put normal development on a broad scale and tell parents that they shouldn't be too concerned if their child is late crawling, walking, talking, or achieving other major milestones.

Yes, children are individuals and therefore unique, and each one develops at his or her own pace. However, this is true only to a degree—and in my experience it is a small degree. Sure, if a child doesn't walk at exactly one year, it's not of immediate concern. But if a child isn't walking by fourteen months, then it *should* be a concern.

Typically, developmental problems are generally not even considered an issue until a child is three years old and not yet speaking. However, most brain imbalances could be identified at least a year and sometimes two years earlier if closer attention were paid to childhood milestones.

In addition to paying attention to the timing of milestones, parents should also take note that the three clocks of development are proceeding in a somewhat balanced way between the right and the left brains.

As you know from Chapter 2, the left and right hemispheres differ in function. For example, happiness, anger, and surprise are positive, or approach, behaviors that develop in the left brain, and sadness, fear, and disgust are negative, or avoidance, behaviors that develop in the right brain. Remember that motor, sensory, and cognitive skills are developing at the same time.

The two hemispheres also mature at different rates. For approximately the first three years, the right brain is developing faster than the left. Emphasis then shifts to the left brain for another three years or so, then starts flipping back and forth about every three years until around age thirteen.

WHEN DEVELOPMENT REGRESSES

There are periods of time when the brain goes through growth spurts. These spurts, which occur at specific times during the first four and a half years of life, are characterized by regressions or temporary changes in behavior and other skills, such as language or fine motor ability, and are often associated with temperamental or difficult times.

For example, children going through normal brain development will experience a regression in their language skills around seventeen or eighteen months. Their handwriting might start to look like it's getting worse. They might even start wetting the bed.

In children who later are found to have autism, this language regression is dramatic. This also happens to be the age for certain vaccinations, which leads parents to erroneously believe that the regression in language is a reaction to the vaccines.

These normal regressions occur at the following ages:

- Five months
- Nine months
- Eleven months
- One year, five months
- Two years, two months
- Three years, one month
- Three years, nine months
- Four years, five months

IS THIS GOOD OR BAD BEHAVIOR?

At our Brain Balance Achievement Centers, we correct brain imbalances in children by stimulating the weak side of the brain through a series of motor, sensory, and cognitive exercises. (You can read more about the Brain Balance Program in Part 3.)

We're finding that some parents and teachers of kids who go through the program and parents who use the Melillo At-Home Brain Balance Program (detailed in *Disconnected Kids*) are confused by the changing behaviors they are witnessing in their children. Almost all parents, we found, judge the benefits of the program by the *immediate* behavioral changes they see at home and in school. For example, a polite and overly demure child who had a right brain deficiency may suddenly start yelling and acting out. This is merely a sign that the right brain is finally in touch with the negative behavioral traits that were suppressed because the brain was out of balance.

The brain cannot leapfrog missed behaviors. It must go through all the stages of development it missed on its way to becoming a fully functional organ, and this includes bad behaviors. They are necessary, expected, and desirable. As in normal brain development, the child will experience the behavior and eventually pass through it. And here's the good news: A child will usually go through these stages rather quickly. A year's worth of catch-up may only take a few weeks.

> A brain cannot leapfrog behaviors. It has to go through all stages on its way to becoming a fully functional organ.

This means that all behavior changes parents are seeing in their child, both good and bad, almost always are a sign of positive change in the brain.

As a child's brain neurology starts to respond to stimulation, behavior definitely does change, and what that behavior will be depends on where the deficits are, the severity of the deficits, and the child's age.

A child with a right hemisphere delay who had too much positive emotion and behavior will exhibit exaggerated negative characteristics while the right brain is catching up to the left. The exact opposite will show up in a child with a left brain deficit. Likewise, there will be similar changes in a child's motor, sensory, and cognitive traits.

These changes will appear to be inappropriate for the child's chronological age, but it's not for the child's current brain age.

For example, a six-year-old child may have the left brain development of an eight-year-old but right brain development of a two-year-old. As we stimulate the child's right hemisphere, her personality suddenly turns into the terrible twos. She is experiencing emotion she never felt before. She'll show a sudden interest in food because she is really beginning to experience taste for the first time.

A seven-year-old child going from imbalance to balance may start displaying emotional outbursts. He may start saying no to everything and come across as oppositional, or he might get obsessive about his toys and compulsive about his looks. At age two you would expect this and not think twice about it, but at age six a parent might think the child is getting obsessive-compulsive disorder. However, the only thing really wrong with the child is that his whole brain is not acting like a six-year-old's—yet.

How to Handle Changing Brain Balance Behaviors

Your quiet six-year-old with a right brain deficit is going through Brain Balance and suddenly starts throwing tantrums like a two-year-old. How should you handle it?

The same way you would handle the behavior in a two-year-old. When a brain imbalance is involved, handle any behavior according to the child's brain age, not chronological age. For example, when a normal six-year-old starts throwing a tantrum like a baby, you should respond by immediately addressing the behavior and then use this as an opportunity to teach the child what they did wrong. Do not ignore the problem; it is a time to encourage the child to self-soothe independently. However, if that six-year-old is experiencing the terrible twos as a result of going through the process of correcting his right brain imbalance, then respond as you would to a two-and-a-half-year-old, meaning you should not react to the situation, because this can reinforce the behavior. Trying to reason with the two-and-a-half-year-old obviously does not work as it can with a six-year-old.

These new feelings and sensations are difficult, if not impossible, for the child to control. Without the knowledge about what is happening with the neurology in a child going through Brain Balance, these behaviors can be confusing and disconcerting to a child's parents, teachers, and siblings, and even to the child himself. It also leaves parents in a quandary as to how to respond to these behaviors.

In fact, parents and teachers can't know if any new behavior is normal or abnormal—or how to handle it—without understanding the progression of behaviors known as developmental milestones.

TRACKING BEHAVIOR DEVELOPMENT

There are both positive and negative behaviors that are normal, typical, and an essential part of brain development. But how do you know when a behavior is normal and when it is not?

From the very first day of life, there are milestones that a child should achieve at or near a certain age in behavior/emotional, motor, cognitive, and sensory development. Parents should be familiar with these milestones and know the progression of behaviors so they can spot a potential problem as early as possible.

I've created charts that offer much more than you'll get from the typical handouts you find in pediatrician offices or the list of milestones developed by the American Academy of Pediatrics that are published in many baby books. These charts will help parents:

- Understand the normal progression of behaviors that correspond with chronological age and other milestones.
- Follow the developmental pattern of the left and right hemispheres.
- Know how to respond to certain behaviors and avoid unwanted behaviors.
- Judge the mental age of a child with FDS.

- Anticipate changing behaviors in children going through the Brain Balance Program.
- Spot a potential abnormality to brain development.

My charts are based on the comprehensive "Physical, Cognitive, and Social/Emotional Developmental Manual" we use in our Brain Balance Achievement Centers. These charts are meant to be a guide for parents, not a diagnostic tool. As a parent, it is very important for you to get familiar with these stages of development so you can recognize what is and isn't normal behavior.

All growth is not simply a left or a right brain trait. Growth is usually occurring on both sides of the brain; however, growth is usually emphasized from one side to the other.

MELILLO AT-HOME BEHAVIORAL
ASSESSMENT CHART

Birth Through Six Months

For the first six months of life, baby does not feel love and affection. The smile you see on a newborn is probably based on brainstem activity and occurs during the stage of sleep called rapid eye movement (REM). Then between six and ten weeks, smiles begin to appear when baby sees something pleasing. Social smiling doesn't begin until ten to twelve weeks. At this time, familiar faces are more likely to elicit smiles than nonfamiliar ones. This is an early sign that memory is starting to develop.

Between three and five months, baby will smile when she begins to notice that she can control her own environment. This is called *mastery motivation*. The pleasure of success encourages her to try harder and to stick to tasks longer. Smiling turns to laughter by around four months, which is initially stimulated by tickling and physical contact.

► **Birth Through Six Months**

BEHAVIOR/EMOTIONAL TRAITS

- Depends on parents for feeding, changing, bathing, caressing
- Attaches to parents
- Is asocial
- Visually fixates on face; smiles
- Is soothed by rocking
- Communicates by crying
- Smiles spontaneously to mother's face, voice, smile
- Responds to one-on-one contact with others
- Enjoys being cuddled
- Responds to facial expressions and social stimuli (around five months)

PHYSICAL TRAITS

- Keeps hands in tight fists and makes only basic random movements
- Later begins to physically explore surroundings to learn about them
- Prefers human faces over other shapes and prefers black-and-white and high-contrast patterns to color
- Repeats infantile reflex movements to master them, which is stimulation for brain growth and inhibition of reflexes
- Doubles in weight (around four months—if this doesn't occur by six months it is a cause for concern)
- Makes jerky arm movements
- Brings hands near face
- Focuses on objects eight to twelve inches away

- Hears very well
- Recognizes voices of parents and some other people
- Smiles at the sound of parents' voices
- Pushes down on legs when feet are placed on a firm surface
- Opens and shuts hands
- Brings hands to mouth
- Grabs and shakes hand toys
- Watches faces closely
- Recognizes familiar objects and follows moving object with eyes
- Starts using hands and eyes in coordination
- Babbles and imitates some sounds
- Enjoys playing with other people
- May cry when playing stops
- Moves head from side to side when lying on stomach
- Raises head and chest when lying on stomach
- Supports upper body with arms when lying on stomach
- Stretches legs out and kicks when lying on stomach or back
- Recognizes objects and people at a distance

COGNITIVE TRAITS

- Vocalizes with intonation
- Responds to voices by turning head and eyes
- Recognizes parents
- Responds to friendly and angry tones
- Locates sounds not made directly at the ear level
- Recognizes own voice
- Vocalizes when sees toys
- Vocalizes at image in mirror
- Makes simple sounds (such as *da-da*, *ba-ba*)
- Begins to fear strangers
- Begins to imitate actions

- Begins to prefer more complex sounds
- Coos (at four to five months)
- Is curious and interested in environment (at four to five months)
- Babbles and starts to imitate sounds (around six months)

PRIMITIVE REFLEXES

Primitive reflexes are part of normal development and should be evident during a baby's first six months. They help baby with automatic functions, such as breathing, heartbeat, and immunity. (Why primitive reflexes are important to normal development is explained in Chapter 4.)

The following chart categorizes the primitive reflexes by age.

PRIMITIVE REFLEXES BY AGE

Birth to 6 months	Breast-feeding Sucking Grasping Startle reflex to falling or loud noise Propping self up with arms Rolling over Playing with food
3 months	Turning head at ninety-degree angle
3 to 5 months	Rolling from side to side
5 months	Purposeful grasp
4 to 6 months	Reflexes should disappear during this time

HOW NEWBORNS PLAY

Babies begin to play through sensory exploration of their own bodies, and they will repeat satisfying bodily actions, such as certain movements and listening to the sound of their own voice.

This type of play begins the experience of approach and avoidance behaviors. Approach, a left brain activity, is displayed as joy, surprise, and interest. Avoidance, a right brain learning, is displayed as distress, frustration, fear, anger, and shyness.

ENCOURAGING ATTACHMENT

Immediately and consistently respond to a baby's cries of distress. The importance of frequent, loving touch—holding and stroking, for example—cannot be overemphasized. It helps a baby feel safe and will encourage her to start feeling her own body. Babies increase in weight and are more social when they are cuddled often. Play with your child as often as possible. Even small infants like games such as peek-a-boo.

> The importance of frequent, loving touch cannot be overemphasized.

Babies don't feel attachment during their first six months. However, attachment disorder becomes a concern if your baby doesn't start to bond by six months.

You know that your baby is attaching to you if she:

- Seeks physical contact when she is in pain or distress.
- Smiles when she sees you and when she starts to make eye contact.
- Cries when you leave and shows joy when you return.

Six Months to One Year

In the second half of the first year, usually around nine months of age, babies become attached to their primary caregiver and begin to show much affection by kissing and hugging.

During this time, your baby will develop full-color vision and have normal distance vision. He will start to drool more and start teething.

Primitive reflexes should be inhibited by this time, and you will notice postural reflexes fully emerging, beginning with crawling on the stomach, then creeping on the hands and knees, then cruising on furniture. Other obvious traits of this transition include the following actions:

- Head lag disappears.
- Can reach for objects.
- Can transfer objects from hand to hand.
- Plays with feet.
- Exercises body by stretching, moving.
- Touches genitals.
- Rocks on stomach for pleasure.

► **Six Months to One Year**

BEHAVIOR/EMOTIONAL TRAITS

- Develops approach (positive) and avoidance (negative) behaviors
- Learns trust in self, caretakers, environment
- Enjoys being near people and being played with
- No longer smiles indiscriminately
- Responds gaily to play interactions with others
- Cries, smiles, kicks, coos, and laughs to attract social attention
- Rejects confinement
- Cries when other children cry

- Recognizes different tones of voice and responds appropriately
- Interprets emotional expression of familiar adults
- Mimics simple actions of others
- Begins to recognize self as an individual apart from mother
- Is learning to cooperate
- Shows guilt at wrongdoing
- Actively seeks to maintain interactions with adult
- Tries to alter mother's plans through persuasion or protest
- Displays separation anxiety when apart from mother
- Is developing a sense of humor
- Teases and tests parental limits
- Demonstrates affection
- Discriminates positive and negative attention
- Doesn't recognize self in mirror; responds as if it were someone else
- Forms attachment to mother (or primary caregiver)
- Expresses fear, affection, persuasion, protest, guilt
- Is curious to explore environment
- Shouts for attention (around eight months)
- Is socially interactive and plays games such as patty-cake (around nine months)
- Develops stranger anxiety (around eleven months)
- Develops separation anxiety (around eleven months)
- Plays alone (around eleven months)

PHYSICAL TRAITS

- Sits up
- Supports almost all own weight when standing
- Supports whole weight on legs when held upright
- Reaches for object with hand
- Transfers objects from one hand to the other
- Picks up dropped object

- Rolls from back to stomach on both sides
- Sits in a high chair with a straight back
- Sits on the floor with lower back support
- Sleeps six- to eight-hour stretches at night
- Uses voice to express joy and displeasure
- Distinguishes emotions by tone of voice
- Explores objects with hands and mouth
- Struggles to get out-of-reach objects
- Enjoys playing peek-a-boo
- Shows an interest in mirror images
- Sits in tripod (around seven months)
- Pushes head and torso up off the floor (around seven months)
- Rakes with hands (around seven months)
- Can go from belly to sitting up easily (around nine months)
- Crawls on hands and knees (around nine months)
- Pulls self up to stand (around nine months)
- Stoops to recover objects (around nine months)
- Can oppose fingers to thumb and can move fingers individually (around nine months)
- Has hand–eye coordination but no hand preference (around nine months)
- Begins walking (around one year)

COGNITIVE TRAITS

- Uses one or more words with meaning (may be fragment of a word)
- Understands simple instructions, especially if vocal or physical cues are given
- Practices inflection
- Is aware of the value of speech
- Follows a fast-moving object with eyes
- Controls own response to sounds

- Responds to own name
- Babbles chains of consonants (*ba-ba-ba-ba*)
- Understands several words
- Says *mamma, papa*, and at least one or two other words
- Understands simple commands
- Imitates animal sounds
- Associates words with objects
- Wants objects not in sight
- Points with index finger
- Waves bye-bye
- May grow attached to object
- Experiences separation anxiety; may cling to parents
- Wanders away from parents to explore familiar settings
- Understands more than can say (by seven months)
- Knows parents from others (by nine months)
- Begins trial-and-error problem solving (by nine months)
- Has a twenty-word listening vocabulary (around one year)
- Begins symbolic thinking (around one year)
- Points to pictures in books in response to verbal cues (around one year)
- Understands object permanence (around one year)
- May use single words (around one year)
- Has more advanced receptive language than expressive language (around one year)

HOW A CONSCIENCE IS MADE

Babies at this age lack a conscience, so they still lack empathy and kindness. To develop a moral sense of right and wrong, babies must first experience the emotions that are associated with the consequences of conduct, such as anxiety, guilt, remorse, and discomfort.

These are the emotional underpinnings of conscience that begin to emerge slowly after the first birthday.

> To develop a moral sense of right and wrong,
> babies must first experience emotions
> associated with the consequences of conduct.

Before this time, babies lack an identity as separate from others. This makes it impossible for them to feel emotions connected to the well-being of others.

When these emotions don't appear, it is a sign of an underdeveloped right brain.

NORMAL LANGUAGE MILESTONES

Age	Milestone
3 months	Cooing begins
2 to 7 months	Vocal experimentation begins, starting with vowel sounds, then consonants
4 to 8 months	Baby begins to babble (note: even deaf babies babble)
8 to 12 months	Babbling starts to sound like language
1 year	Uses one or more word with meaning
12 to 18 months	Begins to parrot parents in attempt to speak

One Year Old

Age one to two is a busy time for baby, as the brain is busy developing the right brain's notorious, but very important, terrible twos. Cognitive learning also becomes very active at this time.

This is the age of learning nonverbal communication, which

leads to language. It is the beginning of the mental steps associated with the problem-solving process. "If I step on this toy, I am going to break it" is an example of consequential thinking, which emerges at this time. Divergent thinking—figuring out that there are many different ways to achieve the same goal—is also developing.

These skills involve physical interaction with the environment and practical exploration. They require a combination of logical left brain skills and creative, abstract right brain skills.

▶ One Year Old

BEHAVIOR/EMOTIONAL TRAITS

- Starts to show independence
- Cooperates by helping put things away
- May become angry if activities are interrupted
- Begins to realize he can't have everything his own way
- Shows anger through aggressive behavior; may hit, bite, or fight over a toy
- Has awkward social relationships with other children
- Engages in social laughter
- Has an almost complete range of emotional expressions
- Seeks comfort from parents—safe-base exploration
- Begins the terrible twos, including being willful and stubborn and throwing tantrums (between 12 and 18 months)
- Displays both types of joint attention (18 months)

PHYSICAL TRAITS

- Engages in imitation, parallel, and symbolic play
- Has one to eight teeth
- Walks holding on to furniture, and possibly a few steps without support

- Walks with help or alone
- Begins to run
- Kicks a ball
- Sits without assistance
- Bangs two blocks together
- Turns pages of book by flipping many at a time
- Has a precise pincer grasp
- Sleeps eight to ten hours at night and takes one to two naps a day
- Gets into hands-and-knees position
- Explores objects in many ways (shaking, banging, throwing, dropping)
- Begins to use objects correctly (drinking from cup, brushing hair)
- Finds hidden objects easily
- Finds an image by name
- Gets on a small chair unassisted
- Walks stairs holding with one hand
- Uses a spoon and cup with help to feed self
- Pulls toys while walking
- Carries large toy or several toys while walking
- Climbs on and off furniture without help
- Scribbles with crayon
- Builds tower of four blocks or more
- Triples from birth weight, and height should increase by 50 percent; head circumference should be equal to that of the chest (by age two)

COGNITIVE TRAITS

- Uses exclamations, such as *oh-oh!*
- Tries to imitate words
- Responds to the word *no* and simple verbal requests
- Has a vocabulary of five to twenty words
- Can say ten or more words when asked

- Has a vocabulary made up chiefly of nouns
- Repeats a word or phrase over and over
- Is able to follow simple commands
- Can name a number of objects common to surroundings
- Combines words into short sentences
- Shows affection
- Listens to a story or looks at pictures
- Identifies one or more body parts
- Frequently imitates
- Can take off some clothes
- Begins to feel a sense of ownership, identifying people and objects by saying *my*
- Picks up objects while standing, without losing balance (by 15 months)
- Learns through imitating complex behaviors (around 15 months)
- Knows objects are used for specific purposes (around 15 months)
- Speaks two-word sentences (around 18 months)

OVERCOMING SEPARATION ANXIETY

The concept of object permanence means children understand that when something is out of sight it does not mean that it disappears and no longer exists. Until they understand this, babies believe that when their parents are out of sight they do not exist. This is the insecurity known as *separation anxiety*.

> Never respond to a child's separation anxiety by sneaking out of the house.

Until they understand this, they may scream and cry and hold on to you for dear life if you are headed for the door. This is normal!

Never respond to this behavior by sneaking out of the house to avoid a tantrum. This affects your child's basic trust and can trigger worse anxiety. If you do try to trick your child, then when you say, "Mommy will come right back," he won't believe you. The best response is to face the tantrum, console your child, and assure him that you *will* be back.

NORMAL STAGES OF FEAR

Age	Kinds of Fear
Birth to 6 months	Loss of support (falling), loud noises
7 to 12 months	Strangers, unexpected objects
1 year	Separation from parents, strangers, injury, toilets
2 years	Separation, loud noises, animals, dark rooms, large objects and machines, changes in environment

PARROTING IS NORMAL AT THIS AGE

Repeating the last words a child hears, medically known as *echolalia*, is a normal stage of language development at this age. Mirror neurons—the foundation of nonverbal communication and the basis of learning emotional expression (a right brain activity)—are just becoming active.

At this stage, a child does not understand words but is learning what you are saying through your body language and will automatically start to imitate and mimic what she sees and hears. This is initially stimulated in large part by a mother's interactions with her baby, which triggers a reflex that makes a child mimic facial expressions. This is how a baby learns that smiling is a happy emotion, and when she mimics it, she's learning to feel her own emotions. This is the foundation of nonverbal communication, social skills, and empathy. Once nonverbal skills have developed, language skills start to emerge, which will include parroting words and phrases.

Children with autism are often echolalic because their brain is stuck at this early stage of development, a sign of abnormal timing in brain growth.

PROMOTING PROBLEM-SOLVING SKILLS

Problem-solving skills develop through trial and error. Children must be given the opportunity to try, fail, and then try again until they succeed.

Persistence is the key to developing good problem-solving abilities, but it can be stifled by overindulgent parents who never let their child struggle with anything. As a result, such children enter adolescence poorly equipped for the frustrations of life. Instead, these children master the skill of getting the parent to solve the problem for them. They throw a fit when something becomes too difficult and will usually quit and give up. After a while, these children become unmotivated and lazy and develop low self-esteem.

> Children must experience how to struggle
> to learn problem-solving skills.

Self-esteem is established by making yourself do something you didn't think you could do—in other words, persistence. Also, studies show that allowing children to take the lead during play leads to the development of persistence.

Two Years Old

Somewhere after the second birthday (and again during the early teens) your child will start to show autonomy—or, in other words, enter the full-blown cycle known as the terrible twos. This is important as this is the time when toddlers are learning to act on their own and think for themselves. It is the reason for the push-pull between dependence and independence that parents and children struggle with.

This is the age when you see your child grow into a little person by leaps and bounds. By age two, children normally are half the height they'll be as an adult, having gained two to three inches and four to five pounds in the previous year. The awkward stage of walking is over, and kids are starting to dress themselves in simple clothing—though their couture selection may give you pause. They should have day and nighttime control over bladder and bowels.

This is the age of abstract thinking. Kids at this age think without acting, but they can now construct a mental image of the world and enjoy imitating what they see. They are now storing these images in long-term memory.

This is an age of key milestones and, once they are achieved, language growth explodes. They'll learn approximately ten new words a day. Age two is when sentences start to form and pronouns, such as *I*, come into play. Children of this age can comprehend verbs, plurals, and past tenses. *No*, a right brain word, comes into use before the word *yes*, a left brain word.

Nevertheless, with all this talk going on, rhythm and fluency are often poor, and volume and pitch are not yet well controlled.

Between the ages of two and three, kids are still egocentric and have not yet developed a clear boundary between themselves and the outside world. They see all property as an extension of themselves.

Toddlers build a sense of self that is very objective: "I am a person," "I am separate from others," "I am a boy (or girl)." Eventually they will build a self-image that is purely subjective—one that may be based on the opinions of others around them.

Mother continues to be very important in baby's life, as separation anxiety may still be apparent at this age. By the time children are near their third birthday, they should be leaving the explosive terrible twos behind and learning to be calm, balanced, lovable, engaging, enthusiastic, and appreciative. They can understand the feeling of pride when they are good and become embarrassed when they have been bad. They are understanding how to empathize with others.

► **Two Years Old**

BEHAVIOR/EMOTIONAL TRAITS

- Is emotionally attached to toys or objects for security
- Defends own possessions but begins to share
- Asks for wants
- Knows gender identity
- Screams, throws temper tantrums for little cause
- Labels self and others by gender (by age two and a half)
- Participates in simple group activity such as singing and dancing (by age two and a half)
- Has a little interaction with other children (by age two and a half)
- May have an imaginary friend (by age three)
- Expresses affection warmly (by age three)
- Develops ritualistic routine (by age three)

PHYSICAL TRAITS

- Turns a doorknob
- Turns a book one page at a time
- Stacks six to nine blocks
- Kicks a ball without losing balance
- Runs with better coordination, even though the stance may still be wide
- May be ready for toilet training
- Should have the first sixteen teeth (the actual number of teeth can vary)

- Can balance briefly on one foot
- May walk up the stairs with alternating feet
- Can easily place small objects in a small opening
- Copies a circle
- Pedals a tricycle

COGNITIVE TRAITS

- Has a vocabulary of 150 to 300 words
- Can count three objects
- Can use two pronouns correctly
- Is beginning to use words *my* and *mine*
- Responds to commands such as "Show me your eyes (nose, mouth, hair)"
- Understands two-step command ("Give me the ball and then get your shoes")
- Can put on simple clothing
- Communicates simple needs (thirst, hunger, bathroom)
- Organizes phrases of two to three words
- Has increased attention span
- Uses more complex toys
- Understands sequence of putting toys, puzzles together
- Outgrows separation anxiety
- Recognizes self in mirror
- Is no longer confused by hiding places (by age two and a half)
- Develops representational thought (by age three)
- Can think without acting (by age three)

TERRIBLE TWOS: WHAT'S NORMAL, WHAT'S NOT

Temper tantrums, meltdowns, obsessive-compulsive behavior—commonly known as the terrible twos—are like a thunderstorm caused by the clash of positive left brain behavior trying to move in on negative right brain behavior. Until the left brain takes over its dominance for the next few years, emotions will swing back and forth during this period of adjustment.

This is the age when kids are starting to get in touch with their bodies and are starting to feel things. They are feeling emotions they never felt before, and they don't quite understand them.

Also, they are now beginning to discriminate taste—they discover sweets—and recognize what they like and don't like.

They'll scream for candy or a cookie and become extremely upset if they don't get it because they want it so badly. They can seem obsessive or compulsive because they want things all the time. They also develop strong dislikes—baths and certain foods are common. They'll scream and yell and get emotional if you try to make them do something they don't like or want. They'll throw an extreme tantrum in a restaurant or store. They'll become extremely oppositional, just like a child with oppositional defiant disorder (ODD), but it is part of normal development.

> A child's struggle to assert independence is an important part of brain development.

Understand that children at this age are going through a major struggle for independence and autonomy. They are trying to establish boundaries between themselves and their parents. The way they do this is to assert their independence and do the exact opposite of what you want. This declaration of independence is a huge step in normal development.

Many parents see this as an act of defiance and view it as a threat to their own authority. They are determined to show their child that back talk will not be tolerated. As stressful as it may be to hear this, punishing typical terrible twos behavior is sending the wrong message because it is saying that a child's desire for independence is unacceptable. This message may delay the development of his or her autonomy. It can interfere with the development of a coherent sense of self.

The Struggle for Independence

The struggle between dependence and independence occurs at two primary stages of brain development: between the ages of eighteen months and three years and then again in the early teen years. This can also be seen as a time of transitioning from right hemisphere to left hemisphere development.

In the toddler years, this struggle will be exhibited as emotional extremes of joy and anger, the classic symptoms of the terrible twos. These tantrums result from frustration because kids can't yet master tasks, communicate their desires, or understand why things are as they are. They feel very intense emotions that they can't express verbally, so they may vent these emotions through tantrums or tics. It is important not to make children of this age repress or feel guilty about anger.

In the early teen years, the brain is once again transitioning to left brain dominance, and children are being pulled between a need for independence and exploration and the fear of the unknown and the need to feel secure. They are not thinking about the consequences of their behavior.

During adolescence, identity is fluid, constantly changing and evolving as teens try to figure out who they are. An important part of the process of forming one's identity is experimentation with different activities and roles, which often includes risky behavior that sometimes includes engaging in crime.

Your best approach for minimizing or avoiding defiant or oppositional behavior is to allow your child to win some of her battles. Allow her to feel as if she is in control of certain situations and decisions.

Children who feel as if they have no control over anything will fight and resist almost everything their parents or teachers want. By allowing them to have some control, you are allowing them to develop their independence and autonomy.

At this age, terrible twos behavior is perfectly normal two or three times a week, and on average, you can expect toddlers to comply with parental commands about two thirds of the time. However, if the behavior is more frequent or continues beyond age four, the behavior switches from normal to abnormal. You should consider having your child professionally evaluated.

LANGUAGE: WHAT'S NORMAL, WHAT'S NOT

These are the signs of normal language development:

- **Eighteen months:** Speaks up to 20 words.
- **Two years:** Speaks up to 270 words and two- to three-word sentences. Uses pronouns, simple adjectives, and adverbs.
- **Two and half years:** Speaks up to 425 words and is using more adjectives and adverbs. Announces intentions and asks questions.
- **Three years:** Speaks 900 words and three- to four-word sentences. Is aware of time and understands stories.

These are the signs of delayed language development:

- **Eighteen months:** No single words.
- **Two years:** Speaks 10 words or less.

■ **Two and a half years:** Vocabulary of less than 100 words; cannot form two-word phrases.

■ **Three years:** Vocabulary less than 200 words; no sentences; clarity less than half the time.

NORMAL PLAY: THE AGE OF MAKE-BELIEVE

Does your toddler or did your child have an imaginary friend? If so, consider it a good thing, as studies show it is associated with better social skills and creativity. An estimated 65 percent of preschoolers have imaginary friends.

Around age two or possibly even before, children start to incorporate inanimate objects into pretend play. Toward the end of the second year, dolls become initiators and recipients of make-believe play.

There are other types of play behavior you can expect at this age:

■ Parallel play or onlooker play (the child plays side by side with other children, but there is very little actual interaction between them).

■ Symbolically uses objects and self in play, such as playing house.

■ Beginning of cooperative play.

■ Imitating mother and using miniature toy versions of household equipment, such as a stove.

■ Participates in simple group activities.

To encourage this type of play, you should:

■ Allow your child to help around the house and participate in the daily family responsibilities.

■ Encourage and provide the necessary space for physical activity.

■ Encourage play that involves building and creativity.

■ Provide safe toy versions of adult tools and equipment.

NEED–REJECT SYNDROME IS NORMAL AT THIS AGE
One minute your child wants to cuddle and the next he's jumping out of your lap to go exploring. One minute he's screaming to be picked up and the next he's yelling even louder about wanting to be put down.

So what's going on?

Need–reject syndrome is a classic symptom of brain development that's transitioning from right brain (avoidance) dominance to left brain (approach) behavior. One minute your child is afraid and has separation and stranger anxiety so wants to be held—and then suddenly left brain behavior starts to rule and he wants to be on his own.

This is another important way a child learns to establish autonomy, and it is an important stage of brain development—one that you'll experience again in an even more intense way in the teen years.

So, how should you react?

You can best secure a loving relationship with your child and foster autonomy by giving him the freedom to move away from you and toward other objects and people. Always welcome him with open, loving arms when he's ready to return to you.

Three Years Old

Between the ages of three and four, toddlerhood is in full swing, and the theme on your child's mind is autonomy. It can be a time of great frustration for parents as their children test the limits on what foods to eat, when play time must end, and when it's time to go to bed.

Behavior is inconsistent at this age and temper tantrums come into play. Children are eager to please. They can be calm, collected, and capable at times and insecure, anxious, and bossy at others. They don't understand that you may have a different perspective than their own, which comes across as being obstinate.

You will find that your little one suddenly finds other people and children more interesting than you. This is the beginning of childhood participation in socialization, and it is a time of stormy self-will, stubbornness, and negativity. The frustration this behavior brings you will be offset by your captivity with your child's vivid imagination and inability to separate fantasy from reality.

You'll notice an explosion in your child's vocabulary, even though about 90 percent of the time you may not be able to understand everything you are being told. Children are now beginning to learn syntax and grammar, and they are beginning to reason: "I know what to do when I'm sleepy, hungry, or cold."

You'll notice a longer attention span, though kids still have a poor understanding of time, values, and sequence of events.

Normal growth continues with the rule of threes: 3 years, 3 feet, and 33 pounds. Kids also are toilet trained. You'll find your child is a little wiggler who can't sit still and always wants to play with something and other kids, but not always in a friendly way.

▶ Three Years Old

BEHAVIOR/EMOTIONAL TRAITS

- Shares toys, takes turns with assistance
- Begins to learn to take responsibility
- Shows affection for younger siblings
- Engages in associative group play
- Interprets emotions from facial expressions and intonation
- Engages in genital exploration
- Plays cooperatively

- Has no sense of privacy
- Has stereotypical understanding of gender roles
- Has a simplistic idea of good and bad behavior; wants to please parents, but behavior is inconsistent (by age four)

PHYSICAL TRAITS

- Has daytime control over bowel and bladder functions (may have nighttime control as well)
- Can briefly balance on one foot
- May walk up the stairs with alternating feet
- Stacks more than nine blocks
- Can easily place small objects in a small opening
- Can copy a circle
- Is starting to get physically active; can't sit still for long
- Throws balls, though clumsily
- Refines complex skills (hopping, jumping, climbing, running)
- Rides big-wheeled and regular tricycles
- Is cutting with scissors and drawing shapes
- Is getting better at handwriting

COGNITIVE TRAITS

- Uses pronouns *I, you*, and *me* correctly
- Uses some plurals and past tenses
- Uses pronouns *he* and *she*
- Knows at least three prepositions (usually *in, on, under*)
- Knows and can point to major parts of the body
- Easily handles three- to four-word sentences
- Has a vocabulary of nine hundred to a thousand words
- Uses verbs more often
- Understands most simple questions
- Asks a lot of questions

- Dresses self and needs help only with laces, buttons, and other fasteners
- Feeds self without difficulty
- Acts out social encounters through play activities
- Fears imaginary things
- Leaves out important facts when speaking
- Draws primitive image of self (by age four)

WILLFUL AND SELFISH? CONSIDER IT NORMAL

With the emergence of autonomy comes independent thinking, and this is the age when you'll see it big-time. Children between the ages of three and four understand that they can affect their environment and will start to exert their will into situations. This can once again show up as temper tantrums and lead to power struggles between parents and toddlers—and toddler to toddler.

As noted earlier, this represents a transition from right (avoidance) to left (approach) behavior. Your child will transition back and forth from needing security to needing to explore and be independent. You can expect your child at this age to comply with your demands and wishes about two thirds of the time. If it is more frequently, consider it abnormal behavior.

Children at this age are naturally selfish and self-centered. They don't care about others' feelings; they care only about their own. Pay attention when you see this and make sure to take the proper corrective action. Studies show that parents who consistently react to this type of misbehavior by focusing attention on the child whose feelings are hurt promote feelings of empathy and altruism in their own children. This is because conscience is beginning to take root at this age and children are beginning to understand things and actions as being good or bad.

Corporal punishment, such as spanking or slapping, is not the answer. It sends the wrong message: that physical violence can get you what you want. Studies show that children are much more likely to internalize their parents' wishes and to follow the rules without having to be reminded when parents treat them with warmth and sensitivity. Explain the rules clearly and don't use physical punishment.

BED WETTING: ACCIDENTS WILL HAPPEN
Most kids should be toilet trained by three and a half years, but it is normal for older kids to have accidents at night. This has to do with development of the frontal lobes—the seat of executive functions, or higher cognitive skills. The earliest area to develop in the prefrontal cortex is the area that controls urination. As this develops, children first develop voluntary control and then involuntary control at night. However, brain activity naturally decreases during the deep-sleep stage called rapid eye movement (REM), and in a child of this age, it drops even more, meaning wetting the bed at night can be expected.

Something else is also happening in the brain at this time. The brain's verbal language center is also housed in the frontal lobe and is built partly on top of this area. As a result, when children go through the language developmental growth spurt common at this age, they may experience a regression in urination control, and bed wetting may temporarily return. Regression of handwriting in right-handers is also common at this age.

A CRUCIAL TIME FOR FUN AND GAMES
Building social skills takes on importance at ages three and four, and you will find that play becomes much more important to children than is clinging to their parents.

It is important that you offer a safe environment in which your children can play and enough room for them to be physically active.

Encourage your children in creative play and in playing with others. Encourage learning by answering questions and providing activities related to each child's particular interests. Encourage children to learn simple chores such as picking up toys and straightening up their room. Welcome their help in small household tasks. Most important, always make sure your children are under constant supervision when playing.

These are the qualities of play you should be observing in children of this age:

- Joins in play with other children (associative play).
- Begins dramatic play—acting out whole scenes.
- Uses imaginative play with dolls.
- Still enjoys imaginary companions.
- Does things wrong purposefully to be silly.

Four Years Old

Children at this age are amazingly curious, though they still cling to Mom and home. Behavior also goes to extremes: They love a lot and they hate a lot. They love excitement, adventure, and anything new, though they still cannot tell the difference between fantasy and reality.

Personality comes through strongly at this age, as children are now more in control of their emotions. They are calm, secure, and balanced. As a result, you should start to see fewer and fewer temper tantrums. However, kids will rebel if your expectations are too excessive. They understand responsibility and will feel a sense of guilt when doing something wrong. This is the age when children start to show a romantic attachment for the parent of the opposite sex.

Children at this age love to talk and will use their extensive verbalization when carrying out activities—they even use words they don't fully understand. They may even lie and use profanity, depending on the home environment. Nothing is secret at this age, and they talk about anything and everything they see at home to whomever will listen.

They ask more questions at this age than any other. Though they are trying very hard to be independent, they still lack the moral concept of right versus wrong.

This is a good age to teach your children social skills and responsibility. Give them small chores, such as helping to set the table. Expose them to different stimuli by visiting local areas of interest.

► **Four Years Old**

BEHAVIOR/EMOTIONAL TRAITS

- Often indulges in make-believe
- Plays and interacts with other children
- Improves with taking turns and cooperating
- Is spurred on by rivalry in activity
- Understands social problem solving
- Shows interest in exploring gender differences
- Enjoys doing things for self
- Plays outside with minimum supervision; likes to be trusted
- Shows increased frustration tolerance
- Is better able to delay gratification
- Has rudimentary sense of self
- Understands concepts of right and wrong
- Has self-esteem that reflects opinions of significant others
- Is self-directed in many activities
- Views self as a whole person involving body, mind, and feelings
- Bosses and criticizes

- Exaggerates and boasts
- Commonly plays with imaginary friend(s)
- May show increased aggressive behavior
- Displays concern and sympathy
- Develops imaginary fears (dark rooms, for example)

PHYSICAL TRAITS

- Continues to improve balance
- Hops on one foot without losing balance
- Throws a ball overhand with coordination
- Can cut out a picture using scissors
- May not be able to tie shoelaces

COGNITIVE TRAITS

- Knows names of familiar animals
- Knows at least four prepositions or can demonstrate their meaning
- Names common objects in picture books or magazines
- Knows one or more colors
- Can repeat four digits when they are given slowly
- Can repeat four-syllable words
- Learns and sings simple songs
- Demonstrates difference between over and under
- Is able to vocalize most vowels, diphthongs, and the consonants p, b, m, w
- Repeats words, phrases, syllables, and even sounds
- Has a vocabulary of more than two thousand words
- Easily composes sentences of five to six words
- Is developing a sense of property
- Can count to six

> ▪ Understands concepts of longer and larger (for example) when the opposite is presented

PLAY MAKES A DRAMATIC LEAP

At four years old, children prefer to play with other kids than play with their parents. Imagination is in full swing. As observer rather than participant, expect the following:

▪ Dramatic play is closer to reality.
▪ Participation in imaginative play with self and others; likes to play dress up.
▪ Plays in groups of two to five children.

As a parent of a four- to five-year-old, you should:

▪ Encourage physical activity and provide the necessary space, both indoors and out.
▪ Encourage creative play.
▪ Teach your child how to participate in group play and how to follow the rules.

STUTTERING AND TICS NORMAL AT THIS AGE

Stuttering and tics give parents anxiety because they can be symptoms of a neurological disorder, but most parents don't realize that these "oddities" are really a natural part of brain development.

Repetitive movements and behaviors are involuntary actions that are done reflexively. Rocking, hand flapping, and clearing the throat are all examples of what is more commonly referred to as stims, or stereotypy.

Stims and tics develop when one side of the brain starts an action and the other side is too slow to stop it. It is especially common when kids get frustrated, angry, or excited.

When stims appear around age four, all kids are doing it so it doesn't seem unnatural at all. It only starts to become a problem when a child is slower at outgrowing them than others. If a child gets stuck in a behavior, it starts to become noticeable to everybody—parents, peers, and even the child. Other kids may make fun of them, and parents can get frustrated with them, causing these children to feel self-conscious.

> Stuttering and tics are natural at a certain
> age. Do not try to correct them.

The worst thing a parent can do in this situation is purposely try to make their child stop. Stims and tics are normal because they give the brain needed developmental stimulation. Initially, the parent should ignore the stims and let the child know it is okay.

If a child seems to be stuck too long, you can help change the behavior by initiating a new action or thought and redirecting the behavior. For example, give your child a ball, beanbag, or stress ball and tell her to squeeze it with the left hand. Tell her to think of her hand squeezing the ball. This will often stop the action but not reduce the stimulation she needs.

If stims continue or come on at an older age, you should speak to your doctor.

Five Years Old

Age five is a big year in the life of a child. It is generally the start of formal education—kindergarten. This is the age when left brain education skills start to blossom. Kids are reading and counting. They're fully engaged in language and can understand some of the more complicated aspects of English. For example, they can grasp the meaning of the doctor is running out of *patience* rather than *patients*. They are attaching words to feelings, which is helping them understand emotions and how to control them.

They are getting socially oriented and forming friendships. They are starting to strongly identify with the parent of the same sex.

They want to do what is expected of them, and they want to please. They are developing a respect for reasonable authority and will display their emotions freely and openly. Suddenly you realize that they are much more interested in spending time with their friends than with you. This is okay because it is all part of social development. They are learning to see themselves as others see them and identify their own strengths and weaknesses. They are finally able to distinguish fantasy from reality. Life is good, and they are feeling secure.

▶ Five Years Old

BEHAVIOR/EMOTIONAL TRAITS

- Willingly plays with most children in school
- Engages other children in play
- Plays fairly
- Engages other kids in role assignments
- Chooses own friends
- Has rapidly changing friendships
- Has situation-specific friendships
- Has one or two best friends of same sex
- Is aware of differences in gender roles
- Cooperates with others
- Leads as well as follows
- Is consistently sunny and happy

- Quarrels frequently but of short duration; forgets quickly
- Has frequent angry outbursts
- Can be disobedient
- May be jealous of classmates
- Can be hesitant, dawdling, overdemanding
- Is sometimes demanding, sometimes eagerly cooperative
- Understands concepts of right and wrong
- Apologizes for mistakes

PHYSICAL TRAITS

- Develops increased coordination
- Skips, jumps, hops with good balance
- Maintains balance standing on one foot with eyes closed
- Ties own shoelaces
- Shows increased skill with simple tools and writing utensils
- Can copy a triangle
- Spreads with a knife
- Gets first permanent teeth (by age six)

COGNITIVE TRAITS

- Can use many adjectives and adverbs spontaneously
- Generally uses grammatically correct speech
- Speaks intelligibly, in spite of articulation problems
- Can express all vowels and consonants
- Has a vocabulary over twenty-one hundred words
- Composes long sentences of eight to nine words and uses all parts of speech
- Understands opposites (big–little, hard–soft, heavy–light)
- Understands number concepts of four or more
- Counts to ten

- Defines common objects in terms of use (hat, shoe, chair)
- Understands three consecutive commands without interruptions
- Knows own age
- Can identify coins
- Understands concept of time (morning, noon, night, day, later, yesterday)
- Properly names primary colors and possibly many more
- Questions more deeply, addressing meaning and purpose
- Responds to why questions
- Accepts validity of other points of view (while possibly not understanding them)
- Demonstrates increased mathematical skill

THE AGE OF LEARNING TO READ

This is the age where brain building switches primarily to the left for the next few years. The fact that it is the beginning of formal education is no coincidence as the left brain is responsible for most early academic skills, such as reading, writing, and arithmetic.

As brain cells grow larger, the speed at which they process information gets faster. Brain cell communication becomes more coordinated, and networks in the brain are busy stimulating genes to turn on and build even more connections.

When a child is first starting to read and learning phonics, the brain has to process all of the rapidly changing sounds and associate them with letters. The brain processing speed of a five-year-old is still relatively slow compared to an older child, which means that kids of this age need more time to hear and process each syllable and match it to letters. This is why phonics is done slowly, accentuating and exaggerating each syllable. It's a skill technique known as phonemic awareness, and at five to six years of age, this awareness is still developing.

If the child's brain is not processing quickly enough, each sound, especially the first sound of a word, can be difficult to distinguish. For example, the only difference between *ba*, *pa*, and *da* is the sound of the *B*, *P*, or *D* in the first few milliseconds. If the child can't process the sounds quickly enough, they'll all look and sound identical. There is no way of distinguishing one from the other. As a result, a child may use them interchangeably. They may transpose letters or reverse letters at first—the classic symptoms of dyslexia. However, in a five-year-old, this phenomenon is not the result of dyslexia; it is normal.

It's common for children learning to read to
reverse letters until they are about age seven.

Almost all children who begin to read will stumble over sounds and letters. Processing difficulties are common when kids first start to read. The brain is not yet mature enough to process words as quickly as is necessary to read.

Read, Read, Read!

The primary predictor of a child's reading ability and success is school is mostly related to one single factor: the amount of books found in the home!

As a parent, the best thing you can do to raise children with healthy brains is encourage reading in your household. Read books to them and with them and encourage them to read on their own. Lead by example: Pick up a book and let your kids see you reading. If you never read a book, chances are your child won't either.

It's common for children to reverse letters up to age seven, especially their *p*'s and *q*'s, because they don't pay too much attention to the way letters are oriented. However, they still should be able to read at age level.

Some parents get anxious when they see their kids struggle with reading. If the problems I just described continue beyond age seven, then you should have your child evaluated for dyslexia or central auditory processing disorder.

WHEN TALKING TO YOURSELF IS GOOD
When adults talk to themselves, people think they're a little crazy. But don't put that same tag on little kids who talk to themselves because it's a positive sign of brain development.

Self-talk is often seen in children with a high level of fantasizing. Such children tend to be better at concentrating on tasks, have better self-control, and come up with new rather than stereotyped responses.

So, if your five-year-old tends to talk to herself, let it be. Do not criticize or try to get her to stop. However, if she is older when she starts talking to herself, you may want to bring the behavior to the attention of your doctor.

NORMAL LANGUAGE PROGRESSION

Age (Years)	Average Words	Average Sentences (Words)
3	900	3 to 4
4	1,500	5
5	2,000	6
6	2,500	7

WHO'S AFRAID OF THE BOGEY MAN?

Just about every five-year-old is afraid of the bogey man! Monsters, robbers, darkness, death, being alone . . . you name it. Fear of just about anything gets in full force at this age.

This is the age when left brain dominance starts to once again shift to the right. The transition sets in a spell of extremes in behavior. As the right starts to dominate, the negative emotions of fear, anxiety, foreboding, and negative thoughts start to creep back. Now that children have better cognitive skills and can verbalize better, these fears become more ominous. At the same time, children this age are well into the fantasy world, so their vivid imaginations can go wild.

Theory of Mind and Autism

At five or six years of age, children develop theory of mind—the ability to nonverbally understand what someone else is feeling or thinking. It's sort of like mind reading.

By age five, children should be able to consider another person's point of view, which allows them to begin thinking about how other people feel. It's how empathy is established. Before this age, all children have diminished or absent theory of mind.

Theory of mind is associated with the development of a sense of self, embodiment, nonverbal communication, and joint attention, which are right hemisphere skills. Simon Baron-Cohen of Oxford University was the first to propose that autism is the inability to develop theory of mind.

Children with autism don't develop theory of mind because they have a maturity delay in their right hemisphere.

Of course, this type of behavior is normal at five to six years old. A child with a right brain delay may get stuck in this transition and will have obsessive fears that can develop into phobias.

PLAY TIME: AN IMPORTANT TIME IN LIFE

When it comes time to play, kids at this age are raring to go. A five-year-old who is not interested in play may be showing signs of depression or autism.

At this age, kids believe rules can change, and they are broadening their skills through active play or role-playing, including fantasy. Play changes rapidly.

At this age, kids:

- Play simple, competitive table games.
- Play games with rules.
- Play in small groups; they are not too highly organized.
- Engage in imaginative play (for example, a trip to the moon).
- Rely on rules to guide behavior and play.

Six Years Old

Six-year-olds have boundless energy, and their emotions can still be all over the place. They'll be silly, brash, critical, and oppositional. They cry easily—almost any behavior that releases tension will come out.

Children at this age understand responsibility and have a strong sense of right and wrong. Being flexible, however, is not a strong trait at this age.

As a parent, you might feel your child getting away from you. Kids at this age are showing more independence from parents and family and paying more attention to friendships and teamwork.

Your child may show a special fondness for a teacher of the opposite sex.

They are developing a keen awareness of the future and are wondering about their own place in it.

▶ **Six Years Old**

BEHAVIOR/EMOTIONAL TRAITS

- Wants to be the first and best at everything
- Considers fantasy as real
- Is less focused on self and shows some concern for others
- Is sensitive to others' opinions about himself or herself
- Has a growing desire to be liked and accepted by friends
- May become infatuated with teacher or playmate of the opposite sex
- Develops positive, realistic self-concept
- Learns to respect self
- Begins to understand own uniqueness
- Gains awareness of own feelings
- Is learning to express feelings
- Participates in groups
- Begins to learn from mistakes

PHYSICAL TRAITS

- Bounces a ball four to six times
- Throws and catches a ball
- Skates
- Rides a bicycle
- Ties shoelaces

- Counts to a hundred
- Prints first name
- Prints numbers up to ten
- Prints a few letters
- Knows right from left
- Can draw a person with six body parts
- Is learning specific sports skills, like batting a ball or kicking a soccer ball

COGNITIVE TRAITS

- Rapidly develops mental skills
- Has great ability to describe experiences
- Talks about thoughts and feelings
- Masters the consonants *f, v, l*
- Properly pronounces two letters with one sound, such as *sh* and *th*
- Speaks intelligibly and is socially meaningful
- Can tell a complicated story
- Understands relationships between objects and happenings

Seven Years Old

Once in second or third grade, children are beginning to be judged on their academic and social progress. They start to show a preference for learning style. Some like hands-on activities (will she be an artist?), others are into science (a budding genius, perhaps?), some love to have a pencil in hand (the creative type?), and others prefer to work quietly and independently (hmmm, what does this mean?). As always, watching your child grow is full of wonder and delight.

At home, you'll find your seven-year-old talking a blue streak—but only if home life is comfortable and safe. Kids this age are beginning to understand perspective and continue to develop a sense of others' feelings. Seven-year-olds should have the ability to understand that intentionally lying and a mistake are two different things and that one is right and the other is wrong.

Their fine muscle skills are developing, and you should start to see an improvement in their handwriting.

They are beginning to overcome some of their earlier childhood fears, but they're still scared of the unknown—and this can include school. For some seven-year-olds, school can be tremendously stressful. Kids at this age are commonly afraid of being in trouble for *something* with their parents and teacher.

You are likely to find your child curious about sexuality and may find her looking at nude pictures in books and magazines.

When Imagination Rules

Could those extravagant plays your child is putting on be a sign that you might have a future actor in the family?

Perhaps—but probably not.

Children between the ages of six and nine have a lot of imagination, and they tend to act it out in imaginative play. They take on the roles of characters and directors, creating their own plots and schemes. The only thing that really changes as they get older is focus.

All children have aggressive and violent impulses that need expression, and playacting is the way they do it. Playing games like cops and robbers or soldier allows them to vent these impulses in acceptable ways. Video games that depict violence with fantasy or cartoon characters serve a similar function and help children vent their natural violent tendencies. However, violent video games that depict real-life characters or people are not appropriate.

► Seven Years Old

BEHAVIOR/EMOTIONAL TRAITS

- Cares for self, room, and belongings
- Takes responsibility for home chores
- Has friendships with kids of same gender
- Plays in larger groups occasionally, but wants time alone
- Has a sense of humor and tells jokes
- Is concerned about rules—good (fair) vs. bad (unfair)
- Likes to belong to informal clubs formed by children
- Draws moral distinctions based on internal judgment
- Has a developed concept of self
- Is self-critical; may express lack of confidence
- Dislikes being singled out, even for praise
- Builds relationships with others
- Develops a sense of responsibility

PHYSICAL TRAITS

- Is becoming more coordinated in activities that use large muscles (swimming, climbing)
- Uses scissors safely
- Can draw a triangle
- Draws a person with twelve body parts
- Uses a pencil to write full name
- Writes and draws with more skill
- Loses four baby teeth

COGNITIVE TRAITS

- Has a solid sense of time (seconds, minutes, hours, days, weeks, months, seasons, years)

- Tells time to the quarter hour
- Is showing preference for a learning style
- Solves simple math problems using objects (such as counting beads)
- Considers issues and problems, using one factor at a time
- Pronounces words correctly (e.g., doesn't say *frough* for *through*)
- Reads for pleasure
- Shows improving reading skills, but sounding out vowels may still be difficult
- Has difficulty with basic spelling
- Performs at grade level in all subjects
- Pronounces consonants *r*, *s*, *z*, voiceless *th*, *ch*, *wh*, and the soft *g* correctly
- Handles opposites well (girl–boy, man–woman, stop–go), including concepts such as alike and different, beginning and end
- Can write or print many words correctly
- Uses language as a communication tool
- Begins to reason and concentrate

Eight Years Old

Eight-year-olds are loving. They have a strong need for love and understanding, especially from their mothers. Some might be called mama's boys, but this is okay—take advantage of it while it lasts.

Kids this age are usually quite sensitive and overly dramatic. You'll see a wide range of emotions that change rapidly. Children can be helpful, cheerful, and pleasant as well as rude, bossy, and selfish.

They may tend to show off and try to appear cool in front of their peers by being rude. This is their natural instinct to be less like their parents and more like their friends—part of their urge to feel accepted. Don't be offended if this is ever aimed at you. Eight-year-olds are trying really hard—at everything.

They are trying hard to master all the skills they're being exposed to—handwriting, arts, crafts, computers, math—and they feel a sense of accomplishment from achieving them. If these skills don't come easily, they tend to exaggerate their feelings of inferiority. Be careful not to criticize and make sure to praise accomplishments.

Everything is black and white in the life of an eight-year-old. Things are either great or awful, ugly or beautiful, right or wrong.

► **Eight Years Old**

BEHAVIOR/EMOTIONAL TRAITS

- Is impatient; finds waiting for special events torturous
- Makes friends easily
- Develops close friends of same sex
- Is uncomfortable with peers of opposite sex
- Wants to be part of a group
- Is influenced by peer pressure
- Acts impatient
- Seeks immediate gratification
- Creates friendships that are inclusive
- Has a know-it-all attitude
- Takes responsibility for actions
- Actively seeks praise
- May undertake more than can successfully handle
- Is self-critical
- Shows resiliency; bounces back from mistakes
- Cooperates and works well in groups
- Is highly social

- Fears speaking in front of class
- Is more likely to follow own rules
- Exaggerates

PHYSICAL TRAITS

- Has quite refined finger control
- Is learning cursive writing
- Has increased stamina (can run and swim farther)
- Organizes a group of objects in more than one way
- Draws a diamond shape
- Draws a person with sixteen features
- Becomes increasingly interested and skilled in hobbies

COGNITIVE TRAITS

- Can converse at almost an adult level
- May read as a major interest
- Seeks to understand the reasons for things
- Begins to feel competent in skills
- Has preference for some activities and subjects
- Displays organized and logical thinking
- Recognizes concept of reversibility ($4 + 2 = 6$ and $6 - 2 = 4$)
- Can relate involved accounts of events
- Has lapses in grammatical constrictions: tense, pronouns, plurals
- Reads with considerable ease
- Writes simple compositions
- Uses social amenities in speech in appropriate situations
- Knows how to count by twos and fives
- Knows what day of the week it is but may not know full date and year

- Completes simple single-digit addition and subtraction problems (1 + 8; 7 + 5; 6 – 2; 4 – 3)
- Has a black-and-white perspective much of the time
- Explains ideas in detail

Nine Years Old

At nine years old your little ones are suddenly starting to grow up. Boys and girls veer off into their own growth patterns, with girls getting taller and weighing more than boys their own age. Boys are full of energy and quite competitive, pushing themselves to their physical limits. As a result they fatigue easily. They can still be a little uncoordinated, so all their excess muscle movement can make them prone to injury.

Kids at this age speak like adults and can converse on an adult level. Nevertheless, when you listen to them talk and joke among themselves, they are decidedly still kids. Friendships are very important at this age, and they are gender specific. Boys and girls play in groups of their own.

Though they'll never admit it, kids this age have a curiosity about the opposite sex but insist that girls (or boys) are yucky or some other unflattering descriptive. There is also other right brain activity going on, and plenty of negatives creep into their language, as in the common declaration, *B-o-o-oring!* They also like taking risks, and they don't like being wrong.

Nine-year-olds are developing socially and intellectually. Their personal interests and abilities are expanding. They comprehend decision making and can make decisions about their own lives.

They are concrete learners and are able to deal with multiple variables in school.

Sleep is still important at this age, and a regular bedtime of eight or nine o'clock should be maintained until age ten.

▶ Nine Years Old

BEHAVIOR/EMOTIONAL TRAITS

- Is both industrious and impatient
- Is competitive
- Has a sense of humor
- Wants to put some distance between self and adults
- May rebel against authority
- Needs to be part of a group
- Seeks independence
- Can express a wide range of emotions
- Is typically not self-confident
- Understands social roles and appropriate behavior and considers them inflexible
- Wants to choose work partners
- Is critical of self and others
- Is easily discouraged
- Can be aloof
- Creates exclusive friendship groups
- Prefers friends of the same gender
- Controls anger
- Demonstrates real empathy for others; wants to help those in distress or need
- Has more stable emotions than previous years and has fewer mood swings
- Overcomes most fears
- Experiences more anxiety to stressful situations, such as school performance
- States things in negatives: ("I hate...," "It's not...," "I don't like...")

PHYSICAL TRAITS

- Cares for self (dressing and grooming)
- Can use simple tools
- Can take responsibility for home chores
- Writes and draws with more skill
- Enjoys active play, such as swimming, running, cycling, games
- Shows increasing interest in team sports
- Likes to paint, draw, build models, make jewelry

COGNITIVE TRAITS

- Holds conversations at close to adult level
- Uses speech patterns similar to adults
- Follows fairly complex directions with little repetition
- Has well-developed time and number concepts
- Can play board games with complex rules
- Worries about things
- Shows anxiety about physical aches and pains
- Knows three thousand words
- Sees inconsistencies and imperfections in adults
- Complains about fairness
- Loves vocabulary and language play but baby talk may reemerge
- Reads for pleasure and to learn about personal interests
- Can think independently and clearly (but tied to peer standards)
- Is concerned about rules—fair vs. unfair
- Has internalized childhood imagination; private thoughts and fantasies
- Has an increasing sense of truthfulness
- Begins to make decisions
- Develops personal interests and abilities
- Is secretly curious about relationships between boys and girls

INATTENTIVE AND UNFOCUSED?
THAT'S A NINE-YEAR-OLD!

"Attention! Ah, boys . . . Can you hear me?"

This is an expression being repeated countless times a day everywhere by mothers of nine-year-olds.

Inattention is the trait du jour of children this age, especially boys, and it tries the patience of even the most resilient parents. It also makes many worry: *Could it be ADHD?* Probably not. Inattention and daydreaming, *within reason*, are normal for a nine-year-old.

Inattention and daydreaming, within reason, are normal for a nine-year-old.

At this age, more advanced areas of the motor cortex and the prefrontal cortex of the frontal lobe are actively developing. The whole purpose of the prefrontal cortex is to guide goal-directed behavior, and it does so by helping plan the outcome of actions before they actually take place.

The prefrontal cortex subconsciously simulates or rehearses a movement several times before the conscious brain is even aware of the movement. In this way, the brain can predict the success of the outcome of that action and get close to the goal. If not, it may inhibit or modify the action and then simulate it again and again until it gets it right. Once this happens, it will direct the frontal lobe to carry the action out.

In an adult brain, this happens fluidly and rapidly all the time, but in a nine-year-old, the brain is just starting to have this capacity. Because the young brain is slower and this skill isn't fully developed, it can get caught up in the process. It's as if the child were lost in a virtual world in his head. This fascination with daydreaming can make a child appear inattentive and unfocused, but it is really part of normal cognitive development.

After this stage of development is over, the child will start to make better decisions and become more goal oriented. He'll be ready to start planning for the future. But for now, you'll have to put up with a little inattentive behavior.

Ten Years Old

Your children are practically growing before your eyes. Growth is steady and rapid in both boys and girls, who gain three or four inches at this age, with girls maturing faster than boys. This is also the age when some kids start getting braces.

Homework, television, computers, and extracurricular activities are making many ten-year-olds sleep deficient, as their growing bodies still require nine to ten hours of sleep a night.

Curiosity about adult life starts to take hold, and they fluctuate between acting as dependent children and independent preteens. They still cling to same-sex friendships, which are becoming stronger and more complex. They are interested in teen culture and may be curious about drugs, alcohol, and tobacco. Television and music will become a way of life for them—if you let them—and they identify with Hollywood and rock stars. Boys emulate sports figures.

This is the age when it is time to start to give your children personal, but limited, space in the home and to begin discussions about the importance of delaying sexual behavior.

► **Ten Years Old**

BEHAVIOR/EMOTIONAL TRAITS

- Shows interest in teen culture (music, videos, makeup)
- Tries to avoid looking childish

- Understands how behavior affects others
- Tends to be obedient, good-natured, and fun
- Is capable of increasing independence
- Becomes more dependable
- Is truthful
- Has improved self-image and acceptance of others
- Has good relationships with authority figures
- Seeks approval from significant people for being good
- Is proud of doing things well
- Shows concern about personal capabilities
- Has internalized standards of right and wrong to some degree
- Finds TV very important and identifies with TV characters
- Is preoccupied with the opposite sex
- Relates to peer group intensely and abides by group decisions
- Succumbs to peer pressure more readily
- Does not want to be different
- Continues to participate in small groups of same gender
- Confides constantly in best friend
- Revels in bathroom humor
- Is increasingly self-conscious

PHYSICAL TRAITS

- Shows better-integrated motor skills
- Uses physical activities to develop gross and fine motor skills
- Is energetic and spirited
- Is usually awkward
- Strives to be physically fit
- Is fascinated with how the body works
- Begins to undergo physical maturation
- Becomes more aware of own body as puberty approaches

COGNITIVE TRAITS

- Solves abstract problems using logic
- Uses logic to argue with parents and other adults
- Accurately recognizes and considers others' viewpoints
- Has an accurate perception of events
- Displays concrete, rational, and logical thinking
- Reflects on self and attributes
- Understands concepts of space, time, dimension
- Retains memories of past events well
- Is more effective at coping skills
- Possesses a surprising scope of interests
- Improves listening and responding skills
- Increases problem-solving abilities
- Is aware of peer and adult expectations
- Is eager to master new skills
- Relies more on intentions

Eleven to Fourteen Years

Early adolescence is a time of many physical, mental, emotional, and social changes in boys and girls. The development of one's sense of self—values, attitudes, belief, and plans—is one of the fundamental tasks of adolescence.

As young as eleven and twelve, kids should be able to take responsibility for their own behavior and decisions. They should also be showing more self-assertion and curiosity. By the next year they should be starting to make their own choices about friends, sports, studying, and school. They are becoming more independent, have their own personality and interests, and are veering even further away from their parents in favor of their peers.

These are years of rapid physical change and maturity. First comes the full set of permanent teeth and many kids are now wearing braces. Many eleven- to fourteen-year-olds feel awkward and self-conscious as they adjust to their changing bodies.

For girls, the tween years of eleven and twelve mark the start of hormonal changes, and they begin to develop breasts, hips, and pubic hair. Menstruation usually begins around age twelve and a half, right after the peak growth spurt in height. Most girls will grow another inch or two before reaching their adult height at around age fourteen or fifteen. By age twelve, most girls can share shoes and some of the same clothing with their mother.

Boys begin puberty an average of two years later than girls and can start to show the first physical signs between the ages of ten and sixteen years, but tend to grow most quickly between twelve and fifteen years. They grow facial hair and their voices deepen. By age sixteen or seventeen most boys have stopped growing in height, but their muscles will continue to develop.

It is also a time of great peer pressure involving drugs, alcohol, and tobacco and experimenting in sex. Girls, especially, can worry excessively about their appearance and especially their weight. This is the time when eating disorders may develop.

Mentally, the ages of eleven and twelve can be emotionally numbing. You may see a wide range of negative emotions like fighting, lying, and outbursts that may include swearing. Socially, their allegiance is changing from same gender to both genders.

As kids hit their teen years, they psychologically distance themselves from their parents and move more toward their peers. They may still exhibit moodiness and struggle with a sense of identity.

Well-adjusted teenagers are generally cooperative and considerate, although they can sometimes be inconsistent and unpredictable. They should be doing well in school and have taken up some creative interests, such as drama, art, or music. By this age, they are enjoying relationships with both sexes and thinking and planning life goals.

► Eleven to Fourteen Years Old

BEHAVIOR/EMOTIONAL TRAITS

- Goes through another version of terrible twos in trying to establish independence and autonomy (in early teens)
- Has sexual fantasies
- Is exuberant and restless
- Talks a lot
- Is self-confident
- Has sense of pride and competence
- Enjoys close interactions with peers, especially same gender
- Enjoys recreational activities
- Recognizes the need for rules and fair play
- Is energetic, enthusiastic
- Takes responsibility for homework with little prodding
- Assumes responsibility for own health
- Is generally cooperative and considerate
- Can be inconsistent and unpredictable
- Tends to gossip and talk about friends behind their backs
- Enjoys socializing in groups of both boys and girls
- Can adapt behavior to fit situation
- Takes on more responsibilities at home
- Has increased interest in team sports, board games
- Tries to avoid punishment
- Flirts
- May engage in kissing, stroking, or other sexual activity
- Is socially expansive and aware
- Is competitive, wants to excel
- May put down kids outside own group of friends
- Exhibits off-color humor and silliness
- Teases and tussles

- Has little impulse control
- Wants immediate gratification
- Has inadequate coping skills
- Is easily frustrated
- May feel out of control
- Can show extremes of emotions

PHYSICAL TRAITS

- Develops pubic, underarm, and increased body hair
- Has reasonable athletic ability or has dramatic, artistic, or musical talents
- May have oily skin and acne

A BOY:

- Experiences voice changes
- Develops enlarged penis, scrotum, and testes
- Experiences ejaculation and nocturnal emissions
- Has increased appetite
- Needs more sleep; may sleep quite late on weekends
- Sweats more easily
- Grows rapidly, which may cause clumsiness and lack of coordination

A GIRL:

- Begins menstruating
- Develops breasts and hips
- Develops more rapidly than boys

COGNITIVE TRAITS

- Believes will do well in endeavors

- Performs at or near ability in school
- Is comfortable in asking parents questions
- Develops personal interests and abilities
- Shows improved arguing skills, demonstrating them often and with great passion
- Has improved reasoning skills
- Can apply concepts to specific examples
- Uses deductive reasoning and makes educated guesses
- Reasons through problems even in the absence of concrete events or examples
- Can construct hypothetical solutions to a problem and evaluate which is best
- Develops focus on the future
- Engages in some fantasy
- Recognizes current actions have a future effect
- Starts to set personal goals
- May reject goals set by others
- Has improved decision-making skills
- Can independently differentiate right from wrong
- Develops a conscience
- Distinguishes fact from opinion
- Evaluates the credibility of various sources of information
- Anticipates the consequences of different options
- May challenge the assumptions and solutions presented by adults
- Has difficulty concentrating
- Finds academic challenges threatening

How Kids Mature Physically	
Growth Spurt	**Puberty**
Girls: 11 to 14 years	11 to 14 years
Boys: 13 to 17 years	12 to 15 years

RISK TAKING: A TEENAGE TRAIT

Teens feel grown up and they may look grown up, but no matter how much maturity they show in their conduct and studies, they definitely are not grown up.

Smart decision making doesn't come easily to teens, and it isn't unusual for teens to err in judgment, especially when it comes to considering the long-term consequences of spur-of-the-moment decisions—like speeding, drinking, and experimenting in promiscuous sex.

Not thinking about the future—what we call future orientation—leads to choosing the fun of the present over the pain of the future. It's also why scare tactics in programs such as Drug Abuse Resistance Education (D.A.R.E.) are largely ineffective. Teenagers engage in risky behavior for several reasons:

- While teens demonstrate that they understand the level of risk associated with a given behavior under ideal (and simulated) conditions, studies show they fail to consider these same risks in real-world situations.
- Teens are reward sensitive and risk adverse—for example, the rush of driving fast compared to the risk of getting in an accident or getting a speeding ticket.
- Teens are impulsive because their brains are still learning impulse control. Teens will have rapid and extreme changes in mood. High levels of emotional arousal, whether anger or

elation, have been connected to difficulties with self-control. The combination of moodiness and impulsivity leads adolescents to have more difficulty in controlling their behavior than adults.

IM: Teen to Parent

Parents do best when they keep in mind the five *I*'s and six *M*'s of the midteen years.

The Five *I*'s
Impulsive
Intense
Idealistic
Immediate (wanting everything now)
Indestructible (thinking nothing can hurt them—they can't get
    pregnant or get into an auto accident or get hooked on cigarettes
    or drugs)

The Six *M*'s
Moody
Messy
Monosyllabic
Mouthy
Money oriented
Me centered

· 7 ·

Setting Family Values and Rules

Perseverance is a great element of success. If you knock
long enough and loud enough at the gate, you are
sure to wake up everybody.

—HENRY WADSWORTH LONGFELLOW

I sit with parents listening to them lament about their children's behavior on almost a daily basis. Usually, tension starts to mount as each parent explains the situation from his or her own perspective. Though there is always a common thread of agreement, parents of children with behavior problems commonly disagree on what's going wrong, how it went wrong, and how to correct it. There is often an underlying tone that one parent is wrong and the other is right. I have fathers tell me how their children are defiant and won't listen while their wives sit there impatiently rolling their eyes in clear disagreement. I've seen it thousands of times.

It's obvious to me that this central theme is an issue that is only exacerbating the problem going on in the family: Moms and dads more often than not are on different pages when it comes to their parenting styles and their children's behavior. In many cases, their parenting styles directly conflict with one another.

The other thing that's become obvious to me is that these parents don't consider this a problem. Or, worse, they don't even recognize that they are not in agreement on most issues regarding their children.

HOW DO YOU WANT YOUR CHILD TO ACT?

When I ask parents to tell me how they'd like their child to act at home and in school, they answer by telling me how they *don't* want their child to act. They are so fixated on the negative that usually it's all they can talk and think about! Or the parents will answer my question in a positive way, but the mother and father will give completely different responses. If the parents aren't on the same wavelength, it's not much of a stretch to understand why they're not on the same wavelength with their child either!

I always ask parents if they have ever discussed with one another exactly what type of behavior they expect and would like to see in their child at home and in school. Sure, they talk plenty about everything that goes and has gone wrong. Sure, over casual conversation and the course of time, they express what they long to see in their children. However, almost all parents admit that they have never formally sat down with each other to seriously discuss and agree on a set of family values, rules, and expectations. Yet, when I ask them if their children know how they expect them to behave, I always get the answer: "Sure, they know."

When I ask, "But how do they know? Have you ever clearly expressed your expectations with them?" The answer is almost always no. They just assume their children know because "We're telling them how to act all the time."

This itself is a problem because the "we" are often saying two different things. What the father wants and says and what the mother wants and says are often completely different. So from the child's perspective, her parents—one supposedly *unified* set of role models and disciplinarians—are sending mixed messages and unintentionally making her take a side (a no-win situation) or, worse, leading her to disobey both parents. I think anyone can see how this can cause confusion, anger, frustration, and even oppositional behavior in a kid, especially as the child gets older, becomes a teen, and wants to express her own ideas and independence.

> The most common reason for negative
> behavior in kids is inconsistent
> messages from parents.

The most common reason for negative behavior in children is inconsistency in the messages they are receiving from their parents. Parents—especially parents of children with behavior problems—must have a set of rules that they establish together, agree on, stick to, and explain to their children in clear, easy-to-understand language. Children should be able and be expected to follow them because *the rules will be in writing*.

I can ask any parent who comes to our centers or attends my lectures if he or she has a written set of rules, and virtually every time the response will be no. I also often find out that there has never been a family discussion on family values and beliefs. I see it across the board in families from all socioeconomic classes and all walks of life and in every type of family structure—from traditional families with a stay-at-home parent to divorced parents sharing custody to single-parent households.

Not having a clear set of expectations not only breeds behavior issues but, I believe, it is core to what goes wrong in many marriages today. When children don't have clearly defined rules and continual communication about your expectations, it not only creates confusion and frustration between children and their parents but also generates conflict between the parents themselves.

> **An ideal family is one in which parents foster family communication.**

I regularly see couples seething over how the other spouse is not doing a proper job parenting, yet they almost never discuss their differences in a meaningful way. As a result, the situation goes from bad to worse. If parents are not in agreement on basic expectations of behavior, if the children have never been told clearly what is expected of them, you can't really blame them or outside influences on their troubled behavior.

Today's ideal family is not the proverbial working dad and stay-at-home mom living in a suburban home with a white picket fence. An ideal family is one in which the parents foster family communication, establish a set of family values, and set boundaries that allow children to grow emotionally and intellectually—all of which can happen whether it's taking place in one household or two (in the case of separated or divorced parents). It's all about being consistent as parents and putting family first, even if the personal relationship between the mom and dad is not ideal. Parents who share common values, agree on what they expect from their children, and communicate that message effectively to their children are establishing the foundation for family harmony and happiness.

GETTING BACK TO BASICS

Having a formal set of rules and values is one of the most basic things you can do to improve the overall behavior of your children and make your house a more positive place to live. It is also the quickest and surest way to establish family harmony, confront and abate behavior problems, and dissolve old resentments. Here's how to go about it.

Get on the Same Page

It is imperative for parents to be in agreement, even if you have to enlist help from a family counselor or other specialist. You and your spouse should plan a time in which you will sit down and actually discuss what to expect from each of your children and how you would ideally like them to behave in all aspects of their lives. You might have to do this in more than one session, and don't go more than two hours at a time—after that, productivity starts to wane.

Design a Set of Family Values

A family is defined as a social unit consisting of parents and the children they raise. Values are defined as the quality or worth of something intangible. Family values means living by a traditional set of social standards. I say *traditional* values because we're seeing less and less of them and more and more friction in families. This is not a coincidence.

Family values means living by a traditional set of social values.

In generations gone by, parents would pass on their values to their children, and the children knew what these values stood for. These days, with extended families often spread out across the country and even the globe, the close ties that were once so precious are lost. Many young parents just starting out don't have the luxury of the wisdom and advice from their parents and older family members.

Do you have traditional family values? What do you stand for? There's an old saying, "If you don't stand for something you will fall for anything."

To design and set family values consider these questions:

- What moral and ethical values are important to you?
- How would you instill these values in your children?
- Do you think your children know the values you stand for?
- Have you communicated your values effectively to your children?

To be effective at parenting, you need to create a common vision of what you want your family to look like, act like, and strive for. This is what a set of values establishes for a family.

Businesses have a mission statement and often create a set of values under which all employees are expected to operate. It creates

---

Sample List of Family Values

The _____ family believes in and promises to always live by and uphold these family values:

- **Respect** for one another
- **Loyalty** to one another
- **Honesty** at all times
- **Consistency** in actions
- **Hard Work** and **Fair Play**
- **Courage** to do what's right
- Be a **Team Player**
- **Persistence** in all pursuits
- A **Positive Attitude** and outlook on life
- **Trust** in self and others

a common ground and a moral compass that has been proven to increase employee happiness and willingness to work for the common good. Why not think of your family in the same way?

Establish Your Rules

Rules are the action steps a family takes to make sure they stick to and stand by their values. Whenever you have a group of people who need to operate together as a team, you need to develop the appropriate tools that enable them to exist together in the same space in harmony and contentment. It greatly reduces the chance of miscommunication and conflict between individuals.

Values create the big picture of what to expect, and the rules are the details or specifics of how you expect everyone to act on a day-to-day basis.

When you play a game like Monopoly, for example, the first thing players always do is establish the rules of the game. Without a set of house rules, individuals set their own, leading to chaos. However, when everyone understands how the game is played, then playing is enjoyable and fun. Consider how much screaming and infighting would be eliminated in the morning if everybody knew what was expected of him or her to get out the door and off to school on time.

Call a Family Get-Together

Once the two of you are in agreement with each other on values and rules, you need to get the buy-in from your kids. The goal is to get them involved and excited about it. After all, they're the ones who have to live by the rules, though you can't lose sight of the fact that you must live by them as well. Then you need to call a formal meeting of your family.

During the meeting, state what you are doing and why. Present what you've come up with in a positive and nonthreatening way.

Family communication is important and should be frequent. The best way I've found to keep it consistent is to have a family meeting once a week. Establish a specific time during the week when everyone in the family gets together to discuss family issues. This needs to be a formal, mandatory meeting, just as you would have a weekly staff meeting at the office. It's impossible to run a business without everyone being on the same page. A family is really no different.

In previous generations, family time often took place at dinnertime. This is where these types of discussions used to take place. This rarely happens on a consistent basis in modern families, unfortunately, because other events have taken priority. Parents work late, kids are at school activities, and so on. So pick a time that works best for your family.

In my household, we get together on Sunday evenings. It is not an invitation, it is a mandate. You need to establish your authority and institute organization so the family can live in harmony.

You need to establish your authority and institute organization so the family can live in harmony.

Come to your first meeting prepared. Have your preliminary set of values and the rules that you and your spouse would like to institute written out. These rules can be modified, added to, or eliminated, based on the feedback you get from your kids.

Work on the Rules Together

Tell your kids what you've done and why and explain what you've come up with. Enlist your children in a discussion around family values. What are they? What do they mean? Why are they important? Ask each of your children to come up with, say, five values.

Give the kids time to think about it and have them write their values down. Ask each child to explain each value he or she has chosen and why. Combine those that are expressed in different words but have the same meaning into a single value. Combine them into a single list to create your set of family values. No list can be too long! The important thing is that you leave that first meeting with a set of family values and rules that everyone agrees on.

Have a similar discussion around family rules. I found the best way to approach this is to go step-by-step through a typical day, starting in the morning. Get specific, such as expectations for wake-up time and getting everyone out the door in an orderly, hassle-free fashion. (Yes, it is possible!) Who gets to shower first, when and how homework gets done, limits on television and computer use, bedtimes, and weekday and weekend curfews for older kids. Again, everything needs to be discussed and agreed on.

Put It in Writing

Once you've agreed on the rules, put them in writing. Create a contract and have everyone in the family sign it.

You Are the Enforcer

Once the rules are written down and agreed on, they need to be consistently enforced. If rules are broken, there must be consequences. It's best to have different punishments for different infractions. The punishment should fit the crime, so to speak, but you must be consistent in handing it out when a rule is broken.

Discuss the Consequences

Have a second meeting to discuss the consequences of breaking the rules. This, too, should also be agreed on as a family. Before this meeting the parents need to be in agreement to ensure that there are consistent responses to every situation. Though it is not readily obvious, this offers kids a form of security. Even though they may complain about rules, they want their lives to be safe and predictable.

Keep the Boundaries Secure

Children need boundaries—need to know their limits. It is impossible to have family harmony without them. Boundaries make kids feel safe. Safe and secure children are generally well-behaved children. They will push against their boundaries to make sure they are there. If they find cracks in the system—a weakness in one or both parents—they will keep on pushing until they find permanent boundaries. Inconsistency from a parent or between parents makes children feel as if the boundaries aren't real. It makes them feel anxious and insecure, and they will act out. Rules are the best way to establish boundaries and to enforce them consistently.

Kids without boundaries will feel anxious and insecure. They will act out.

RULES ARE ORDER

Everywhere you look in society, there are rules. Imagine what life would be like without them. It would be chaos. Family life is no different. Without rules, there's strife. I'm sure this makes perfect sense to you. In fact, you are probably wondering why you didn't think of it before. I can guarantee that once you have a set of rules, you'll wish you would have done this sooner.

Once you get your values established and your rules in motion, you'll see a big difference in family life very quickly. This is especially true for families with challenges, such as divorce, a one-parent household, or a child or children with a learning disability or a behavioral or developmental disorder.

All families can benefit from having a written set of values and rules. Neither marriage nor children come with instruction booklets. Most of us just do what we were taught or follow the lead of our parents, mistakes and all. Things are too difficult today to just leave these things to chance. Parents need to take control and work with their children to find family harmony.

Sample List of Family Rules

Post your rules in a place where everyone can see them. As the family grows, the rules can and should change. Here is a sample set of rules that would apply to a family that includes teens:

1. Get out of bed as soon as the alarm goes off.
2. Limit morning shower to five minutes. Make sure to use soap and shampoo.
3. Get fully dressed—pants, shirt, socks, and shoes—before breakfast.
4. Eat a healthy breakfast; take vitamins.
5. Check backpack to make sure nothing is missing. Add lunch or make sure you have lunch money.
6. Make sure all notes, permission slips, homework, tests, and so on are signed before leaving the house.
7. Get to school on time and attend each class promptly.
8. Use school agenda to carefully, in detail, note all homework, projects, and test dates.
9. Sit near the front in each class, be attentive and respectful, ask questions, take detailed notes.
10. Do not leave school property at lunch without permission from parents.

11. After school, go immediately to scheduled activity or go directly home.
12. Eat a healthy snack after getting home and start homework. There is no TV or computer time until all homework is done.
13. Homework is to be done at the kitchen table or in the library only.
14. No iPod, music, phone, social networking, or texting is allowed while doing homework.
15. After homework is complete and checked by a parent, you can have free time.
16. When weather is nice, free time must take place outdoors until it starts to get dark or dinner is called.
17. Screen time—television, computer, video games—is limited to one hour, fifteen minutes each weekday, and two and a half hours per day on weekends. Extra screen time must be earned.
18. You can listen to music, but music with foul, explicit, or negative language is off-limits anytime and anywhere.
19. There will be no cursing or inappropriate language used in the house at any time.
20. There will be no inappropriate pictures, images, or language on the family computer.
21. Come in for dinner immediately when called.
22. The family will eat together when possible. Each family member will wait for everyone to be finished before getting up from the table. Don't ask to be excused without a good reason.
23. Prepare backpack and select the next day's wardrobe before bedtime.
24. Bedtime during the week is ____, meaning lights out. Weekends and holiday bedtime is ____, unless extra time is earned.
25. No phone or texting after ____ p.m.
26. There is no going out on a school night without permission. Weekend and holiday curfew is ____, meaning in the house. No excuses!

27. No making expensive purchases or eating junk food without permission.
28. Never borrow someone else's belongings without permission.
29. If you damage property belonging to another family member or the house, you will pay for replacement or repairs.
30. Treat and speak to others with respect.
31. Respect each other's privacy.
32. Physically hitting another family member is never acceptable.
33. Fighting of any kind is never acceptable, unless it is to defend yourself or a member of the family.
34. Treat others the way you would like to be treated; never speak unkindly of others.
35. Always clean up after yourself. If you remove something you must put it back and clean up any mess.
36. Study for at least two days before a test.
37. There is never a reason to get below a B+ on any test or in any class or for any project.
38. If you need help, ask for it. You will get the help you need as long as you are trying hard on your own.
39. All projects will be completed a day before they are due.
40. No using cell phone or texting during class.
41. No friends are permitted in the house without specific permission when parents are not home.
42. Using alcohol, cigarettes, or drugs is absolutely forbidden.
43. No boyfriends or girlfriends are allowed in bedrooms, ever.
44. If alone in a room with opposite sex, lights must always be on.
45. Sunday night from 8:00 to 9:00 is family meeting hour. Nothing else is scheduled during that time.
46. Every Sunday everyone will write an action plan for the week. These items will be added to your schedule as necessary.

Part 2

THE FAMILY
EMPOWERMENT
PROGRAM

· 8 ·

The Secret to Family Empowerment

Forget about all the reasons why something may not work.
You only need to find one good reason why it will.

—DR. ROBERT ANTHONY, AUTHOR AND PERSONAL
PERFORMANCE TRAINER

No one to date has come up with a program guaranteed to get kids' behavior in line. If one existed, we'd be seeing many better-behaved kids out there, and schools would have significantly fewer discipline problems. We know, of course, that this isn't happening.

The reason, I believe, is because the scores of programs currently in existence—and it's likely you've tried some or even several of them—are aimed at fixing behavior only *in kids*. This makes sense only if you believe that children are 100 percent to blame for their own bad behavior. However, I believe that fixing a behavior problem in kids usually warrants a change in their parents as well.

The flaw in behavior programs is that they're set up as a positive and negative reinforcement system that parents or a therapist uses to redirect a child's anger and frustrations, but they don't address the behavior and attitude of the parents. It's not rocket science to understand that it's virtually impossible to have a well-behaved, focused, motivated, and happy child if the parents are unhappy, angry, frustrated, and not models of good behavior and character.

I've become acutely aware of this over the last several years as a result of my work with children with neurologically caused behavior issues. Now, parents can't be blamed for the behavior associated with these conditions, which include attention deficit/hyperactivity disorder (ADHD), autism, obsessive-compulsive disorder, and oppositional defiant disorder. Their unruly and abnormal behavior can be blamed only on a brain imbalance caused by one hemisphere of the brain either growing too fast or too slow. I started to notice, however, that after we corrected the imbalance in some of these kids, different negative behaviors started to emerge that had nothing to do with a neurological problem, new or old, or a psychological one. These kids were displaying what we call *secondary behaviors*, and it became obvious that their bad acting was a defensive attitude caused by living in a negative environment or as a response to poor parenting skills.

This doesn't mean that these kids had bad parents. Far from it. The parents, understandably, were troubled by their children's behavior and felt frustrated, angry, and at the edge of their rope. Some of them were among the most loving and caring parents I have ever met and were totally unaware that their emotions were creating a negative home environment for their kids. In most cases, they weren't even aware of how unhappy they themselves were!

I initially developed the Family Empowerment Program to help parents like these work on creating a healthy, *positive* environment that would get their kids' behavior in line and put them on a path in life that would give them the opportunity to achieve their best potential. However, after I started teaching it, I realized that it is a program that can benefit *all* parents, especially parents of misbehaved kids, whether their behavior is a result of a brain imbalance or not.

Children who do not have a neurological or psychological problem but behave poorly—and this is the majority of kids who behave badly—are not doing so for no good reason. They are picking it up at home, and it's usually not because they have mean, uncaring parents. Many parents just don't realize the impact a negative environment or parenting style, no matter how subtle, can have on their children.

THE VIEW FROM A GLASS HALF EMPTY

A badly behaved, disruptive, and disrespectful child is a parent's worst nightmare. All parents feel this way, but parents of kids with real behavior-oriented disabilities take it the toughest.

It's natural for parents of limited means to sacrifice for the sake of their children, but some parents take it to extremes. Parents of kids with diagnosed mental disorders, particularly, sacrifice a tremendous amount and are willing to sacrifice even more "just to make their child right" or "get peace and quiet in the family." Most eventually resign themselves to the idea that they will have to sacrifice a lot for the foreseeable future for the sake of their child. They put their own lives and dreams on hold and, unwittingly, some of the dreams of their other children. They put aside their plan to move to a better home in a location with a better school system. They stop saving for their dream vacation. They can get so absorbed in their fears of what the future holds for their family and their disruptive child that it interferes with their job performance. Some parents tell me they are so deeply in debt trying to help their child that they don't think they'll ever be able to retire. They also give up on the dreams they have for their problem child—academic achievement, a sport's scholarship, a prestigious college, a great job. They have prepared for and accepted a life filled with sacrifice and many unknowns.

They are prepared, and they have accepted it, but it doesn't mean they are happy about it. Deep down, how can they be? Life isn't fair, and they're on the receiving end of a bad deal in life. I see it in the faces and hear it in the voices of parents all the time. They are fearful, bitter, angry, unhappy, and often even depressed that their life has taken a rocky road.

As I said, all of this is completely understandable. There is, however, a problem with this kind of attitude. If parents are negative, then the family whole family environment is negative. Any child living in a perpetually negative environment is going to adopt negative reactionary behavior, whether there is a neurological problem or not.

There's a lot of truth in the old-time sayings, "The apple doesn't fall far from the tree" and "He's a chip off the old block." Negative parents breed negative attitudes in their children. There is only one cause for a negative environment—parents.

> There is only one cause for a negative
> environment at home—parents.

You might be thinking these are the kinds of parents who don't care about their kids, so they wouldn't even want to read a book like this. The reality is, however, that many loving, caring, and well-intentioned parents *are* like this. In fact, parents who care the most are the ones who suffer the most and can become the most bitter. They just aren't conscious of it and can't see it in themselves. Negativity can get so ingrained in your personality and attitude it just seems and feels, well, normal.

Take a look at yourself and consider if you are unhappy, frustrated, or dissatisfied with any aspect of your life. If so, you can bet it's rubbing off on your spouse and kids.

If you can relate to this or you are thinking that this might sound like you, I want you to know that it does not mean you are a bad parent. It only means that you are *human*. Truth is, it is not as easy to see the glass half full as it is to see it half empty. But it is absolutely possible to change the way you view the world.

THE VIEW FROM THE GLASS HALF FULL

Chances are you're familiar with the bestselling book *The Secret* by Rhonda Byrne or the movie she produced by the same name. The secret to getting what you want in life, says Byrne, is through the universal law of attraction, which posits that we all have within ourselves the power to use conscious and unconscious thoughts and actions to transform any weakness into strength, power, and perfection. In essence, like attracts like. You can get anything you want by thinking positive thoughts about whatever it is you desire. Think negatively, and you attract negativity into your life. It's not quite as simple as that, but let's just keep with this thought for a moment.

> Think negatively, and you attract
> negativity into your life.

It's akin to the placebo effect in medicine. People who think they are getting a medicine to cure an illness but are actually given a sugar pill start feeling better because they believe they are getting a pill that is going to make them well.

Byrne, an Australian movie producer, made the documentary before writing the book, which became its own best example of the law of attraction. The book brought this metaphysical philosophy into the mainstream as the author made the national talk show circuit, including Oprah Winfrey, and attracted the interest of more than four million book buyers.

You could say that the secret really isn't much of a secret, however. Byrne was hardly the first person to talk or write about the law of attraction. The first person to ever use the phrase *law of attraction* was Charles F. Haanel in his 1915 book *The Master Key System*, in which he described the law as a powerful force of nature. Haanel states that to get anything in life, be it material wealth or well-behaved kids, you must first create a clear and powerful vision in your mind of what it is you want. The more powerful the vision, the quicker you will attract it. Reportedly, *The Master Key System* is the book that inspired Microsoft's Bill Gates to drop out of Harvard University and pursue his dream of putting a computer in every household.

In addition, *Think and Grow Rich* by Napoleon Hill, *The Power of Positive Thinking* by Norman Vincent Peale, and the numerous works of Anthony Robbins, who has been the motivational adviser to many of today's great leaders, all focus on using the power of a positive mental outlook to engage the law of attraction.

I believe there is a great deal of truth in this. I believe that if you consistently focus on what it is you desire, it will physically manifest in life. I believe it because I have seen it happen in myself and other people.

Now don't misunderstand me. I am not pushing a "think and it will happen" philosophy. This isn't magic. To make the law of attraction work in your life you need, as Haanel says, a vision of what you want and the motivation to take the necessary actions to make it happen. In other words, it needs to be part of who you are.

I believe this because I have studied all of these great authors and speakers. I have taken something from each of them and have been applying many of their principles to my own life for years. My persistence in exploring and perfecting Brain Balance and writing my books came from applying these principles daily in my own life.

Let me give you an example. Before my career in childhood neurological disorders, I worked with patients in some of the worst pain imaginable. These people needed to be in a rehabilitation program but were in so much pain and so depressed about it they didn't have the motivation to go through the grueling hours of rehab that were necessary to make them better and get on with their lives.

I wanted desperately to help them. I reflected on the insights I had gained from these great motivational leaders and the law of attraction and used those insights to design a motivational program that would help my clients think beyond their pain so they could get better. I was amazed (but not surprised) how people in so much pain made the connection—like attracts like. Good things can come from making an all-out effort. Motivation is a powerful fuel that can propel you to your goal. The Family Empowerment Program is based on the same principles, only it is designed for parents to attract positive thoughts and outcomes to their own lives and the lives of their children.

IT'S MORE THAN A BELIEF

If you're like me, it is not enough to take on face value that something works, especially something as esoteric as the law of attraction. I always need to know on the most basic level why things work, happen, and behave the way they do. When I first started reading about the law of attraction and how it is the secret behind some of the world's most successful motivational programs, I wanted to find out exactly how it worked. It wasn't enough for me to just take it as faith, so I don't expect you to either.

Considering that the law of attraction has been written about and debated among some of the most brilliant minds for centuries, I'm going to attempt to explain it at its most basic level. I'll preface it by saying there is probably more that we don't understand about the law of attraction than we do understand.

The law of attraction is based on the principles of quantum physics, which state that matter is too small to measure and comes in discrete particles of energy that form waves that are completely random in the universe. Therefore when we attempt to look at or measure the smallest particles in the universe, we affect those particles as beams of energy. However, we can never be certain that a particle is where we are measuring it because the simple act of measuring may change its position in space. As a result, we can only estimate where it may be at any given time.

This is why Albert Einstein believed that nothing in the universe is random. He also believed everything happens for a reason. The point being that at the smallest level, all matter can be reduced to waves of energy. Likewise, thoughts can also be related to waves of energy. At their core, they are the same as matter.

Universal laws tell us that like energy attracts like energy. So when we think of something or someone, the thought consists of the same basic energy vibrations as the actual thing or person we are thinking about. We set up a unique pattern of energy that is the same as the energy pattern of the actual object. So, according to quantum physics, thoughts attract the things and people we are thinking about. Thoughts really do become things!

When you think about it in terms of behavior, it makes a lot of sense. Like attracts like, and mental attitude is like a magnet. We behave in certain ways because we create certain electrical patterns in our brains that can be broken down into measurable patterns or waves of energy that are put out into the universe. This not only creates behaviors in ourselves but will also affect the behaviors of those around us.

> A positive attitude is like a magnet. It will affect a positive attitude in your children.

To me this has profound implications—and practical applications. Life is purely a reflection of where you consistently focus your thoughts. Positive thoughts attract positive actions and positive results. Negativity attracts more negativity. The more powerful your thoughts, the more powerful the energy you send out and the more powerful the feedback. It really is within our power to attract what matters most in life.

Now think of the changes you can implement if you apply this philosophy as a parent.

My Story

I became acutely aware of the power of the universal law of attraction early on when I started practicing this program on myself. I was coming up on my thirty-fifth birthday and was just starting to explore the principles in some depth.

My health and fitness were of major concern, as it is to many people of that age. As a health professional, I know the importance of personal health and I knew I had to make it a priority. So, I decided I was going to run the New York Marathon that year, in November just before my birthday.

Now, I had been a pretty good athlete in college. I was a quarterback on my college football team, and I considered myself to still be in pretty good shape. However, I knew I was setting myself up for a challenge. With just ten months to train, I sat down with my empowerment plan and wrote a clear vision of what I wanted, why I wanted it, and how I was going to attain it.

I imagined in vivid detail how it would feel to accomplish an athletic feat that I had never attempted before. I could already feel my focus and productivity soar as I envisioned myself running farther and farther. Picturing my family, especially my kids, cheering me on pushed my motivation in gear. I imagined their pride and excitement standing on the sidelines watching me run by. I also saw what a great example I would be setting for them, how it would influence them to take care of their own health as they got older. I hoped they would learn that sports and athletics do not have to always be about winning and losing; they can be about challenging yourself, pushing yourself beyond what you once thought was possible.

I used my empowerment plan to set my goals—my training schedule, my diet. I had absolutely no doubt that I would be running in the New York City Marathon come November. I was all prepared, except for one thing. I had incorrectly assumed that it would be easy to register for the marathon.

As with other shorter races I'd participated in, I figured you just registered a few days before the race. Boy, was I wrong. In April, seven months before the race, one of my associates mentioned that he had heard that the last day of registration for the marathon was just a few days away. I realized I had no idea how to go about the registration process. Then I found out the most devastating news: Something like a hundred thousand people try to register for the race each year, but only thirty thousand are chosen to run. Plus, there are rules and regulations, including having completed three previous marathons.

I didn't plan for one of the most obvious things, and it was going to prevent me from fulfilling my dream. After all the hard work, I felt I had screwed up royally!

A week later, I happened to run into a colleague who asked how my training for the marathon was going. I told him my story. He could see my disappointment and said, "I think I might be able to get you in." It turns out he ran a small running league for a group of public service workers that gets a certain number of guaranteed spots in the race. "If they're not all taken, I might be able to get you in." Sure enough, I got my spot. I was so happy, I gave him a giant hug.

Immediately I recognized that this was no accident or coincidence. I realized I didn't have the perfect plan, that sometimes, even if you don't know how it will happen, you just have to have a strong vision, purpose, and faith, and the universal law of attraction will get you what you need. It worked for me that November.

As I ran past my family, I could hear their cries. They were just as excited as I was. I couldn't help but go over to the side of the road and give them a hug. My kids were hugging me so tightly it almost hurt. I looked into their faces and I saw the expressions I had imagined months ago. This moment was almost exactly as I had envisioned it.

Now years later, my children are all into exercise and are in great shape. They often remind me of the times they saw me run the marathon and how that made an impression on them. They also tease me about how it almost didn't happen. I am convinced that because of my positive thinking through those long nine months of training, the law of attraction got me in the race.

FEAR, OUR NATURAL TENDENCY

Think about how the law of attraction is affecting your life as a parent right now. Consider the basic universal truth that your life is purely a reflection of what your mind is focused on consistently. Or, to put it another way, you are ultimately responsible for everything in your life that you don't like.

Here's another basic truth: Most people are consistently focused on their fears—what you're afraid is going to happen. It's like a self-perpetuating prophecy. Your thoughts are like a welcome mat inviting negativity into your life. It's not unusual for us to focus on our fears because our brains are wired to look at the negative first. It's part of our survival instinct—fight or flight or, in terms of how the brain works, approach (a left brain trait) or avoidance (a right brain trait). Negative emotion is also a right brain activity, which is hard to change because the positive left brain likes familiarity and doesn't like transitioning to something new. This is why it is so easy for us to wallow in our fears and see the glass half empty rather than half full.

People have a tendency to spend so much time dwelling on their fears they almost never clearly think about what they do want in their life. To attract what you want, you must stay focused on what you want and not what you fear.

> To attract what you want, you
> must stay focused on what you
> want and not what you fear.

You see, when you focus on your fears you automatically draw other negatives into your life. Anxiety, frustration, anger, a bad attitude, negativity, lack of drive, and so on are all part of our focus on fear. It becomes our environment—an environment of our own creation, and the environment we create for our children. Living in a negative environment perpetuates negative emotions in our kids. They act badly because it's a negative emotion elicited by a negative environment. They act by what they know, and what they know is fear and negativity.

Most people have to spend a tremendous amount of energy to force themselves to be positive and motivated each day. My goal in designing this program is to make it much easier than that. After all, if it's so hard for an adult to do, you can't expect your children to do it.

If you have a child with a neurological disorder, the negativity is going to be even more pronounced because it is going to create the secondary behaviors I mentioned earlier. This is avoidance behavior, and it is a child's natural tendency as a protective mechanism.

So, if this is a natural tendency, if we're driven by natural instinct to respond this way, is it possible to change?

Absolutely.

RECONNECT WITH *YOUR* DREAMS

I know from working with parents of children with functional disconnection syndrome (FDS) that finding motivation and sticking with it doesn't come easy. These are often parents in deep emotional pain or depression who have been told many times by teachers and doctors that their child will never be like other children and that the best they can do is cope. Well, Brain Balance has shown that children with neurological problems can get better and even be like other kids. And Family Empowerment has shown other parents how to make positive change in kids who, excuse my bluntness, simply behave badly.

I've found, however, that motivating parents isn't as easy as motivating kids. Motivation in parents is often short lived. It can last a few hours, a few days, or maybe a few weeks until the next almighty explosion comes crashing down.

This was my challenge in coming up with this program. The reason it works is because it starts with the parents first. You will work on the Family Empowerment Program as parents, looking at what you want out of your lives and reconnecting with your dreams. Once making positive change in your life starts feeling natural to you, you'll be ready to start teaching your children how to do the same.

Parents tend to be selfless when it comes to their children, so when I tell them that they have to focus on fulfilling their own dreams and making themselves happy first, they act like I'm asking them to commit treason. At least at first, until they begin to understand the philosophy behind it.

Keep in mind that you are your child's role model, so if you have forsaken your hopes and dreams in life and have abandoned your goals for the future, chances are your children will follow in your footsteps. To create a positive environment at home and to help your child create noticeable positive change in behavior and/or school performance, you must create an environment of possibility in which your children can believe in themselves. This starts with changing the attitude within you.

You must create an environment of
possibility in which your children
can believe in themselves.

By instilling the right attitude, you are engaging the law of attraction and drawing on positive energies. Once you harness those energies in your own life, then you can manifest them in your children by coaching your children to do the same. Don't attempt to skip the parent part of the program and go straight to the children part of the program, because you'll be wasting your time. It's not going to work—it would be like trying to build a house without a foundation.

This program is designed to work for all families:

- Parents of kids who are in and have already been through the Brain Balance Program.
- Parents of children with a psychologically based behavior problem.
- Parents of kids who behave badly for no organically known reason.
- Parents of kids who are struggling in school and behind in their studies.
- Parents with no issues but who want to help their children reach their best potential in life.

In the end, helping your children model good behavior and reach their full potential is what the Family Empowerment Program is all about. It empowers parents and teaches them how to empower their children. I can assure you that if you use the principles and the tools I am about to share with you, you will see positive change in every person in your family. You will free yourself to find and follow your own dreams and set the same example for your children so that they can follow their own dreams. The way to lead is by example.

Let's get started.

· 9 ·

The Power of
Positive Parenting

When you determine what you want, you have made
the most important decision of your life. You have
to know what you want in order to attain it.

—DOUGLAS LURTAN, AUTHOR

If you've gotten this far, I assume you're ready for change. You're
ready to empower yourself and your family to pursue family harmony and a future filled with potential.

Family Empowerment is an interactive program. I will be asking
you a series of questions, and you will write down the answers. You
will also perform a series of empowerment exercises that you will
put in writing. In fact, you will be doing a lot of writing, so I have
provided Family Empowerment Worksheets in the back of the book
(beginning on page 283), where you can write your answers. If you
prefer something more private, you can use a personal notebook.
To help you along, you will find similar downloadable forms at the
Brain Balance website (www.brainbalancecenters.com).

Your written answers are essential to get you to where you need
to go. Physically writing down your innermost thoughts actually

engages the left brain motivation you are going to need to make the Family Empowerment Program work on your behalf. So, when I ask you to write, you must write!

GET IN A RIGHT BRAIN STATE OF MIND

If you are having behavior issues in your family, it means something must change to make them go away. By definition, change means creating enough motivation to move someone to act. The way you're going to motivate yourself to change starts with looking at your life honestly and with no illusions.

We generally don't do this. Most people tend to assuage the bad situations in their lives by rationalizing. It's all part of human nature. We have a tremendous ability to rationalize almost any situation so it never looks as bad as it truly is. If you need an example, think about kids screaming in a restaurant who are annoying everybody within hearing range except their parents. It's a credit to the human spirit and to perpetual hope (even if it is a reflection of bad manners)!

> We have a tendency to rationalize
> almost any situation so that it never
> looks as bad as it really is.

There are really only two primary motivators in humans: pain, a right brain response, and pleasure, a left brain response. The most powerful of the two is pain because it is associated with the primary imperative of survival. To survive, we must have a fear and/or withdrawal drive strong enough to motivate us to fight or run away, depending on the situation.

When survival is threatened, the right brain responds by triggering neurotransmitters to release hormones that turn on the gut-wrenching, heart-pounding emotion we know or dread as fear. The brain recognizes this fear or withdrawal instinct as emotional pain. It gives us powerful negative reinforcement. It responds by causing subtle contractions of the gut muscles that make us feel uncomfortable or even slightly sick in the stomach. This is the gut feeling we get when we are fearful or when we know we are doing something wrong. It is designed to make us feel bad so we are strongly motivated to stop, withdraw from what we are doing, or never do the same thing again.

It is also a powerful motivator to get us to change our behavior and to act immediately. However, the rational and positive, or approach-driven, left hemisphere, can justify almost any situation as long as it isn't immediately life threatening. It sees the bright side of a situation so that you can continue to move forward even when your gut instinct is telling you to stop.

So, the first step to motivating ourselves is to quiet the left brain, stop rationalizing, and let the right brain and our gut lead us. We must feel the fear fully so that we are driven to finally change our behavior. The more fear, the more we will be driven toward action.

Change does not come easy to humans, and the reason is the left brain loves routine and familiarity. It hates transitioning to new things. So to change from being in a perpetual state of negativity you must train your brain to inhibit left brain emotions. You inhibit left brain emotions by feeling the fear and the pain so the right hemisphere can motivate the change. So to set you up for your transition, I'm going to ask you to wallow in your misery for just a little bit.

To do this, I am going to ask you a question, and I want you to think about it carefully and answer it with brutal honesty:

What is it about your life that you dislike or absolutely hate?

Think about your life and where it is today. Think about all the things you are unhappy about—the things you wish didn't exist and could just disappear.

I know it is painful to look at life in stark reality, but if you want to change it, you need to feel the pain. List all the things you feel you cannot take anymore, the things you say you are sick and tired of, things and even people who you wish you could get out of your life.

Most parents find this difficult to do. However, I tell them and I'm telling you: Don't be hesitant or afraid to answer truthfully. Give yourself time to think about it, as much time as is needed. Write it on the Family Empowerment Worksheets or in your notebook.

When you have completed your list, take a look at it and answer the following two questions:

How important is it to change this situation?

What are you willing to do to change what you don't like about your life?

If you're not willing to make change happen, stop now and give it more consideration. I've seen many parents, when considering their family situation, rationalize, "It's not that bad. I can live with it." However, "it's not that bad" isn't good enough when it comes to your family. It's not going to cut it, if improving your home environment and changing their children's lives for the better is your top priority. The it's-not-that-bad attitude is a negative attitude.

I see it and hear it from parents all the time. And I tell them that creating a positive environment at home and changing behavior and/or their children's academic performance must be their number one imperative. Being satisfied with mediocrity when it comes to family isn't going to get them to their goal.

You should never settle for less than what's possible when it comes to your children, and that starts with not settling for unsatisfactory circumstances in your own life.

Once you've taken a look at your life, warts and all, and you've committed to creating change, you'll be in the right mind-set to generate the motivation you're going to need to make the positive life-altering change that will help you realize the potential in yourself and in every member of your family. Before you can change and help your family you must first create the change and realize the potential in yourself.

CREATING YOUR VISION

I can't help but notice how frequently undertones of negativity come into casual conversation. That's how natural and prevalent it is. People grouse about their jobs, their relationships, their kids. It's not like they're complaining—at least it's not their intent—it just comes out as a natural statement of life.

When I hear parents go on about what's wrong with their kids, their families, and their lives, I can't help but ask, "So what is it that you *want*?" It usually causes a quizzical look or a change of subject. But I never really get a straight answer. It's more often, "I don't know what I want." People know they're unhappy and what they're unhappy about, but they don't know or consider what would make them happy.

> We're so fixated on our fears we have no room to think about what makes us happy.

They're so fixated on what they fear is going to happen as a result of their current situation that they never even think about what it is that would make them happy. They are getting exactly what they're asking for, what their unconscious mind is attracting. It happens automatically. What you consistently think about happens. It's the law of attraction. So why not use the law of attraction to get what you *want*? Put a positive force in your thoughts and visualize where you want to be.

To help you tap into this power and replace negative thoughts with positive, I am going to ask you three questions. Write down your answers as you did before.

What do you want?

Why do you want it?

What do you have to do to get it?

The answer to your first question will be your *Goal*, the answer to the second question will be your *Purpose*, and the answer to the third question will be the *Actions* you will take to get there. Together they create your GPA Plan.

When I throw these questions out to parents in an empowerment class, I see faces change from enthusiasm to overwhelming bewilderment in an instant. Really, where to begin!

The way to begin is by compartmentalizing, or chunking, your life into specific units, or what I call areas of focus.

Areas of Focus

Most people's lives are divided into little lives: family life, work life, and personal life. Within each of these units of your life, you actively spend time in certain pursuits. These are your areas of focus.

Take a big-picture look at your life (a right brain activity) and pull out the things that are most important to you. Is it your family, friendships, career? Maybe you wish you could spend more time with your children. Maybe you have a friendship that has fallen by the wayside because your life has gotten too busy. Perhaps you love sports or wish you were more outgoing, or maybe you want to be thin and physically fit.

Material things? This is a fine goal, too, if it's what is going to make you happy and feel fulfilled. We're all different, so anything is game. The key is, What would make you happy? Maybe you secretly want to own a fast car, or even race one. Maybe you want to rekindle your love life with your spouse, or you're a single parent wanting companionship. What about your job? Is it really what you always dreamed about or would you really rather be doing something else?

Think about the areas of your life that are important to you, because this is what you're going to be focusing on for as long as it takes to make your dreams reality. Keep in mind, it has to be *your* dream, something you want for yourself, not for someone else.

To help guide you, I've provided a list of some general areas of focus that are close to the desires of many people. Use it to brainstorm the areas of your life that are most important to you. It's a starting point for you to design your own list. The sky's the limit. Give yourself time to think about it. It is your life and your dream, so don't hold back. There is no room to be judgmental.

Remember, it is essential that you actually write your answers down.

► **Sample Areas of Focus for Parents**

- Family
- Friendships
- Career
- Personal health
- Fitness
- Emotional health
- Money and finances
- Body image
- Spirituality or church
- Social life
- Love life

- The environment
- Sports
- Material possessions
- Education
- Hobbies
- Home improvement
- Creative pursuit
- Giving back to the community

SEARCHING FOR BALANCE

Life is a series of ups and downs, highs and lows. There are good days when everything goes great and other days when nothing seems to go right. Sailing through life on a straight reach and even keel sounds wonderful, but it's not reality. Also, wouldn't it make life a little boring?

Ups and downs are part of human nature, but we only get stressed and down in the dumps when there are too many downs and not enough ups. And when this happens, we tend to exaggerate them. This happens a lot when kids are acting out.

In this next exercise you're going to assess your path along the rocky road of life. To do this, you're going to take the areas of focus that you have just identified and rank them according to how satisfied you are with them now in relationship to where you want them to be. This represents the balance in your life.

Turn to page 285 or download the "Area of Focus Balance Graph" from the Brain Balance website. In the spaces provided across the bottom, fill in your areas of focus. The numbers on the left, from 1 to 10, represent your current level of satisfaction with each of these areas, with 0 representing rock bottom and 10, nirvana. Place a dot next to the number that matches your level of satisfaction for each area of focus. Then connect the dots to form a graph. The graph represents the life path you are now traveling.

Here's an example of what one might look like:

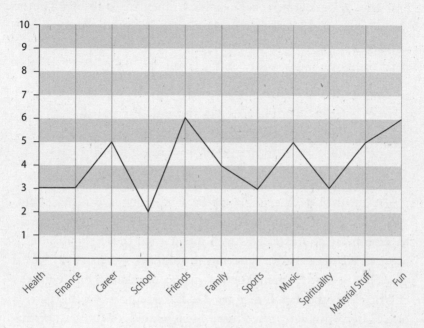

Is the road on which you're traveling smooth and straight or is it jagged and filled with ups and downs? In my experience working with parents with family behavior issues, the path can look mighty treacherous with some highs but lots of lows. Now you can see why you get stressed. It's no wonder so many of us feel like we are stumbling through life!

If you're like most people, certain areas of your graph are ranked higher in your satisfaction rating than others. And guess what? If you're like most people, these are the areas where you already focus most of your time. They're your comfort zone. You tend to avoid or ignore the areas on the lowest end of the scale as much as possible. They represent pain and fear. But this is your life. You've already recognized all of these areas as important to getting what you want out of life. This means you have to focus on *all* of them.

Think of the parents who focus on a child with a disability to the exclusion of work or personal happiness. They are so absorbed in the fear of what might happen that the rest of life suffers. Some people struggle at work and become dispensable in the eyes of the boss. Next thing you know, you're on the layoff list.

Parents out of balance and out-of-balance parenting create a negative family environment.

As altruistic as this might appear, it is really parents out of balance and out-of-balance parenting that create a negative family environment, no matter how well intentioned those parents are. It also exacerbates negative behaviors in children, whether they have a disability or not. It strains the marriage and relationships with the children and other family members. In fact, studies show that parents of children with autism are three times more likely to have financial problems or lose their job. A one-dimensional life—everything for one while forsaking others—is a life out of balance. In reality, nobody benefits.

This is why the Family Empowerment Program focuses on the parents first. When you are on an airplane getting the routine instructions from a flight attendant on what to do in the case of an emergency, remember what she says about the oxygen mask? Put your face mask on first before putting it on your child. A child isn't going to be securely safe unless the parent, the caretaker, is equipped to handle the situation.

This goes against our natural instinct to make sure our children are safe first. The lesson here is clear. Your children cannot be safe if you are not safe. Your children cannot be happy if you're not showing them how to be happy.

ONE MOTHER'S EXPERIENCE

I've seen all too often how a parent can unintentionally cast a negative pall onto a child's life. I remember in particular one child who I was treating who had been diagnosed with attention deficit/hyperactivity disorder (ADHD) and oppositional defiant disorder (ODD). Though his mother, whom I'll call Catherine, was making a major commitment by enrolling him in our Brain Balance Program, it was pretty obvious that she was skeptical. She had a negative attitude about everything.

Despite his ODD diagnosis, Brian was a nice boy and was quite cooperative with our staff. Testing showed he was intelligent but had the classic unevenness of skills common in all children with FDS. Testing also confirmed a right brain deficiency, which fit his ADHD and ODD diagnoses. In talking to his mom, we also pieced together that his behavior problems started to escalate about a year earlier when she and Brian's dad were getting a divorce.

I sat down with Catherine and explained what we found and how we could help him. She agreed to enroll him in our program but said openly that she doubted it would do any good.

As is our policy and philosophy, I met with the mother every week during the three-month program. At our first meeting, I told Catherine that Brian was already showing progress in all areas, and I stressed the importance of carrying out certain activities at home in order to continue seeing improvement. Every week she'd come back and complain that Brian refused to do the exercises with her, even though he willingly did as instructed when at the center. "I knew he wouldn't do as I ask," she said, "and I let him know that I wasn't surprised and was very disappointed."

We also had designed a diet for Brian based on a nutritional analysis and laboratory testing. We found he was sensitive to wheat and dairy, which was contributing to his problem. Our nutritionist spent a significant amount of time with Catherine explaining the need to avoid these foods and showing her how she could make foods that he would enjoy. For example, Brain loved to eat waffles for breakfast, so she gave Catherine an easy-to-make gluten- and dairy-free recipe that was a hit with kids in our program. Catherine pushed it aside. She said she was a single mom and only had time to give him commercially made waffles you can pop in the toaster. "I have a waffle maker, but I never use it," she noted.

I finally sat down to have a talk with her. I told her I understood how difficult it must be as a single mother to make Brian's breakfast and lunch, but I stressed that it was important that she prepare his meals as we instructed if she wanted to see a real change in her son. I explained that there are ways to find the time, that other moms and dads have overcome the same problem. I asked her what time she had to be at work in the morning and, to my surprise, she said she didn't work. It turns out that her ex-husband made a handsome income; she got a large alimony and child support settlement and was able to keep up her substantial home without having to work. It was obvious that she was not motivated to commit to Brain Balance, even though we were gaining ground.

As we talked more it came out that she was bitter over her husband leaving her for another woman. It turns out she and Brian's dad fought constantly. To make matters worse, they often carried out their arguments in front of Brian, and Catherine made no bones about how she felt about her ex to anyone who would listen, including Brian.

She told me Brian's dad spoiled their son out of guilt. "His dad is hopeless. He'll never go along with any of the stuff you're asking," she said.

Well, we can change a neurological problem like the one that was causing Brian's behavior problem, but it's almost impossible to make a kid feel happy—and therefore have a change of attitude and behavior—living in a perpetually negative environment. Brian was surrounded by anger, bitterness, and resentment.

We were making progress at correcting the imbalance that was manifesting itself as ADHD and ODD, but even if he was neurologically healthy, we worried that psychologically there wouldn't be much of a change in his bad behavior, unless his mother decided to change, too. I knew I had to try to get both of Brian's parents into our Family Empowerment Program. Catherine said it would be hopeless, but she gave me permission to call Brian's dad, Kevin.

When I spoke to Kevin, he was very pleasant. He said he was more than willing to do whatever he could to help his son. He was very frustrated with his ex-wife's attitude and confided that her negativity and hostility led to their divorce. He said he felt frustrated because he saw what was happening to their son, and he felt guilty about it.

It turned out that Kevin was more agreeable to attend the program than was Catherine. During the classes, all the parents were very upbeat and eager to give the program a try, except Catherine. She would comment aloud that the whole idea was nonsense and complained it was a waste of her time. Her anger toward her husband was palpable.

Other parents were frustrated by her bad attitude and many asked her to just trust the process. Catherine didn't realize it but, ironically, she was acting like the poster child for every point I was making. Being a parent like Catherine is what I wanted people to make sure they would avoid. It was impossible for Catherine to focus on what she wanted because she was drowning in negativity. She feared her son would continue to be a problem, but it was she who was making it a self-fulfilling prophecy.

I spent a lot of extra time with Brian's parents, especially his mother. As I got to know her better, I could tell that deep down she desperately wanted to be a good mother. She was so paralyzed with fear about what was to become of Brian that everything she could envision was not good.

I finally convinced her to get serious about Family Empowerment and give it a try. I knew it would work and I told her so. Kevin got on board, too, and I was able to help direct them to create a unified vision of what they wanted for their son and what they needed from each other to make it work.

The vision helped Catherine slowly dislodge her fear. Months later, when I was doing a follow-up on Brian with Catherine I could see a big change of attitude. She said she finally realized that if she really wanted to help her son she had to be more upbeat about her own life and she needed to build a positive relationship with his father. She said she was now focusing on her own dreams and desires.

She told me how she had dropped out of nursing school to get married. She got pregnant almost immediately and wanted to stay home with her baby. She said she realized now that she was jealous of her husband's success and resented the time he spent away from the family. Then when her son was diagnosed with ADHD and ODD, it drove her from resentment to despair.

The Family Empowerment Program was a life-altering experience for Catherine. It reawakened her dream to become a nurse, and she had plans to go back to nursing school. It was too late to save her marriage, but she and Kevin were able to develop a close bond where their son was concerned.

As for Brian, Brain Balance turned out to be everything it is meant to be. His parents tell me that he is no longer a discipline problem at home or school and that he's getting straight A's. Though dad's not usually there, all three of them work on their action steps on Sunday night at their own home. Kevin made sure, however, that he was able to take his son to watch Catherine graduate from nursing school.

AIM HIGH

What is the potential of any person? Every time I ask this question, I get the same answer: unlimited.

Most of us believe instinctively that all people are born with unlimited potential. But look around you. How many people do you know who are living up to their full potential? I bet not very many.

We are all placed on the same path in life, but it is up to us to choose the direction. You can take the high path to success or the low path to defeat. Obviously, everyone wants the path to success. Now that you've started this program you are already on your way.

· 10 ·

See Results Before They Happen

Great minds have purposes, others have dreams.

—WASHINGTON IRVING, NINETEENTH-CENTURY AMERICAN HISTORIAN

What would you try if you knew you wouldn't fail? I love asking people this question because it opens up a universe of possibilities.

If you've ever worked for a successful profit-driven company, you have seen how results drive motivation. It's contagious. Success breeds success. Think of Apple, Microsoft, or any other great company. These companies are powerful not only because they have great leadership but because they know how to motivate employees to make things happen and produce results.

One of the best things about success is that it is motivating. It means that when you start reaching for your goals, you can visualize actually attaining them. You start believing in yourself and your potential.

You become even more inspired. You believe even more in your potential. You take even more action, and you get even greater results. Positive results reinforce beliefs and motivation.

Positive results reinforce
beliefs and motivation.

But you say that's not you? You've already felt disappointment. You've believed in yourself in the past and you failed. You have no faith in yourself. Well, keep in mind the law of attraction. You can change your attitude by creating results in advance.

So, how do you find the contagious motivation to make your life successful and happy, if there isn't much to be happy about to begin with?

By creating your results first!

This is the core of the Family Empowerment Program. You will create your results first by creating a powerful vision of what you want your results to be. You will create a vision of the results you want for each area of focus you have identified. Each vision needs to be so powerful that it excites you. It's so exciting that you think about it all the time and you can't wait for it to happen. You feel like a kid at Christmas. In fact, this is exactly how I want you to feel—beside yourself with excitement and expectation. Just like a kid at Christmas.

DARE TO DREAM

What do I want?

Thinking about our heart's desires comes naturally when we're children, but real life and its disappointments happen on the way to adulthood and dampen our childish dreaming. Only I don't think it's childish at all.

I love talking to kids and asking them what they want to be when they grow up. They don't hesitate and light up when they answer—an astronaut, a famous singer, a doctor, the president of the United States. They believe anything is possible.

As we grow up we are taught to be rational, to not expect too much from life, that we will only be disappointed if we hope for too much.

For this next exercise I want you to find the child in yourself. Don't think as an adult with adult expectations. Think as a child would, believing that anything is possible.

Create a vision for your ultimate goal in each area of focus you have identified. Write it down in the appropriate space on your worksheet. Give yourself enough time to craft your perfect vision.

Write as if you were writing a story, *your* story. Create the story you want for your life in each area of focus. Don't hold back. When you get to the point at which you can actually see and feel it happening vividly in your mind's eye, you are creating the result.

Think about how you become absorbed in a story when reading a good book or watching a good movie. You get so involved in a character's emotions that it almost feels as if the plot were happening to you. Think of the times you've woken up from a pleasant dream and for a moment you don't know if it was real or not. This is the mind-set I want you to create when writing your ultimate vision. Use descriptive and exciting words. Make it amazing.

You need to do this in each area of focus, but you don't have to do it all at once. Some people get so involved and in such a great mind flow that their imagination becomes flooded with possibilities and they just write and write. Others like to ruminate and complete the exercise over a few days or a few weeks. It doesn't matter how quickly you finish this exercise, but it's essential that you do it.

Select a time when you are alert and in a positive mind-set. If you are stressed or agitated, you're not going to be able to get to the place in your imagination that you want to be. Some people find it helpful to do this in a quiet place; others listen to soothing or inspiring music.

Enjoy the process. Think of it like taking a vacation from your problems. You are escaping to a place that has always been in your dreams.

Don't worry about how you're going to make this happen. I will show you how soon enough. For now, just dream, and dream big!

To help get you started, here is a sample of what I wrote many years ago as my ultimate vision for health and fitness:

> I am a lean mean energy machine! Each morning I awake rested and energized. I bounce out of bed excited to start my day. I look in the mirror and I love the way I look and feel. I feel powerful, and I know I can accomplish anything I want. I love to exercise, I eat well, I am the envy of my friends and an example to my children.

THE POWER OF WHY

Why do I want it?

The answer to the question of why is probably the most important step in this process because it is what will create the motivation you need to make the results happen.

This is your *purpose*, and it is a powerful motivator. Purpose is the reason to want something. In many ways it is more important than the vision you just worked on because purpose gives you the motivation to attain that vision. Motivation creates the positive energy waves of the law of attraction. Purpose is what will keep you motivated when the going gets tough and will sustain you when it gets even harder.

Motivation goes hand in hand with self-esteem. Many people believe that what we already have or already have achieved is what gives us self-esteem, but this is not true. Research has proven— and we have seen the aftermath in many public personalities—that neither money, material wealth, nor fame bring self-esteem. Having purpose is what builds self-esteem.

Doubt is the negative mind-set that fights purpose. Sadly, too many people have the attitude that says why bother pursuing something you know you won't get? You might want to ask that question to the millions of people who play the lottery every week! Somebody's eventually going to win, right? You can't be a contender unless you get in the game. You see, purpose is a powerful motivator.

Purpose, however, is often clouded by the negatives in our lives. We've all accomplished something important at some time in our life: Maybe it was getting a job, being promoted, developing a patent, running a marathon, or making an incredible sale. How often do you think about the wonderful and meaningful accomplishments you've achieved compared to the times you think about what is going wrong or could go wrong in your life? Probably not nearly as often.

You see, many of us are in the right brain frame of mind that allows us to dwell on what isn't possible rather than visualize what can be possible. We're more prone to brood over our failures than to celebrate our successes. It's like the law of detraction. Shake it out of your system. Get it out of your head.

You've already created your results in advance by creating your vision. Your next step is to focus on your purpose. *Why* do you want to realize your dream?

For parents, there is no greater purpose than the well-being of their children.

For a parent, there is no greater purpose than a child. If you have a child with a disability, you have an even more compelling purpose. The mere fact that you have this book and are working on this is proof that your children are a prime motivator in your life.

Now I'd like you to think about how achieving the results you've visualized will enhance your life and the lives of everyone in your family.

Here's some food for thought. Let's say your goal is to make a million dollars and the idea of it excites you and drives you to take massive action. You achieve the goal of making a million dollars—but then what? If there was no purpose behind making a million dollars, your goal was really only superficial. Goal isn't your prime motivator, *purpose* is.

You don't work like a dog for a million dollars so you can sit and look at it and stuff it under the mattress. You're more likely to work even harder, though, if your purpose is to buy a beautiful house, send your kids to a great college, or secure a financial future for a disabled child. The purpose will always be there. Giving your children the means to achieve their full potential is the ultimate purpose of the Family Empowerment Program.

I want you to now look at each of your visions and ask yourself *why* it is important to you. This is your purpose. You might have one purpose, three, or even ten. It doesn't matter how many purposes you have in mind as long as you write them all down. Again, put your purpose in words using descriptive, powerful, motivating language.

To help you along, here is the purpose I wrote for my health and fitness goals:

Without my health, I have nothing. Without energy, I am useless.
I have tremendous responsibilities to myself and my family. They
depend on me to keep them safe and secure. I must be able to do
my best every day, and I cannot do my best if I don't feel my best.
I need to set the best example for my children, so they grow up to
be healthy and fit adults.

GETTING TO YOUR GOAL

The next step is to actually select your goals. Review your vision and purpose and think about what it is going to take for you to achieve your results. I suggest aiming at no more than three goals in each area of focus.

If the results you desire are long range, then set your goals in achievable increments. Most of us are more motivated when we aim at achieving an immediate goal. It is also less overwhelming. I find three months is a good incremental goal time.

For example, let's say one of your areas of focus is health and fitness and your goal is to lose sixty pounds. That's a lot of weight and certainly should take as much as a year if you do it in a healthful way. This means that fifteen pounds would be realistic in three months, or five pounds a month. You can see the results, because you chose them in advance. You can almost feel what it would be like to be fifteen pounds lighter. You can envision what you'd look like fifteen pounds lighter, then thirty pounds, then sixty. With each five pounds lost, you're building confidence and fueling motivation.

Goals must be specific and measurable. For example, the goal "I want to lose weight" is not specific and measurable. However, the goal "I want to lose sixty pounds in the next year" is specific and measurable. You cannot manage what you cannot measure. Measuring your progress is motivating in itself. It also makes it more fun, like you're in competition with yourself. Have you ever played a game where no one kept score? That wouldn't be much fun, would it? You may have enjoyed the game, but the only games you ever remember playing are those where there are winners and losers.

Think carefully about your goals. How much time is it *really* going to require for you to attain them? Be realistic and make sure they are measurable. Write them down in the space provided on the Family Empowerment Worksheets (page 283).

As an example, these are the top three goals I came up with in my health and fitness area of focus:

Time Frame: 3 Months

- Lose 12 pounds.
- Reduce my body fat to 10 percent.
- Do 10 full pull-ups at once.
- Bench press 225 pounds one time.
- Run an average of 10 minutes per mile.
- Do 6-mile runs.

Make sure your goals are challenging but also attainable. I often come across parents who are reluctant to talk about their goals. They fear that if they talk about them and don't pull them off, then they'll look foolish or disappoint someone, especially their kids. Well, talking about them reinforces them in your mind just like writing them down. You're committing to them. Not talking about them is negative thinking, and your reason for not wanting to talk about them is just more negative thinking. So, keep those negative brain waves out of your achievement plan!

The next step is the big one—make those goals reality. This is the heart of the Family Empowerment Program and where the work really begins. Let's get to it.

· 11 ·

Making Your Goals

Goals are dreams with deadlines.

—DIANA SCHARF-HUNT, AUTHOR

Would you attempt to start a business without a business plan? Would you plan a trip without some sort of itinerary? So then why should you live your life without a plan?

It is not enough to just wish for something to happen. No matter how positive your thoughts, you're not going to experience the law of attraction unless you take action and maintain a powerful commitment to stick it out. That means you must have a plan. You need to plan your life around your goals. This is the most important part of the Family Empowerment Program. Having an action plan to carry out your goals is what will make the visions you just created for every important area of your life become reality.

Most people don't center their daily lives around their goals. A lot of people barely give them any thought at all, except possibly on New Year's Day, when they make a resolution: "This is the year I'm going to _____." For the first few weeks of January, gyms are crowded because people resolve to get in shape, and restaurants are empty because people resolve to trim their waistlines. By mid-February, the gym crowd has thinned out and restaurants are humming again.

The resolutions don't work because there was no plan to make them work. People lose their focus and go back to dwelling on their fears. It's a testament to the law of attraction, or I should say the law of *detraction*.

Now, let's take a look at what would happen if you took your New Year's resolution—a goal like the ones you just planned—and scheduled it into your everyday life so you'd work on it as sure as you eat breakfast, lunch, and dinner. This reminds me of the principle in neurology that says frequency of activity is more important than intensity when it comes to having a lasting and powerful effect.

If you'd connect with your goals simply by looking at and reviewing what you wrote out once a month, you'd increase the likelihood of achieving those goals by 1,200 percent because you would reinforce the idea of taking action. If you were to sit down and review your goals just once a week, your chances of meeting them would increase 5,200 percent. If you reviewed them once a day, your chances would increase 36,500 percent! I think we all like these kinds of odds.

By the same token, the chance that some negative event would occur and take you away from your goals goes down by the same percentages. So the more committed you are to your goals, the less likely something will interfere with your effort in achieving them.

Centering your life around your goals will make your life more efficient and less stressful.

BENEFITS OF A GOAL-CENTERED LIFE

I accomplish a great deal in my daily life because I center my life around my goals. They are scheduled into my life just like my appointments with my patients. I have plenty of free time and I rarely feel stressed. It's all because my life is efficient. I am doing what I am supposed to when I am supposed to, and I do it 100 percent. Most important, it gives me time for the top priority in my life: my family.

Writing this book at this very moment is among my goals. It started as a vision, with a strong purpose and a list of action steps. I knew it would happen. I saw it advance along with all of the other things in my life I am doing at the same time. None of my other goals is being sacrificed because of it.

If I'm going to the gym, I commit a time to go and I go. The time is there because I planned it that way. Think of how many times you throw your gym bag in the backseat of the car in the morning and come home at night with it untouched. If you're like a lot of people, this happens more often than you'd like.

Hitting closer to home, how often do you promise to be at your kid's soccer or Little League game or school play only to show up at halftime or barely making it at all? But if you scheduled in your appointment book to be at soccer at 5:00 p.m. and considered it as important as a meeting with your boss, you wouldn't be late. Can you think of a reason why showing your support for your child isn't as important as a meeting with the boss? Of course not. Yet teachers tell me all the time that kids who are trouble in the classroom have parents who are too busy. It always seems that the children can wait while other matters take priority.

Going to your child's game or school play is just as important as a meeting with your boss. You don't ignore a meeting with the boss, do you?

I have never met someone who has consistently kept their focus on what they clearly wanted who has not eventually accomplished their goal.

I remember one woman who came to one of my empowerment

programs several years ago. Marjorie was an accomplished, pleasant, and attractive woman who seemed to have everything going for her. She seemed to be very happy, and I sensed she had a strong marriage and family life. I remember even thinking to myself, *How am I going to help her?*

In her own quiet way, Marjorie delved into the empowerment process. She was very attentive, and I could see she was deep in thought as she explored the three key questions, designed her vision and purpose, and developed her areas of focus and action steps. At the end of the last session, everyone in the class had an exact GPA Plan for their life and eagerly talked among themselves and shared their dreams. But not Marjorie. She just smiled, thanked me, and said good-bye. I often wondered what was in her plan and what she was doing with her life.

A few years later, I found out when she dropped in on one of my sessions. She told me life was great.

"I am actually living out my dreams because of you and what you taught me," she said. "Going through the Empowerment Program made me realize that my lifelong dream was to live in Las Vegas. It's always been where I wanted to live, but I was too afraid of change. I never even told my husband. We both had great jobs here, a wonderful house in a beautiful neighborhood, and our kids were in great schools. I never saw how changing all that was possible. So I pushed it to the back of my mind. After taking your class I realized what I wanted, and I connected with a very strong purpose. I didn't know how it was going to happen, but I knew what I wanted and why I wanted it and I was determined to make it happen."

She told me how she finally approached her husband about what she really wanted and why. "I was so afraid of what his reaction was going to be, but it turned out he was just as eager to move away as I was." They sold their house, bought their dream house in Las Vegas, and they both landed great jobs. Their kids were excited about the new venture, too, and settled well into their new school. "Within six months of taking your class I was living my dream and I am so happy," she said. She gave me a big hug and a kiss on the cheek. "I just wanted to say thanks."

I would have never guessed in a million years that anything was missing in her life, that she yearned to live, of all places, in Las Vegas. It goes to show that you can never know what someone else's dreams might be.

What makes us happy is doing what we once thought was impossible.

What makes us happy is doing what we always dreamed, getting ourselves to do what we had once thought was impossible. Knowing what you want and why is motivation. Action, however, is what will make your dream reality.

CREATING YOUR ACTION PLAN

The main reason people waste time and never get things done is because they don't plan. Most people jot down a to-do list and feel they are accomplishing something by ticking off items one by one. To-do lists don't work because they have no structure. And they can create stress. Think of how many times you've gone to bed at night with a to-do list still incomplete.

Think about your life now. Do you feel stressed out all the time? If so, why? Do you even know?

Most of the stress we feel is because we don't feel like we are doing enough with our time. The old cliché of feeling overworked, underpaid, and underappreciated is hovering in our brains. We can see no light at the end of the tunnel.

You get stressed because all day you carry your to-dos around in your head. You are thinking about all the other things that are coming up that must be accomplished, but you don't know what or how they're all going to happen. You're stressed because you worry about how you're going to fit it all in. You can't sleep because you are afraid you won't wake up in time to accomplish everything that needs to be done. The first step to relieving that stress is to keep an action list and keep it with you at all times. Whenever you make an appointment, or you think of something you need to do, write it down. You don't have to be too descriptive; the main thing is to get it recorded so you can plan to do it. To make sure I always have my list with me, I use the notepad on my cell phone.

Your list is important because it is what you will use to help make your *weekly action plan*. When you have a clear vision, a strong purpose, and an action plan and you schedule that action plan into your life and make it a priority, your stress level goes down dramatically. You feel fulfilled. You know you are doing the most you can, and you believe you will ultimately get everything you want, which eliminates the rest of the stress.

It also allows you to enjoy the moment. You know that whatever you are doing at that moment is exactly what you should be doing. That alone gives you a feeling of satisfaction and accomplishment—and there's no stress in that!

If you follow these steps, you will connect with your goals on a daily basis. They have a purpose and are goal directed. They are measurable and designed to be constantly evolving so you can continually move toward achieving your visions.

Make a vow to yourself that you will follow these steps and you will realize your dreams.

Commit to It

Set aside one hour a week as your planning hour. This is the most important step in the process. Schedule a day and a specific time each week to devote to your action plan. This is when you'll review and organize the action list that you've been keeping and decide what actions you must take during the upcoming week to achieve your goals. Next, you'll schedule a specific day and time to do them. Most people, myself included, do this on a Sunday night.

You'll need:

- Your action list.
- A weekly planner, calendar, or a datebook.
- Your written vision, purpose, and goals.
- Pencil and paper.

Set aside one hour each week to plan your action steps for the coming week.

Write Up an Action List

Review your vision, purpose, and goals and then look at the list of action items you have compiled to do in the coming week to achieve your goals. It doesn't have to be anything more formal than this sample.

► **Sample Action List**

- Go to gym.
- Grocery shop.
- Talk to financial adviser.
- Practice language.
- Go to soccer game.
- Go to dance practice.

- Find tutor.
- Speak to teacher.
- Check on life insurance.
- Play basketball.
- Call travel agent.
- Call parents.
- Call, Jim, Jane, and Bill.
- Go to church.
- Call car dealership.
- Make doctor's appointment.
- Go to dentist.
- Go to health food store.

Chunk and Prioritize

If you have a busy life, as most of us do, your action list might be very long and a little overwhelming. So to make it more manageable and less intimidating, you will take all of those action steps and group them by your area of focus. For instance, go to gym, make doctor's appointment, go to dentist, and go to health food store are all related to your health area of focus. Organize your actions by your areas of focus; now instead of fifty actions you have maybe ten groups of five actions or even five groups of ten actions, making your weekly plan much less intimidating and much easier to manage.

The next step is to prioritize them. Number one is your top priority, the things that you absolutely must do no matter what. Number four, for example, might be something that can be pushed into the next week if, when you get to scheduling your week, you realize you've overbooked yourself. It's also an action that can slide if some unscheduled event comes into your week. For example, if your boss needs you to see a new client during the time you're scheduled to go to the gym—a number one priority—then your can reschedule the gym at the time you were planning to go to dance practice—a number four priority.

Prioritizing is important because you don't want to loose sight of *any* of your goals. So, if you do miss dance practice one week, you'll move it up to a number one or two priority the next week so it doesn't slide again.

▶ **Sample Priority Action List**

AREA OF FOCUS: HEALTH AND FITNESS

- Go to gym: 1
- Grocery shop: 3
- Make doctor's appointment: 2
- Go to dentist: 4
- Go to health food store: 5

AREA OF FOCUS: CHILDREN

- Find tutor: 2
- Speak to teacher: 1

AREA OF FOCUS: PERSONAL FINANCES

- Talk to financial adviser: 2
- Check on life insurance: 3
- Go to bank: 1

Commit the Time

Look at your list again in terms of time commitment. How much time will each action step take up during your week? Consider them in real time. If it's the gym, for example, consider travel, changing, and shower time. If it's grocery shopping, figure in the time it will take you to get to and from the store and also the time it will take you to put the groceries away. Write the time next to the priority.

- Go to gym: 1   1 hour
- Grocery shop: 3   1½ hours
- Play basketball: 2 2 hours

Schedule It

Now, look at your weekly planner and schedule each item on your action list, taking into account the time you've estimated it to take. Plan the actions around the other obligations in your life, such as your job. Start by scheduling in your number one priorities and go down the line until your week is filled.

As I noted earlier, I find that the easiest place to keep my schedule is on my cell phone. It is the one thing we all seem to carry with us everywhere we go. Almost all phones today offer some sort of datebook and a notepad for writing reminders to yourself. If you don't have a phone like this, get one. It's a very worthwhile

---

Set Your P.A.C.E.

- **Plan:** Create your vision, purpose, and actions and carry them with you.
- **Act:** List and prioritize all your goals and plan them into your schedule each week.
- **Commit:** Devote the time and resources required to make your vision a reality.
- **Evaluate:** Measure your successes weekly and update actions to stay or get back on track.

investment. If you're not electronically inclined, then get yourself a professional day planner.

Most smart phones have calendars that also synch with your computer. So you can do your list and calendar on your computer and synch it with your phone or vice versa. However, keeping your schedule only in your computer isn't a good idea. You can carry a phone or day planner with you. A computer isn't as convenient.

Revise and Improvise

Doing a schedule only once a week means it isn't going to be picture perfect. Your child gets sick and you need to get him to the doctor. A client is on the brink of pulling her account and you have to hop a plane as soon as possible.

As the week moves on, unexpected things are always going to come up. Don't let these surprises create stress. Take a deep breath, look at your schedule, and revise. Something has to come out. So is it your hairdresser appointment or the miniature golf you were planning to play with your son? Consider your action steps and your priorities. Obviously, you cancel the hairdresser appointment.

Consider your action steps your top priority.

You can help keep your life organized by being aware of what your day is going to be like, hour by hour, by reviewing it the night before. Make it a part of your nightly ritual to take five minutes to check your calendar for the next day. Do it at the same time every night, such as after you brush your teeth, so it becomes habit. This will avoid a lot of stress if you somehow get overbooked. If there literally aren't enough hours in the day to do what you want to do, pare your list down to what you need to do. Your action steps, as always, take top priority.

Measure the Results

As I said before, no game is fun if you don't keep score. So as you accomplish more and more with this system, it is very important to measure your results. Each week, review your success and evaluate your mistakes. Remember, results are a great motivator. We can create them in advance with a powerful vision, purpose, and action plan, but it's when we get real measurable results that we start to feel unstoppable.

Refine, Refine

As you are moving forward, you will need to refine your action steps to reflect what is going on in your life at the present time and keep on the road to progress. You may need to add more action steps and replace steps. Think of it as an ever-revolving process. The important thing is to keep negatives out of your life and to keep moving forward.

Focus, Focus, Focus

Scheduling your action plan and other requirements of your life means that you can focus 100 percent on what you're doing because you aren't thinking ahead to a laundry list of items that somehow randomly need to get done. Imagine being able to eliminate all that stress and finally be able to focus 100 percent on your children. All this will happen if you just simply commit and schedule it.

Imagine being able to eliminate all the stress
so you can focus 100 percent on your children.

Savor the moment. You'll see how much you'll enjoy your down-time because everything else has been taken care of and you are doing exactly what you're supposed to be doing right now. You won't be saying to yourself, *I should be doing . . .* , and feeling guilty about it. That's just needless stress. Putting structure in your life so you can accomplish your goals and focus on what's important to you in life is the ultimate stress-release technique.

When you are with your kids or your spouse, you are with them 100 percent because you're not worried about what didn't get done and what needs to be done. Imagine how this alone will improve your children's behavior!

Don't Expect Perfection

If you let yourself think about getting it perfect all the time, you'll be generating a negative thought process. So don't let it happen! The point is to be consistent in aiming toward your goal. If you goofed—say, walking two miles a day just isn't enough—then modify your action plan. Trial and error isn't trial and *failure* unless you give up.

You should also be prepared for setbacks. If you expect smooth sailing right to your goals, you're setting yourself up for disappointment. Distractions happen, and you will get thrown off course. The key is to get back on track as soon as possible.

When you don't, you are reinforcing the mentality that you will never get what you want. Your vision will become cloudy, your purpose will weaken, and you'll end up right back where you started, focusing on your fear. Don't let it happen.

Reach Out

You want to thoroughly think through the entire scenario of what your life will be like on the way to your goals. It should look exciting and doable. Brainstorm ideas with your family. Think about snags and how you can work around them. And don't be afraid to reach out when you need help.

Many people make the mistake of making their goal so big that it's overwhelming, and their immediate reaction is that it can be accomplished only by a monumental effort. However, if you look at a large goal as individual smaller goals instead, you'll get a different perspective.

Also, keep in mind that you don't have to make everything happen all on your own. Enlist help if you need it, just as you would in other aspects of your life. Let's say that your goal is to be a Girl Scout leader because it will be an enriching program for your daughter who is kind of shy and timid. However, you haven't a clue as to how to go about it. Then, reach out to other Girl Scout leaders for help. In fact, this becomes your first action step!

Or maybe your dream is to write a play. Same thing. Talk to others who may know a playwright with whom you can talk. Or you may need to take a writing class.

The Internet has put so many sources at our fingertips, it is almost impossible not to find the help you're looking for! Whatever you need, you should be able to find on the Internet—a consultant to write a business plan, a nutritionist to help you plan a diet, a coach to teach you how to play golf. If you don't have a computer, go to the library and use one there. Many resources at our disposal, such as the library, are free.

And don't forget to enlist the help of friends and colleagues. Some of your best resources may already be people you know. Most people will be flattered that you thought of them.

AN ORDERLY LIFE IS LIBERATING

Some people may feel like the weekly action plan is too structured, taking away their freedom and spontaneity. They like to be able to do what they want, when they want. Nothing could be further from the truth. Having a plan is freedom.

Organization is crucial to accomplishing results and living a stress-free life. In fact, it is so important there are seminars, experts, and a whole genre of books aimed at helping people organize their lives. Disorganization creates tension in the family environment. When you're disorganized, everybody around you feels the tension. And the effect on kids is the same as getting conflicting messages from their parents: It creates anxious, insecure children who will act out and will most likely be disruptive and oppositional.

Everyone talks about taking control of their life and how liberating it would be. Having organization in your life, having a plan, is liberating. I guarantee that you'll find it will make your life so much easier. You'll feel less stress. You won't be running around at the last minute in a frenzy and snapping at the kids. When you are efficient and everything you are doing is moving along as planned, you are at ease. You're smiling, so your kids are smiling, too.

If you feel life is starting to unravel and keeping up with your goals is getting impossible, pause and consider the following thoughts:

Stuff happens. In the real word, things will come up that you do not anticipate and possibly that you do not want. Having and following a plan does not mean there's no flexibility in the schedule to adapt to life as it comes your way. In fact, you are better prepared to deal with the unexpected because the rest of your life is organized. When you're in control of your life during the routine of life, you're less likely to swing out of control when something unwanted suddenly comes your way.

Negativity breeds negativity. A positive and negative thought cannot exist in the same space. Keep in mind, however, that negativity isn't always blatant. It is both conscious and unconscious. Just as the universal law of attraction says motivation, both conscious and unconscious, can cause great things to occur, the opposite is just as true. Negativity is its own self-fulfilling prophecy. If you start thinking that everything is going wrong, that's exactly what's going to happen.

Stay focused on your vision. Each week when you're planning your schedule, take a few moments to reconnect with your vision and purpose. Write them down on a piece of paper and carry it in your purse or wallet. Turn them into a screen saver on your computer. Have them printed on a piece of cardboard that you can use as a bookmark. If you read before going to bed, it'll be the last thing you see and read before going to sleep.

By staying focused on your vision, you are connecting with your goals frequently. Each time you review your vision, you activate the law of attraction and harness its energy.

In my area of focus for family, I have my wife and children. My vision is what I want my relationship to be with each of them. I write down how I can help each of them achieve their goals and become the person they want to be.

There are two areas of life that no one ever really teaches you how to manage, and they happen to be the most precious and dear: your personal life and your family. Yet, people rarely if ever develop a plan to make their life and their family the best they can possibly be.

To manage your relationship with your family, you must first be able to manage your own life. Once you have this in check, you're ready to move on to make life for your family more meaningful.

· 12 ·

Becoming Your Child's Coach

Hope sees the invisible, feels the intangible,
and achieves the impossible.

—UNKNOWN

You now have a vision of your future and a purpose for achieving it. You have created your own goals and implemented your action plan. And now you'll soon be ready to help your children change their behavior and their lives in a meaningful way.

How soon? Well, that depends on you.

And how? In the same way you're making changes in your own life. You're going to teach this process to your kids and coach them through it so they will embrace it as eagerly as the start of a new day.

The only way you're going to truly engage their interest and get them positively involved in the process is to do it yourself first. This program is much too important to involve your kids until you are completely confident about doing it yourself. *You learn by doing and teach by example.* If you can't coach your children through this process with the conviction that it is fun and pivotal to their future, they'll pick up on it easily. You'll lose their interest right away.

The way to get comfortable and confident is through practice. You must be able to handle your own experiences—the accomplishments and letdowns—so that you can counsel your kids with empathy as they go through the ups and downs themselves. You need to be able to relate to the process so you can feel their frustrations. If not, their interest will wane.

The time to start involving your children in the Family Empowerment Program is when you yourself start to feel the power of the program. When I teach the program, most parents click into it and feel the excitement fairly quickly. Once they get started, they recognize its value almost immediately. And once they get really involved, most parents say they can't imagine not doing it.

Imagine the benefits your children will reap from finding direction in life at such a young age. Imagine what they will be able to accomplish. The possibilities are limitless.

SETTING AN EXAMPLE

When you first start the Family Empowerment Program (or shortly thereafter), let your kids know what you are doing, but don't let on that your ultimate intention is to do this as a family. Not even a hint! Your strategy is to subtly engage their curiosity and interest by letting them watch you.

Make sure your kids notice what you're doing. You want them to see you in practice—doing your planning session every week, taking up new interests and pursuits, and sticking with them. Most important, let them see that you are enjoying yourself in the process.

Tell them about your goals. They'll be interested in what you're doing and will probably ask a lot of questions.

By watching you plan and achieve
your incremental goals, your kids
will want to get involved, too.

You'll be creating a lot of positive energy, and they'll be able to see it. As you get happier, you should start to see a change in them, too. But this isn't your primary goal. It is just the beginning. Witnessing the changes in you will help your children see that the same is possible for themselves. They'll be imagining themselves doing as you're doing.

As I've said before, you are your child's role model. Your child will realize that these positive changes you are making in your life are, by extension, changing their lives. They should notice that:

- You're focused because you've become more organized.
- You're calmer, so you respond rationally to an unwelcome situation rather than yelling and blaming.
- You're happier because you have a vision of the future and a purpose.

This is the point at which you'll want to bring them into the process and make it a family program. You'll now be teaching by example.

So, let's get started.

THE GROUND RULES

When the time is right—when you're confident and at ease with what you're doing—you'll know it. Don't involve your kids a minute sooner. And when you do, you're going to do it subtly. Do not propose it as a formal program with a sudden proclamation, "Okay, gang, this is it. Starting Sunday we're going to have weekly family meetings and you're going to start setting goals." If you want to squash any prospects that your kids will actually participate and think it's going to be fun, this type of approach will do it.

Actually, the first thing you're going to do is a little behind-the-scenes planning because it is important that both parents be on the same page, especially if you live in separate households. Children can live by only one set of rules.

> **Your greatest chance of success is if both parents are involved in the process.**

Your greatest chance of success is if both parents are involved in the process. It's fine for you and your spouse to have individual visions and goals as long as they don't conflict or compete in any way. Ideally, they should complement one another, but your goals for your children should be the same. Remember, inconsistency of message from the parents is the number one reason for behavior problems in kids.

If you can't interest your spouse (or former spouse) in getting personally involved in the program, you at least need to get him or her to buy into it and show interest in your children's involvement.

Both parents should also be present, if at all possible, when you bring this to your children. If you and your spouse have had problems in the past and your children have witnessed it, that's okay. If either one has been considered (or is) a bad role model, that's okay, too. Your children don't expect you to be perfect, but they expect you to practice what you preach. In fact, if you've had past flaws as a role model, this is a powerful opportunity to change your image.

Before you start to work with your kids, the two of you must get together and come up with a shared vision and purpose for your family and each of your children. Use the same process you used to come up with your individual visions. Discuss and agree on specific goals that you, as parents, want to achieve with each child *and* with each other.

Once that's done, you're ready to go. Chances are you have one child, or even more than one, who has behavioral issues or learning problems. More and more families today have multiple children with disabilities. This plan should be done with every child in your household, disability or not.

THE KICKOFF

The scene: Your kid's favorite space.
The time: When opportunity knocks.

You want to introduce your children to the process in a totally casual way. You want to involve all your children, but you're not going to do the kickoff as a team. Rather, do it one on one.

Find a quiet time in which your child is in a comfortable spot amusing himself and casually join in. Maybe he's watching television or playing a game. Perhaps the two of you are relaxing on a Sunday afternoon reading a book together and your spouse comes in to sit with you. When I have these kinds of conversations with my kids these days, I like to sit in front of a fire, play some enjoyable music, and just start talking.

With each of your children, wait for the right moment and then start the conversation by asking them about their dreams and wishes. Simply ask, "What do you want to do with your life?" Just let them talk and make sure to listen attentively. The beautiful thing about children is that, unlike adults, they know exactly what they want. All you have to do is ask. You'll be amazed how eager they are to tell you.

I remember the first time I did this with my daughter. She was about six. We were sitting on my bed, and I simply asked, "What do you want to be when you grow up?" She looked at me with the kind of smile I used to see when Santa had arrived on Christmas morning. She was so happy describing all her dreams.

I was amazed how such a simple question brought forth such amazing ideas and emotions. I feel I know my children really well, and you probably feel the same way about your kids, but I can tell you from personal experience and what other parents tell me that you will learn things about your children you never knew.

Whatever they say, listen patiently without judgment and listen carefully. Then simply ask, "Would you like me to help you make your dreams come true?" Of course you know the answer will be yes, most likely followed by a question for you: "How?"

At this point I usually produce a cool-looking journal of some sort and say, "What if I told you this was a magic book, and everything you write in this book will come true. What would you write?" If the child is very young, you may have to write it for her, but otherwise let her do the writing. Then I say, "This is actually how it works. If you write down your answers to three questions, you can make all your dreams and wishes come true." This really gets her attention and, of course, she's eager to hear them. Then casually ask her the three key questions that you now know by heart.

Your children haven't realized it yet, but
you have just transferred ownership
of their behavior to them.

This is how you get your children started and this is how you get them hooked. They haven't realized it yet, but you have just transferred ownership of their behavior to them; their behavior is now their own responsibility.

THE STRATEGY

Parents have a tendency to tell their children what they should want, how they should act, and what their goals should be. This is especially true of parents of a child with a disability. In this process, however, you are going to listen to what *your children want* and help them develop a plan to make it happen.

Parents tell me all the time that they have tried to engage their children in all different types of behavioral plans, but their kids refused to go along with them. These plans didn't work because somebody else—you or a counselor or a psychologist—was in charge and made your child feel intimidated and helpless.

This plan is different because it offers children the opportunity to be in charge of their own destiny. They'll create their own plan, so they'll be eager to follow it. It will give them direction and teach them responsibility. They also have security and support from you.

If you find your children are resistant or oppositional, it only means that they are craving and fighting for independence and autonomy. The best way to address this is by allowing them to make some of their own decisions. Tell them this is part of the program. This tactic can immediately turn the most obstinate child into a more compliant one.

If you follow the program correctly, you will be pleased with the results. These are the rules that will make it work:

- ■ Your job is to coach and guide (an important job!), but you can't dictate or try to persuade your kids to take a different direction.
- ■ You can direct your children toward the areas in their lives that need improving, but be subtle. Ultimately, the decision with be theirs.
- ■ Your children will set their own goals with your *help*, not your *advice*. There's a distinction. Offering help goes like this:

"Honey, what do you think you'll have to do to achieve this goal?" Advice is the natural parental instinct as in, "Here's what you need to do," or worse, "Don't you realize what you're going to have to do to get this!?"

■ Your kids will establish the rules and the punishment if the rules are not enforced. This is an extremely effective tool because if they fail at something and there is a negative consequence, you're no longer the bad guy, because your child will be carrying out the punishment of her own choosing. The punishment children choose for themselves often turns out to be harsher than what you would have chosen. Trust me, I've seen it hundreds of times!

■ You'll have your children go through the process just as you did, including putting the plan in writing. True power comes into play when they write it down. It is important to instill this in your children. Get them used to writing their plans.

> True power comes into play when you get
> your children to put their goals in writing.

At this point you can reveal to your child that this is a family program, that everyone in the family will be involved in the same program you and your spouse are doing. Many children eagerly go along, but others are likely to pose the obvious question, "Why do I have to do this?" And this brings us to the final rule:

■ Be positive. You don't want to say, "Because it's time to bring some law and order into this house." Give them an honest answer: "We'll all be shooting for what we want. We'll be rooting for each other. We'll get closer as a family. We'll be happier, and you'll have the best opportunity to make the best of your life."

Rules of the Game Plan

Through a child's eyes the Family Empowerment Program should look like this:

- Wow, what a dream come true! I don't *have* to do this; I *get* to do it!
- This is going to be fun! Keeping track of my goals is really cool.
- My mom doesn't tell me what to do anymore. She advises me when I need help.
- My parents aren't yelling at me all the time and what a relief! I feel totally different around other kids. I feel as good as everybody else.
- School suddenly feels a lot more fun. I like going to school.

GETTING STARTED

You're going to guide each of your children into selecting their areas of focus and then answering the three key questions:

- What do you want, either now or in the future?
- Why do you want it?
- What do you have to do to get it?

Areas of Focus

Help your children focus on the most important areas of their lives. Tell them about the thought processes you went through to come up with your own categories. Elaborate and be descriptive. Show your kids how passionate you are about your areas of focus so they will emulate you and be just as ardent about their own.

Again, it is not your job to select their areas of focus for them. But you can ask them questions that will help steer them into making the best choices for themselves. Some of these questions might be the following:

- What is it you think about most during the day?
- What do you wish for when you blow the candles out on your birthday cake?
- What do you like most about school? Why?
- What do you dislike about school? Why?
- What would you like to change about your relationship with your friends if you could?
- What's your favorite fun thing to do?
- What do you want the most for your brother or sister?

It is best to give your children a list of choices that you can generate based on their individual interests, relationships, and academic status. Explain that they will answer these three questions for each category they select and that they must write everything down in their journals. Explain the GPA Plan:

- What do I want? becomes the *Goal*.
- Why do I want it? becomes the *Purpose*.
- What do I need to do to get it? becomes the *Action*.

Your children shouldn't pick too many areas of focus, as you do not want to overwhelm them. Children naturally have fewer areas than adults because their lives are not yet so complex. I recommend no more than four to six for children five to ten years of age and six to eight for older kids.

The best thing is to give your children choices. Show them the following list or create your own:

▶ **Example Areas of Focus for Children**

- Health and fitness
- Food and nutrition
- Behavior
- School
- Athletics
- Music
- Social skills/making friends
- Physical environment/cleanliness
- Chores
- Family relationships
- Fun and excitement
- Following directions
- Hobbies
- Emotional control
- Spirituality
- Focus and attention
- Personal appearance

Once your children have chosen their areas of focus, you will simply ask them to answer the three questions. One area of focus children always select is school. Just ask, "What is your vision of your perfect life at school?" Offer to brainstorm with them if they can't come up with something right away or if you sense their response is tentative or unsure.

A typical example of what a child may come up with is this:

- I want straight A's.
- I want to make my parents proud.

What Do Kids Pick?

When it comes to picking areas of focus, children most frequently choose these:

- Sports
- Dance, music, theater, and so on
- Physical environment
- Health
- Personal appearance
- School
- Family
- Organization
- Social relationships
- Activities
- Material stuff
- Fun/entertainment

- I want to hang out with the smart kids.
- I don't want to get in trouble in class.

Then use what each of your children came up with to help them craft a powerful vision.

Sample Vision Statement

I'm going to study real hard and do my homework every day right after school, start my projects ahead of time so they will be the best they can possibly be, and study two days for a test so I can become a straight A student.

Then you are going to ask them the second question, "Why do

you want this?" This is the purpose. Now take what your kids say and help them create an ultimate purpose statement.

Sample Purpose Statement

I want to make my parents proud, hang around with the smartest, most popular kids, and get an academic scholarship to an Ivy League college.

Setting Goals

Time seems longer to children than to adults, so you want to make sure that you set short-term goals that can be measured on a weekly and, when necessary, daily basis. Most children, especially those with attention problems, cannot plan out too far in advance, so the time frame must be manageable. The long-term goal should be no longer than three months or three-month increments for a large goal. And as you learned with yourself, the goals must be measurable.

> The goal is to achieve success that will reinforce the new behavior and will build the child's confidence.

For each area of focus, the goals should be simple, just enough to make an impact but not too much to be overwhelming. The key is to achieve success that will reinforce the new behavior and will build the child's confidence. Again, guide your child but make sure that he is selecting his own goals.

► **Sample Goals**

AREA OF FOCUS: HOME ENVIRONMENT

1. Clean room without being told.
2. Make bed without being told.
3. Put clothes away and keep room neat without being told.

AREA OF FOCUS: BEHAVIOR

1. Willingly attend and participate in school activities.
2. Show respect for parents and teacher at all times.
3. Cooperate and do chores without making a fuss.

AREA OF FOCUS: SOCIAL SKILLS

1. Play with others without being mean or disruptive.
2. Make playdates with at least two new classmates.
3. Listen to others and do not interrupt them when they are talking.

ONE FAMILY'S STORY

A few years ago a well-known couple approached me after coming to listen to one of my Brain Balance lectures in New York City. I recognized the husband immediately, as he was a fairly popular writer whose books I enjoy. They said they got what I was talking about and asked if they could bring their seven-year-old son to our center on Long Island for an evaluation.

The couple, whom I'll call John and Rita, told me the school and other specialists told them their son should be on medication for attention deficit/hyperactivity disorder (ADHD). However, they were resisting taking this monumental step. "That's why what you had to say piqued our interest and curiosity," they said almost in unison. They seemed to be on the same wavelength.

Our tests found that their son, David, displayed the characteristics of ADHD with Asperger's syndrome tendencies. Though quite bright, he was impulsive, hyperactive, and did not respond correctly to social cues. As a result, he was somewhat of an outcast in school and got in trouble a lot. At home, he acted strangely aloof. They were considering homeschooling because his classmates bullied him often, and his teachers were frustrated with him. His parents had already been called to the principal's office a dozen times that year, and he was only in second grade! I could tell this was heartbreaking to his parents. They saw Brain Balance as hope for David and signed him up for a session that upcoming summer.

During our initial meeting, I could sense tension between John and Rita, and I got the impression the cause was deeper than what was happening with their son. Rita played the role of caregiver and brought David to his daily session. John showed up when he could.

During one of our weekly meetings, Rita implied that John had attention problems himself and seemed depressed. She said he was going through a long spell of writer's block, and it was creating some financial strain on the family. She hesitated, then said, "John's a great guy and willing to do anything to help our son, but he seems really lost when it comes to parenting."

Once that was off her chest, she let the rest spill out. She complained that John got uneasy when their son acted out, and his usual response was to do nothing rather than take corrective action. "When he does do something about it, his response is too extreme and totally inappropriate," she said with a sigh. She resented having to be the sole disciplinarian.

David did remarkably well in Brain Balance. The principal and his former teachers noticed a dramatic change in his behavior when he entered third grade. John and Rita laughed when they told me how the principal approached them during a parent school function.

"We thought, uh oh, what did he do now," Rita said, "but actually he was coming to us to praise David. He said, 'I don't know what you did, but I have to tell you I can't believe how much your son has matured. He is a completely different child.'"

That was at school. At home, however, David was not much different from how he had been before, even though our tests confirmed that he no longer fit the criteria for ADHD or Asperger's syndrome and had age-appropriate skills in all functions.

This was a clear sign to me that something was amiss in the home environment. Without voicing my suspicion, I suggested that the two of them might want to attend the next Brain Balance Family Empowerment Program. "It's a natural progression for parents in your situation," I said. They eagerly agreed.

Right from the start, Rita was a willing participant, though perhaps a little skeptical, but John looked like a deer caught in the headlights. He was taken aback that the program was more about the parent than the child. The notion that he could be contributing to his son's problem came as a big blow. However, as soon as he got the drift of what I was attempting to do, he got totally into it.

As a writer he was in his element. I could see how he was tapping into his natural ability when it came to answering empowerment's three key questions. He could visualize well. He wasn't the nervous, tentative, and somewhat morose person I had observed on previous occasions. I was fascinated watching him. As he was writing his dreams and connecting with each purpose, a different person emerged. He sat tall and looked the picture of confidence. For the first time I saw a real smile on his face.

As if through osmosis, I saw the same change happening in Rita. I had always noticed an angry edge in her. I remembered that in our meetings she'd make me kind of nervous because it often seemed like she was ready to scream or cry. I remember watching them as they were writing their visions. One time I caught them smiling at one another and exchanging a wink. They left that session arm in arm, and I could see that they adored one another. I was still puzzled as to what was going on at home that was impeding David from behaving well. I still wasn't sure when the session ended. Their only comment to me was, "Thank you."

So, what *was* going on at home?

A few weeks later I met up with Rita at a follow-up Brain Balance meeting to discuss David's home behavior. I asked how things were going since taking the empowerment class.

"Your program actually changed our lives," she said. "John's a totally different father. And we're a much happier couple. We're a team. David's a much calmer child."

> John was second-guessing himself when it
> came to discipline and would respond the
> way he thought his wife wanted him to act.

It turned out, she explained, that John was always second-guessing himself when it came to disciplining David, and he would respond in the way he thought his wife wanted him to act. Only he always got it wrong. Rita, however, didn't know this and figured he was just ineffective at parenting. It created an undercurrent of resentment that their son picked up on. David sensed the tension he was causing, which made him sullen and irritable at home. Even though he was neurologically better, tension at home was creating a psychologically based behavior problem.

"It turned out that it wasn't hard for us to get on the same page because we were actually much more in sync with each other than we realized," Rita explained. "We had just never before, shall we say, compared notes."

John had been drifting emotionally. He had lost his focus. He was in a slump because of his fears. He didn't want to be an incompetent father and he worried that his writing might not always be adequate to keep up with his growing financial responsibilities. He also had a hunch that he himself had had ADHD as a kid and felt guilty that he might be the source of his son's neurological problem. He hadn't recognized his own emotional baggage until he got immersed in the self-reflection that is part of the program and was forced to really consider what he wanted most in life.

Shedding his fears allowed John to pick up on a dream he had had for such along time he had almost forgot about it. He wanted to write a historical novel. "The program showed me the way to do it," he told me when we ran into each other recently. His book became a bestseller and was even optioned for a movie.

In one year, their life had completely turned around. David's behavior at home changed as markedly as it had in school. John's book success gave the family financial freedom, and John and Rita had renewed their romance.

The last I heard from them was a thank-you note Rita dropped off at my office. "How can I thank you enough," she wrote. "You not only gave me the son I knew was always there, but you gave me back my husband and my marriage and you helped us to fulfill our wildest dreams. How does someone repay that?" Our eyes welled up as we gave each other a hug.

It's happy endings like this that make me feel like I have the best job in the world.

· 13 ·

Family Action Patterns

Crystalize your goals. Make a plan for achieving them and
set yourself a deadline. Then, with supreme confidence,
determination and disregard for obstacles and other
people's criticism, carry out your plan.

—PAUL J. MEYER, FOUNDER OF FAMILY MOTIVATION INTERNATIONAL

In my experience working with children, I find that they love having goals. It offers them a challenge, gives them something to
work toward, and gives them an awesome sense of accomplishment
when they succeed. It also gives them amazing focus, so they chan-
nel all their energy on their goals. Even children with focus problems find they can block out some of the distraction around them
when they have *their own set of goals* to think about.

This isn't meant to say that it's always going to be easy or, depending on your family situation, that it will be easy at all. But you've
already taken a monumental step, so there's no turning back now!

This is about the time you're going to get your entire family on
board. You're going to move from your individual children's personal journals to a giant family scoreboard. This is where the process
becomes fun because your children can see their goals in action.

THE MEASURES OF SUCCESS

The ability to track and measure the success of your children's goals is the backbone of the Family Empowerment Program.

Before the process starts, you must find out where your child currently stands in relationship to his goal. The best way we've found is to tie each goal to a number on a scale. This number becomes what we call the *baseline*.

This can get a bit touchy when it comes to addressing problems such as behavior, motivation, and attitude because they are hard to measure and subjective by nature. However, you can objectify and measure anything if you have the right tool.

The area of health and fitness is probably the easiest category in which to establish a baseline because it is measurable. If your fourth-grader's goal is to compete in high school gymnastics and he wants to be able to do twenty-five sit-ups but can only do five, then five becomes the baseline. Other examples of a measurable baseline are these: how much you want to weigh compared to how much you currently weigh, and how fast or how far your child wants to run versus how fast and far she can run now.

So how are you supposed to know how your children are doing in areas of life that you are not always there to witness and measure? By enlisting the help of coaches, teachers, and other important people involved in your childen's nurturing.

We do this all the time at our Brain Balance Achievement Centers. We have "goal cards," similar to school report cards, that we give to parents, teachers, coaches, instructors, and other adults involved in the goals children set for themselves. You'll find samples of these forms, which you can copy, beginning on page 295 or you can download forms from our website (www.brainbalancecenters.com).

Essentially, this is how it works: Meet with each adult involved in your child's life and tell him or her the purpose of the process and what you are doing. Each person who plays a part in your child's goals should get a feedback form listing your kid's goals. For example, a coach would be given a form listing your child's athletic goals, a teacher would get a form with his academic, behavior, and other related goals.

Ask the coach or teacher to rate your child as she currently stands in relationship to where she wants to be on a scale of 1 to 10. However, you'll notice the sample forms contain a lot of numbers, with some going as high as 50. This is important because you want to have plenty of room for your child to grow and you want your child to be able to see her progress. If you make the scale too simple with too few numbers, it can appear that progress is moving too slowly.

Discourage the teacher or coach from being too generous. This will only be counterproductive. However, if the adult picks a number leaning toward the low side, then your child will find it easier to see progress early on. This is very important in keeping her motivated. The number the teacher or coach fills in will be considered the baseline.

If the child sees the person every day, like a teacher, then the adult should file a grade on a daily basis. If it is once a week, such as a dance or music teacher, then ask him or her to fill in a grade after each meeting with your child.

Don't hesitate to meet and discuss this with teachers and coaches and ask their support. I have yet to come across a teacher or another adult involved with children who is not willing to participate. Mostly they will be impressed with what you're doing and will participate wholeheartedly.

Also, keep a goal card of your own for each of your children with all their goals and baseline numbers. This will be the form you will use when you sit each week to review each child's progress. (Sample forms are available beginning on page 295.)

Once the goal cards are filled out, sit down with your child and review them just as you would a school report card. In this case, however, no matter how onerous the score is, do not lecture your child. This should be a pep talk. Encourage her "you can do it" attitude, even if at the moment she doesn't have one. With your coaching, she will.

Remind your children that the goal cards are designed to help them achieve the goals of their own choosing. You may have slightly directed your children to focus on areas important in their lives that need improving, but these are the goals that will lead them to their ultimate vision. Ask your child, "How far up the scale do you feel you can get in three months?" Tell her to select a number that is challenging but realistic. You should have a basic idea what your child can achieve (though she could surprise you!). If you think the number she chose is too aggressive, gently influence the scale down a few notches. If you think the number is too low, let it be. Allow her to get a feel for the system. She may feel scared and lack confidence. Let her build confidence with success. No matter what, this should always be a positive experience.

> No matter what, this should always be
> a positive experience for your child.

Baseline to Perfection

Here's a way to establish your child's incremental goals:

1. Take the baseline number as determined by the teacher, coach, or other authority figure and help your child determine the percentage of improvement that he should realistically shoot for in three months. If the baseline is 10 and the scale goes to 50, a 50 percent improvement comes in at 30.
2. Divide the number by 3. Your child has to move up 10 points a month, or approximately 1 point every three days, to make his goal.

Break the goal into months and weeks. Set it up in a way that a child can see progress on at least a weekly basis. Some things can be measured on a daily basis. This goes a long way in improving your children's confidence and self-esteem because he can see his goals as much smaller and more achievable.

You have now created results in advance! Your children can see their goals, and they believe they are achievable. They have a clear vision and a strong purpose. Now they're ready to take the actions necessary to achieve them.

TAKING ACTION ON YOUR KIDS' ACTIONS

Here are a few examples of how you and other adults working on your children's goals should use the report cards.

AREA OF FOCUS: MY ENVIRONMENT

1. Make my bed and clean up my room daily.
2. Put toys and other stuff away after I use them.
3. Clear school desk at the end of the day and keep my cubby clean.

Determining Baseline

Let's take your kid's room. It's a mess. Currently you are telling him multiple times a day to clean up his room. On a scale of 1 to 50, you rate him low—a 2.

He almost never makes his bed no matter how often you ask. Low again—a 4.

Your kids' teacher says his desk is a mess. On a scale of 1 to 20 he gets a 5.

You'd think measuring how clean your boy's room is would be

somewhat subjective, but it doesn't have to be. Think about how many times a day you have to remind him to make his bed or pick up after himself. If it's 10 times a day and the goal is to get to 0, you have a measurable goal.

Initially you might want to rate him daily, but as time goes on and he improves, you can rate him only every few days or every week. If things start slipping, so does the report card, and monitoring gets strict once again.

The strategy you are working toward is to permanently change your child's behavior by reinforcing it with measurable success. Initially, this takes a lot of work because it needs to be measured daily. Eventually, as the child's behaviors become reinforced and modified, he won't need to be reminded as often and the ratings can become less frequent. The idea is that, eventually, he will use a plan like this as a type of self-discipline for the rest of his life.

> The strategy is to permanently
> change your child's behavior by
> reinforcing it with positive results.

GETTING WITH THE PROGRAM

Now comes the final question. Ask your child: "What do you have to do to get what you want?"

This is the crucial process and you want your child to answer thoughtfully. Tell her she needs to come up with three actions in each area of focus that will help her achieve her goals. You can help her talk through and brainstorm ideas, but in no way lead the conversation.

Children expect to be told what to do, so your children might be quiet or cautious, expecting you to make suggestions. Don't do it, even if they ask. If they truly get stuck, then recommend choices but offer lots of options, so they can choose. When they select three it will be your job to ask, "Are you sure you can work on these action steps each day?" When you get to a yes for all of them, you're ready to roll. They can see their results in advance, they have a clear vision and the best support group—their parents—to help lead them to success.

Parents often tell me that the worst night of the week in their household is Sunday. The kids work at the last minute on their homework and then end up acting out because they don't want to go to bed. Somehow the night ends up in a fighting match before everyone finally calms down. But this doesn't happen until it's late and everyone is tense. It's not a great way to prepare for the week ahead.

The main reason for Sunday night bedlam is that children with behavior and learning problems are anxious and afraid. Monday is the start of a new week of struggling in school. They don't know what to expect, and they fear the unexpected. They fear what they can't control, and to a child with a disability this means just about everything.

Even adults go through a degree of Sunday night anxiety, wondering, *What's going to happen this week?* or *I can't wait until this week is over*, just before dozing off. It's all because we fear the unexpected. For some people it is like they're waiting for an impending disaster to strike. But not if you have a plan. When you have goals you want to reach, you'll find you can't wait to get up on Monday morning. It's the power of the program and you will feel it. When your kids get on board, they will feel it, too.

There won't be bedlam in your household if you sit down as a family on Sunday nights and prepare your goals for the week just like you have been doing for yourself. I find it to be a great family hour—no computers, cell phones, TV, or video games. Just 100 percent family time.

Keep a running action list for each child during the week. If one of them has a test, a recital, a project due, or a party coming up, just jot it down on that child's list. If they are old enough, encourage your children to keep their own list, using their school agenda. Then on Sunday:

- Take out each child's weekly list of action steps.
- Categorize them by area of focus.
- Prioritize them.
- Allocate a time to each of them.
- Schedule them in writing.

Once you get the entire family involved, you should consider making the scheduling process more elaborate by putting a big calendar on the wall in the kitchen or mudroom in which everyone call fill in his or her goals. Use erasable markers with each person assigned to a different color. Kids love this. This way it is easy to track progress, and all of you can see it—a subliminal reminder!—as you walk by.

Another option is to post your family's goals on the family computer. You can even make it the screen saver. If your kids have a cell phone with scheduling capacity, show them how to use it. (Or maybe they can show you.)

I've found that kids love this kind of family interaction, and it proves to them how much fun the process can be. It also is great for family bonding.

Before doing your action steps, each family member should connect with his or her ultimate vision and ultimate purpose. Reading them aloud helps to affirm your commitment. It's positive pressure—shared support among people who love each other, the people in your life who matter the most. If your children are too shy to read them aloud, then don't push it. Let them read silently or you can read to them. Remind them that by doing this once a week, they will increase their chance of success by 52,000 percent. How's that for a last note of encouragement before turning in! Not only will you be experiencing a new kind of Sunday night, Monday morning will kick off with a bunch of happy faces.

> Until the goals are scheduled, they
> are nothing but a wish list.

Remember, until the goals are scheduled into an action plan, they are nothing but a wish list. Schedule it, and it will happen.

TAKING PRECAUTIONS

If you've ever seen kids with their new toys at Christmas, you have seen how easily they can lose interest in something new if it doesn't appeal to them. To help them keep their interest up and stay on track, you should be a model of consistency.

Kids are constantly getting confusing messages about what is expected of them from teachers, coaches, siblings, friends, and mostly from you, the parent. Now things are different. Everyone in your children's world knows what is expected of him or her. Possibly for the first time in your children's lives, everyone is on the same page as to what their needs are and what their plans are for themselves.

Most important, your kids know what to expect of themselves because they have a plan. They created it, and they'll want to live by it. These two realities in and of themselves will go a long way in reducing their anxiety and will give them a sense of certainty, possibly for the first time in their lives. They will feel safe, secure, and supported. And here's the bottom line: In no time you will see better-behaved, more confident, and less anxious children in your household.

And don't forget to give yourself a pat on the back for a job well done. You have:

- Redirected your children's behavior by showing them that they are in control of their own life, actions, decisions, punishments, and rewards.
- Focused them on their future.
- Helped them create a powerful vision of what they want in their lives.
- Set up their daily schedule to draw their focus every day toward what they want, not what they fear.
- Eliminates fear, anxiety, and uncertainty in their life.

Congratulations on a job well done!

A Plan for a Low-Functioning Child

Some of the most difficult behavioral issues are found in the lowest-functioning or most immature children. This program can work very well with these children, too. It just needs a few modifications.

Because these children can't express their desires, you will have to make decisions on their behalf. Select your child's areas of focus based on the focal points of her life. Come up with a vision and purpose for each area. Then choose the action steps based on her capabilities.

Use pictures of the action steps in place of words so your child can recognize them. You'll also want to use some sort of token as a reward system. It can be something simple, such as a penny or a shiny object she likes. You'll know best what works for your child.

Start with fewer categories and only a few simple action steps. As your child improves and builds confidence and learns the program, you can add more categories and action steps.

By doing this together you are creating a positive focus by direct-
ing your child toward the same goals. When both of you are focusing
on the same thing, the power is doubled (or tripled if both parents are
engaging in this process). This will draw everyone's attention to what
you want for your child, and it is drawing all of you away from focusing on your child's negative behavior and what your child cannot do.

Parents of severely disabled children tend to lower their expectations for them. They don't want to challenge their children because
they feel it is cruel or mean. However, quite the opposite is true.
Understand that these children will never grow if they are not pushed.
You'll make the difference by working with your children in the con-
text of a positive, supportive environment.

Don't be afraid to challenge your child and expect her to meet that
challenge. It may take time, and consistency is the key. Create a secure,
consistent environment that challenges your child, and you will see
great results.

REINFORCEMENT PLAN FOR GOOD BEHAVIOR

By now it should be obvious that actions are reinforced by results.
As your kids experience the results of their actions, they'll work
harder and harder to continue to move in an achievable direction.
This is the power of the Family Empowerment Program. You are
teaching them that they are ultimately the ones who control their
own destiny. They are learning that they can overcome any obstacle
and you are there to encourage them and believe in them. You are
connecting them to their ultimate purpose in life and showing them
that achieving what's important is what life is all about.

Parents often err because they use a reward and punishment system with their children based on what the parents want their kids to
do and how they want them to act. By the same token, the parents

also select what the rewards and punishments will be. If the child does what the parents want, the child gets a reward of the parents' choosing. If the child doesn't do what the parents want, then the child gets the punishment of the parents' choosing. This may be the way parenting works in a lot of homes, but I believe this is not the way to create a positive family environment. It is not the way to get children to take responsibility for their own actions and it is not the way to build a good relationship between children and authority figures. I'm not just talking about parental authority figures, but *all* authority figures children inevitably will greet in their lives. This kind of dictatorial approach breeds resentment, anger, and frustration and robs children of using their creativity and experiencing their individuality.

There is nothing wrong with a reward and punishment system. In fact, it can work splendidly, but only if it is approached in the correct way—by basing it on what each child wants, with the rewards and punishments decided by the child (with your subtle guidance, of course). But it can only work the way it is supposed to if you're already leading by example and you've displayed a unified front to your children that is consistent and stable. By doing so, you have helped tremendously to reduce or eliminate the fear, anxiety, and uncertainty that triggers misbehavior in children.

Now, don't misinterpret the idea of allowing your kids to choose their own rewards and punishments. It doesn't mean they should be allowed to watch television or play video games all weekend because they made their beds and ate all their vegetables every day that week. I've lost count of how many parents lament, "But this is all my kids want to do!" I tell them that they're wrong. Kids who think this way only do so because they haven't learned that there is more to life than TV and video games. To be blunt, it's not their fault; it's the parents' fault.

I spend each and every day with children who have issues, and I know without a doubt that all kids want to accomplish things and be successful. They want their parents to be proud of them. They want to have friends. They want to do well in school and sports. If they choose not to try to achieve any of these things it is because they believe they will fail. The natural state of childhood is to dream and dream big.

Think back to when you were ten years old and someone asked you what you wanted to be when you grew up. You had a ready answer—baseball player, movie star, doctor, fireman, or whatever. It was something big in your mind based on something or someone that made an impression on your young life. That is the natural state of a child's mind. If a child doesn't have goals and dreams, it is because they have been knocked out of him by the negativity or inconsistency in his world. If he is used to failing and those around him have low expectations of him, he will have low expectations of himself. He feels he can't make anyone happy, so he retreats to his video games where he can win and nobody yells at him. He is escaping. The virtual world may feel safe, but the real world is where he really wants to be. Even if it isn't obvious, trust that your child has very powerful wants and desires.

Getting children on the right track requires more reinforcement than simply doing things right and getting parental approval, at least at first. All children need feedback, and it is essential for kids who lack motivation. Kids have short attention spans and focus and they live in a world of instant gratification. At the Brain Balance Achievement Centers we have developed a goal-driven reward and punishment Reinforcement Plan that plays into their world of instant gratification. Kids and their parents love it because of the way it so easily measures progress. It helps parents monitor their children's achievements, and it teaches kids how to plan for the future and understand the benefit of delaying gratification to receive an even larger reward.

The system requires children to choose their short-term and long-term rewards and punishments that are tied to their goals.

Again, this means that each child will set his own rules of the game. Your job is only to enforce the rules. You are simply the umpire and referee.

This doesn't mean your kids won't get angry with you from time to time. In fact, you can expect it. It's another reason why this facet of the Family Empowerment Program works so well. You don't end up in a fight with your kids when they aren't staying on target. All you need to do is remind them that these are the rules of their own choosing, as are the repercussions should they disobey them. It's all designed to help them take the action steps that they have determined will lead to their goals. If they fail on any given day, you are there to remind them that they only have themselves to blame—not you or their teacher or their friends. In addition to keeping them on track with their goals, there is a valuable learning in all of this. It teaches them about consequences and instills the reality that they ultimately control their own destiny and how others treat them.

On pages 236 and 237 you'll find an example of what a Reinforcement Plan Worksheet looks like. Once you get the basic idea you can design the chart any way you like. Or, you can download the worksheet from www.brainbalancecenters.com.

Here's how it works: Across the top of the worksheet, enter your child's areas of focus. For each day of the week, you'll put a 1 if your child achieves the action step properly. If he doesn't accomplish the action step, then enter a 0. At the end of the day, you will add up each area of focus to get a daily total. The total represents a certain number of points that can be cashed in right away or saved for later. At the end of the week, add up all the daily totals to get a weekly total. If the weekly total is at or above the baseline, a reward is in store. If it is below the baseline, then it's punishment time, meaning rewards will be taken away. Weekly totals can be added to get a monthly total. Points can be saved and accumulated over time to get a bigger reward.

Each point represents something of value, the reward of the

SAMPLE REINFORCEMENT PLAN WORKSHEET

	Physical Environments	Hygiene	Organization	Diet/Exercise
Action Steps	• Cleans room/house • Cleans up after oneself • Cleans up school environment	• Takes daily shower • Washes hands • Brushes teeth	• Ready and prepared for day • Fills out agenda • Makes capture list	• Takes vitamins • Eats healthy/allowed foods • Exercises
Sunday	1	1	0	1
Monday	1	1	1	1
Tuesday	1	1	0	0
Wednesday	1	1	1	0
Thursday	0	0	1	1
Friday	0	1	0	1
Saturday	1	1	1	1
Weekly Total	5	6	4	5
Goal	Baseline 10 Want 100% increase • Month 1: 11–14 • Month 2: 15–18 • Month 3: 19–21	Baseline 20 Want 80% increase • Month 1: 21–26 • Month 2: 27–32 • Month 3: 33–36	Baseline 1 Want 500% increase • Month 1: 2–4 • Month 2: 5–7 • Month 3: 8–10	Baseline Body Fat 35% Want 30% decrease • Month 1: 35–31.5 • Month 2: 31–27.5 • Month 3: 27–23.5

School	Family	Socialization Skills	Activities	Daily Total
• Respectful behavior • Studies for all tests • Finishes all work/projects	• Respect for parents and the rules • Cooperates • Exhibits kindness	• Kind to others • Respects others' space/ body • Shares with others	• On time • Respectful toward coach/others • Never gives up • Works hard	
1	0	0	1	5
1	1	1	1	8
0	0	1	1	4
0	0	0	0	3
1	1	1	1	6
0	1	0	1	4
1	1	1	1	8
4	4	4	6	38
Baseline 5 Want 200% increase • Month 1: 6–10 • Month 2: 11–15 • Month 3: 16–20	Baseline 25 Want 60% increase • Month 1: 26–30 • Month 2: 31–35 • Month 3: 36–40	Baseline 15 Want 100% increase • Month 1: 16–20 • Month 2: 21–25 • Month 3: 26–30	Baseline 8 Want 100% increase • Month 1: 9–11 • Month 2: 12–14 • Month 3: 15–17	• Month 1: 39–42 • Month 2: 43–46 • Month 3: 47–50

child's choosing. It could represent additional minutes of playing on the computer, watching television, visiting friends, or staying up a little later. Conversely, if the child fails to achieve his daily goals, time is taken away. The key is to let them have limited amounts of what they want. Don't let them deviate from the basic time allotted or the reinforcement will have no meaning.

The Reinforcement Plan works immensely to circumvent an argument when you remind your kids of what they are working for and why. For example, if each point is worth an additional five minutes of computer time, the maximum amount of additional time the child can earn each day is five minutes multiplied by the number of areas of focus. If there are eight areas of focus, it represents a maximum of forty minutes of computer time.

For younger children, it helps to have a tangible object represent the points. Some children find pennies, play money, or stickers as motivators in themselves. They will work very hard for these objects, which they can cash in for their reward.

For a reinforcement to be effective, it must be immediate. Here are examples of reinforcements that work well:

- Computer game time
- Television time
- Game time with family or friends
- Extra allowance money
- Extra time to stay up before bedtime
- Extra privileges
- Extra treats, but always keep them healthy

Examples of weekly reinforcements are:

- More computer, television, or video time
- Watching a movie
- Money

- A family outing to something like a water park, miniature golf, or festival
- A special playdate with a friend

There are a few caveats. Do not permit unlimited, unsupervised access to the computer, television, cell phone, or video games. This means keeping them out of the hands of your kids and in a place where they can't access them without your knowledge and permission. This is important. You must create a value system for what they are working to achieve and stick to it no matter how much they complain. Remind them that they set the rules and you are simply enforcing their own rules.

The Family Empowerment Program can work for all children to tease out what they want and who they want to be. It's all deep inside, but it is up to you to work to get it out. Your job as the parent and the coach of this process is to be patient and positive and, of course, lead by example. Your job is to encourage your children to believe that they can be whoever they want to be—that nothing is impossible and that they will achieve what they focus on. But first, *you* have to believe it. This is why the whole process starts with

---

Family Empowerment Program

All forms and directions for implementing the Family Empowerment Program can be found on the Brain Balance website (www.brainbal ancecenters.com). You can access the site to do the entire program with your family. It includes everything from designing a vision and purpose to setting goals and establishing action steps to implementing a daily Reinforcement Plan. It will even keep score for you. Our plan for the future is that you will have the capability of synching it all with your phone.

you. Once you are utilizing the law of attraction—once you are creating your ultimate vision and have connected with your ultimate purpose—you will have no doubt that you can show your children how to believe in themselves. Even if there is just one child in the family who needs direction, it is that much more important for both parents and all siblings to be involved. Remember, you set an example through your own actions.

· 14 ·

Just Do It—But Give It Time

*Those who try to do something and fail are infinitely better
than those who try to do and succeed.*

—LLOYD JONES, AUTHOR

I think the real secret to success is failure. Not failure itself, but how you handle it. To so many of us, failure is our number one fear. It occupies the vast majority of our time and attention. We lie awake at night and worry about failing in the most important aspects of our lives. This is never more obvious than when it comes to struggles in a growing family. I see it every day in parents who come to our centers. Most often, parents wind up at one of our Brain Balance centers because they've experienced failure time and time again in other programs.

When you look at it historically, failure has been the driving force to achieving success. The biggest difference between those who live their dream and those who do not is fear of failure. History tells us that making it in this world does not necessarily require intelligence, money, good breeding, education, or other tangibles. Many of the world's most prominent people have said that learning from their failures was the key motivator to their success. Unfortunately, most of us don't recognize the positive influence that failure can have on life.

I know what you're thinking. This is a cliché, and you've heard it a hundred times. But I'd like to explain it from a different perspective.

You may consciously and intellectually know this, but emotionally most people are deathly afraid of failure and will do everything they can to avoid it. They don't take actions they fear won't work because previous experiences have left them disillusioned. They rationalize that they don't have enough knowledge, experience, time, or money. There's a family to support and a mortgage to pay. Whatever, there is always some kind of excuse.

Excuses are not hard to come by—we exude excuses. However, if you knew for sure that in the end you wouldn't fail, that you would eventually get what you want even if at first you had to fail, I bet you'd go for it. You'd be in hot pursuit.

Well, I don't mind going out on the limb to tell you that if you follow the actions in this book, you will see dramatic improvement in your children's behavior, your family's quality of life, and your personal happiness. Most important, you'll get your kids pointed in the right direction for success.

This doesn't mean it's going to be easy and that you're not going to feel failure from time to time. I know from personal experience that it's not always smooth sailing. I've strayed from the process more times than I can count. Like everyone else, I've encountered bumps along the way. Events, both good and bad, creep into my life and tempt me away from the process. When I let go of the process, my life and perspective get out of kilter. Getting back on course truly is my salvation. Feeling empowered keeps me centered.

Truth is, when I look back on the fifteen years that I have been using this program myself, I realize that almost all of the important things I have accomplished and have helped others accomplish are a direct result of this very process that I am teaching you.

A PERSONAL LOOK AT FEAR

I personally learned the importance of overcoming fear the one time I let my GPA Plan slide egregiously. This time it wasn't for just a few weeks or a few months, but for a few years.

I had been through a couple of really stressful years. At the time, I told myself that this is what everybody goes through at my age— my judgment confirmed by the fact that all my friends seemed just as stressed as I was. I told myself I was just too busy to take the time to really concentrate on my life goals and formally work on them. I had a practice, three young children, a wife, and a mortgage. My weekends were pretty much eaten up by taking classes and lecturing. I stopped exercising, and my eating habits got out of hand. I was heavier and more out of shape than I had ever been in my life. I pushed through my fatigue to get through my busy days.

All this, of course, nagged at my conscious. I felt guilty about not following my GPA Plan, but I rationalized that maybe it really wasn't all that important to get so formal about it. Of course, I was dead wrong. My negative attitude toward my body was about to attract some nasty negativity into my life.

It started one day when, my mind preoccupied in a thousand thoughts, I got into a fender bender. Nothing serious but the next day I felt a little back pain. I mentioned it to one of my partners, who suggested I get a sonogram. At first I resisted, saying it was just muscle strain, but I eventually gave in.

As I was getting the test, the technician asked, "How are you feeling?"

"Just a little tired and a little back pain," I answered. "Why?"

"I think I see something," she said. Turns out there was a renal cell carcinoma on my right kidney—cancer.

I remember sitting with my wife in the surgeon's office at the age of forty not knowing if I was going to live or die and wondering, *Why me?* Then it hit me like a wave. What was happening in my body was the manifestation of all my fears and stress over the previous few years. I had gotten away from my core beliefs. I did this to myself.

The doctors were baffled by my cancer. It was highly unusual in a young, healthy man with no risk factors or family history of the disease.

They didn't understand it, but I did. It was the law of attraction at work, and the voice inside me started to get louder: *You're not done yet. You have important work to do. Get back to what you know.* It was a moment of reckoning. I knew as surely as I had attracted my cancer that I could also control it. I refused to wallow in my fear; instead, I set out to conquer it.

That was ten years ago, and today I am still cancer free. During that decade, I accomplished more in my life than all my previous years combined. I believe it all wouldn't have happened if I hadn't defied my cancer by conquering my fear. It was my family and this process that got me to do it.

WHO'S CALLING THE SHOTS?

I'd like you to think of failure as a necessary step to ultimately getting what you want for yourself and for your family. Think of the difference it would make in your motivation if you didn't fear failure along the way, but rather you embraced it as the first step to success.

Think of failure as a necessary step to getting want you want in life.

Imagine a basketball player standing at a foul line and *not* taking a shot because he might miss. Truth is, in life almost everyone misses his or her first shot. In basketball, winning the game means shooting that ball in the hoop, but more shots miss than go in. Yet, every basket that is made is a step toward success. Every miss calls for a new strategy, so you'll get a better shot next time. You'll get closer to scoring. It's challenging, it's enjoyable. It's *fun*.

View life in the same way. You'll miss a shot, maybe even drop the ball a few times, but so what. Each miss is a learning experience. Next time you'll line the shot up better. You must believe in yourself, believe that you can do it. If you have a trail of failures behind you, it only means you are closer to achieving success.

I am constantly giving this pep talk to parents who have spent years hearing from other doctors that there is no hope for their child, that what they see is about as good as it's going to get. Only, it's not true. Life *can* get better. Much better.

I have a friend whose life's dream is to write a novel "some day." One day over lunch he went on and on about how he has a story in his head and how he plans to someday take time off to write it. He got so excited talking about it that I didn't have the heart to tell him that I had planned to write a book, too, but I was already doing it. In fact, he didn't know anything about my dream until *Disconnected Kids* hit the bookstores.

He was floored. "When did you learn how to write a book?" he asked. "As I was writing it," I replied.

"Weren't you afraid that it wouldn't get published? That it wouldn't be good enough?" I simply said, "No. I knew I had important information to get out to parents, and the only way it was going to happen was to write a book. I'm not a writer by profession but I can *write*, and I'd never written this kind of a book but I've read plenty of them. So, I figured I'd learn how to write a book by just sitting down and starting it."

My friend is a very creative guy, and I don't doubt he has a great story to tell, but I realized as we talked that all the questions he was asking were the fears he was facing himself. They are the reason he had never even taken the first step in writing his book. He feared rejection.

I confided that when I first started writing my book I wrote it only for myself. I never expected that my first shot at it would be good enough to get published (which it wasn't). I expected it would take a couple of tries to get it right (which it did), but the only way to get there was to just start writing (which I did).

After it was published, people said to me, "That book must have been a lot of work. Where did you find the time?" I told them it never seemed like work to me. It was actually fun. Like shooting baskets.

The process, I'll admit, was overwhelming at times but I was determined to succeed. Quitting was not an option.

You need to look at the processes I am recommending in this book the same way. They are not only important, they are essential to reaching your goal of family harmony. And I promise that when you look back on it, you'll say it was actually fun. Like shooting baskets. Maybe it was rough going at first. The scoreboard didn't always look so good, but in the end you achieved victory.

I have seen countless parents succeed using the Family Empowerment Program, though at some point, many were ready to give up. They were ready to call it quits because they were feeling defeated. Their kids weren't advancing as they wanted them to, everyone complained about writing up their action steps, or they themselves just let the process slide. If you experience these failures—and it's likely you will, especially at first (most parents do)—promise yourself that you will consider it a good sign because *you'll learn something from it*. Sit down as a family and review the past, analyze what went wrong, discuss solutions to fixing it, and pick right back up where you left off.

When you look at your family's life this way, it won't feel so stressful. In fact, when you get the program right, family life won't be stressful at all. That's why I call this an *empowerment* program.

Instilling the idea of empowerment
in children at a young age opens
up a world of possibilities.

Imagine what this success will mean to your kids as they grow up. If you can instill the empowerment attitude in your children at a young age, imagine how it will open up the possibilities for what they will be able to accomplish in their life. Imagine the amount of fear and worry they will never have to experience.

WHAT TO EXPECT FROM EMPOWERMENT

Why am I spending so much time dwelling on this point? Because when you start this process you are not going to get it perfect the first time out. Getting to Family Empowerment is not easy, especially if you've never experienced it before. You're going to miss a few shots. Expect it and embrace it. Or, as others might put it, just get over it.

At first, venturing into the Family Empowerment Program may feel uncomfortable, even awkward. This process is a skill that must be learned and developed. It takes practice. The more involved you get, however, the better you will get at it. Just like shooting baskets.

I've taught hundreds of parents this technique since I initiated it into our Brain Balance Program. Time and time again, a parent comes back with the same old story. "Well, I tried it but it didn't work." Some even describe it as a "disaster."

So, I ask them, "How long would you give a child to learn how to walk?" The answer, of course, is always, "As long as it takes."

"Of course," I say. "You would never tell them, 'You fell too many times, so your time is up. No more chances for you, little guy. Just crawl for the rest of your life.'"

This process is a lot like learning to walk. It will seem quite unnatural at first. Expect it. You need to commit to this process for as long as it takes to get it right. This is also why you, as parents or a single parent, must begin the Family Empowerment Program for yourself first. You must give yourself time to master the process until it feels natural—until you recognize its value, until you see the results, until you are having fun.

Embrace failure so it propels you to success.

When you develop this mind-set, you will have adopted the mind-set of people who succeed—in particular, the parents who succeed in this program. Embrace failure so it propels you to success. Be fearless when it comes to knowing want you want and why you want it and be prepared to take action to get it.

I like telling the old story of a famous Hollywood agent who tells his clients that they will be successful and make it, but he knows from experience that it's going to take a good ten years of hard work before it will happen. Every one of his clients who listened to him and stayed committed for ten hard years became Hollywood stars— all 10 percent of them. The other 90 percent got sick of waiting and never attained their dream.

What would you have done?

Most people, of course, say, "I would have stuck with it if I knew for sure I would become a star." With the same attitude, you will succeed. All it takes is a clear vision, a strong purpose, powerful action steps, and faith and patience.

Be like the minority 10 percent and stick with the program. Try not to lose faith, but if you do, try to always come back to the program as quickly as possible. Consistency, persistence, and tenacity are just as important to your ultimate success and happiness. Set the example for your children. They are your ultimate purpose—and you can also become theirs. One of the greatest rewards of parenthood is to see your children work hard because they want to make their parents proud. There is no stronger motivation for a child. With your support, love, and motivation, your kids won't need anything else.

To borrow from a famous company with a clear vision and powerful purpose, *just do it*.

Part 3

THE
OUT-OF-BALANCE
BRAIN

· 15 ·

Brain Balance: How and Why It Works

Not too long ago, common wisdom held that most childhood learning and behavior disorders were genetic and therefore little could be done about them. Scientists believed that unless we could figure out a way to reengineer or influence genes, these disorders were not curable.

To my way of thinking, and other experts agree, these disorders cannot be blamed solely on genetics. It is not a child's fate to get autism, attention deficit/hyperactivity disorder (ADHD), dyslexia, obsessive-compulsive disorder, or any of the other neurological problems that are becoming more and more common today. The logic of this argument simply can't be supported.

WHY THE GENE THEORY DOESN'T FIT

There is no such thing as a genetic epidemic. Science has yet to find any significant genes that are mutated, damaged, deleted, or altered in their physical makeup in children with most of the major neurobehavioral disorders. We have yet to find any "bad" genes associated with any of these disorders.

There is no question that genes are involved in these disorders, but not in terms of a certain gene determining a child's fate. Genes can be turned on or off, depending on external influences. A new area of science called epigenetics has demonstrated that environmental factors play a major role in the way genes are expressed. This means that even if there were a bad gene that could turn your child into an uncontrollable terror, it doesn't mean that the gene would be expressed and your child would have problems with behavior. Epigenetics has opened up a whole new way of looking at childhood neurological disorders by examining how and why genes become activated, or turned on.

In the brains of children with these neurological disorders, we can see that certain genes—ones that control normal development—are not being expressed. It's as if they were stuck in the off position. So genes that normally get turned on at a particular time to create brain-building networks stay dormant.

Just because a gene was turned off
and didn't respond on cue doesn't
mean it will always be turned off.

We can help alter gene expression during any stage of development. Just because a gene was turned off and didn't respond on cue doesn't mean it must stay this way. If we can turn the gene on, we can then alter the potential of that child. This does not mean, however, that if we can turn the gene on, everything immediately becomes or returns to normal.

I like to use the analogy of a child who breaks a leg. The leg is put in a cast for a period of time while the injury mends. When the cast comes off, the leg is fixed but it is smaller and possibly even a little shorter than it was before. If nothing specific is done to strengthen the leg to catch up to the other one, it will always be this way, a little out of balance, a little lopsided.

Why? Because lack of environmental stimulation to the muscle prevented the expression of genes that would have been turned on to create more protein to build a bigger muscle. This is an epigenetic effect.

Once the cast comes off, stimulation can go back to normal, and from that point on, the leg develops normally. However, because it missed a window of time when genes were not being expressed, the leg will always be different, unless some type of intervention takes place.

For example, the leg can be exercised in specific ways to strengthen it and pick up speed until it reaches the same size and strength of the unaffected leg. This is because training that moves muscles stimulates gene expression. Genes will produce more protein than normal in order to advance muscle size to match the undamaged leg.

This in essence is what Brain Balance is all about.

ENTER BRAIN BALANCE

At one time scientists believed that the brain was hardwired at birth, but we now know that this is not the case. The brain is actually malleable and has the ability to change throughout life.

This is why it is now commonly recognized that genes are not a child's destiny, as was once previously thought. We *can* alter genes' expression.

This is what we believe we do in Brain Balance. We turn on the genes, and then choose the proper stimuli to correct the areas of the brain that are underdeveloped.

Brain Balance is based on the now accepted theory that the myriad problems we are seeing in children—from autism and Asperger's syndrome to dyslexia and obsessive-compulsive disorder—are in fact variations of just one condition. We call the condition functional disconnection syndrome (FDS), an umbrella term for mental disorders caused by a developmental weakness in either the left or right side of the brain. The problem is the same—an imbalance in either the right or the left side of the brain—but the symptoms are different, depending on the side affected and the severity of the imbalance.

In children with FDS, some environmental force, either before or after birth, caused a gene or genes to miss their cue to enlarge the neurons and spawn the synapses that grow the brain at specific times to correspond with physical growth. As a result, certain areas or circuits on the affected side of the brain are smaller than the normal side, just like the example of the broken leg.

Like the growth of the repaired leg, just turning on the genes that missed a window of opportunity on the developmental track is not enough to compensate for the delay in growth that occurred. But when a specific area of the brain is stimulated with the proper and sufficient level of training, gene production increases, so the slower side of the brain will catch up to where it should have been all along.

> The ability to balance the brain
> means these disorders no longer
> need to be a lifelong challenge.

The ability to balance the brain through stimulation to the affected regions means these disorders no longer need to be lifelong challenges.

The changes we achieve with Brain Balance are dramatic and quick—in most cases a matter of three months or even less. It is not unusual for a child who had been clinically diagnosed with autism or Asperger's syndrome to get an independent diagnosis of no neurological problem after going through the program.

New research shows that environmental factors have a big influence on a wide range of other conditions. It's why diseases such as heart disease, diabetes, and cancer are now considered lifestyle disorders and why, for the most part, they can be prevented. Evidence is building that neurodegenerative disorders such as Alzheimer's disease and Parkinson's disease are also related to lifestyle. It means that our lifestyle choices—how much or how little we choose to exercise, our food choices, whether we smoke, how much we drink, the amount of stress we let into our lives—all have the potential to turn on a bad gene or turn off a good one at any point in life.

Lifestyle choices play a role in turning genes on and off—both good and bad ones.

Childhood neurobehavioral disorders, however, are a little different. They aren't just influenced by a child's lifestyle, but also by the parents' lifestyle. Poor lifestyle choices can alter a mother's or a father's genes and affect the genes a child inherits and how they will be expressed. For example, stress or trauma during pregnancy, parental exposure to toxins, and other environmental factors that affect a parent's health can affect the genes passed on to his or her children.

ADDING TO THE PROBLEM

In the last twenty-five years, we have witnessed the most dramatic lifestyle changes that the world has ever encountered. Technology has forever dramatically altered our lifestyle more significantly than anything that has ever come before it. Studies show that when kids are playing computer games, there is brain activity going on in the parts of the brain that control vision and movement, but there is no activity going on in the frontal lobes, the area that controls intelligence. More recent research shows a correlation between the amount of time kids spend on a computer and an increase in inattention problems that define ADHD.

Computer technology is having a negative impact in other ways, too. Not only does it promote sedentary behavior, but for many families it has completely disrupted family time. Kids *and* parents spend more time communing with their computers and cells phones than with each other.

> The impact that technology is
> having on the growing brains of
> children is extremely harmful.

I find the impact this is having on children frightening. Children and their developing bodies and minds are extremely susceptible to environmental changes. Their brains and their genes are waiting for instructions on cue, and if those instructions don't come at the right time, a child's development will forever be delayed. The most significant effect is on the genes that build the human brain.

Around twenty-five thousand genes make up the human genome, and almost 85 percent of those genes are believed to be responsible for building our brains. What parents often forget is that when a child is born she doesn't really have a brain yet. Her brain stills need to be built, and DNA is the blueprint. DNA, however, depends on a set of instructions from the environment. I've already explained what happens when this doesn't unfold on schedule.

When we look closely at the brains of children with various neurodevelopmental disorders, we don't see injury, damage, lesions, or degeneration. We see a brain that looks immature, underdeveloped, or delayed. We see that certain networks in the brain are immature for their age while other networks in the brain seem to be advanced in their maturity and development. The core problem is not just a delay in development, but an *imbalance* between one side of the brain and the other. The whole brain is not developing equally. This is the classic description of FDS.

More and more clinicians are now accepting that it is the foundation to the whole spectrum of childhood mental disorders:

- ADHD
- Asperger's syndrome
- Autism
- Dyslexia
- Learning disabilities
- Nonverbal learning disability
- Obsessive-compulsive disorder
- Oppositional defiant disorder
- Processing disorders
- Tourette's syndrome

An imbalance between specific centers in the right or left hemispheres of the brain can account for all of the symptoms these children express. Skills and functions that are too strong or overdeveloped on one side of the brain combined with skills and functions that are too weak or underdeveloped on the other side of the brain is the only way to fully explain all of the issues faced by these children. It is truly the only universal theory of developmental disorders and is the only one that makes completes sense.

WHAT THE CRITICS ARE SAYING

As I mentioned in the introduction, *Disconnected Kids* raised a few eyebrows. That's not unusual because the establishment condemns just about every great new theory at first. When Einstein proposed his theory of relativity, he was unknown to the establishment. Most mainstream physicists laughed at him because he was going against Isaac Newton's universal law of gravity, which at the time was considered doctrine. It was blasphemy to think or say otherwise. The people who condemned him were eventually proven wrong, and we recognize his theories as some of the most profound in the history of science.

Today's establishment is no different. There will always be naysayers who criticize anything new and innovative that goes against long-held beliefs. In the professional world of childhood mental disabilities, there are people who will tell you that the rise in autism is not real, that we are just better at diagnosing it. They'll also tell you that the best way to deal with these problems is to learn to cope with them because they are genetically caused and thus there is no way to improve the condition or make it go away. They stand by the long-held belief that there is little connection between the physical body and cognitive, academic, or social skills. They dismiss the connection between these conditions and digestive problems, immune issues, chronic infections, and exposure to toxins. They write them off as purely coincidental.

Some have even charged that it is unethical for me and my ever-growing supporters and professional staff to give hope to parents, even though there are now thousands of families that can prove otherwise. To be ethical, these experts believe you must be honest with parents and tell them there is no hope that their children will ever be normal.

In reality, the methods doctors, psychologists, and educators have been using to deal with childhood neurological disorders have not changed in fifty years. They obviously are not working, yet many experts would have you believe that we should just keep on doing the same thing. They say the only correct approach is to compensate, not remediate. They claim that "there is no scientific evidence" that a program using muscle movement can improve cognitive skills, though we are seeing it happen every day.

The idea that we can only compensate for, and not correct, the neurological problems so many children are confronted with today is incorrect.

The idea that we can only compensate for, and not correct, the behavioral and learning problems that so many children are confronted with today is simply incorrect. Despite all the evidence to the contrary, mainstream doctors, therapists, and educators generally continue to rely on a purely compensatory approach to dealing with the issues. Mostly, these methods involve medication and helping the child and family learn how to cope.

There is still much we don't know, but we do know that motor and sensory development is foundational to the brain. At the end of the nineteenth century, most neurologists maintained that there was no relationship between cognitive function and motor activity. They said the two were separate and humans were unique because we are innately (genetically) blessed with these amazing cognitive abilities. That bias continues today among many in the fields of psychology and education, even though it has been disproven.

Cognitive and academic ability is built on top of our motor-sensory development. Areas of the brain that control both are not as separate as once thought; they are actually one and the same. In children, these areas are not developed yet. They have to be built from the ground up.

If a child has failed to develop a cognitive, academic, or social skill, it is often not for lack of exposure but rather a failure to develop the foundational motor or sensory skill.

Truth be known, once you understand how the brain develops,

you realize how naive it is to think that we can develop cognitive and academic skills by exposing a child to educational and behavioral training alone. Rather, it is necessary to work on foundational skills through motor and sensory stimulation, and then use them in conjunction with cognitive skills. Most significant, the coordination of effort must be focused on the areas of weakness in the deficient side of the brain to properly establish balance and coordination and get the two sides in sync and working as a whole brain.

This means that to help children with FDS, we must work on strengthening areas of weakness and ignoring the strong areas. This smacks in the face of conventional programs. Conventional behavioral therapy says there is nothing that can be done about the weaknesses, so we should focus only on a child's strengths because it will help give the child a sense of accomplishment. This comes from the viewpoint of psychology. My program is based on what we know about neurology. And from the viewpoint of neurology, ignoring the weakness and focusing on the strength is the worst thing we can do.

> Similar therapy is helping awaken dead brain
> areas in people who have had a stroke.

Another example to prove this point is the cutting-edge work taking place in rehabilitating people who have had a stroke. Traditional rehabilitative treatment says the best way to help stroke victims—especially those whose injury is more than a year old—is to focus on the person's strengths and ignore their weakness. A subspecialty of medicine called rehabilitation neuropsychology believes that the injured areas of the brain are not dead, as once believed, but have been traumatized into a state of dormancy, as if they were in a drug-induced deep sleep. Rehabilitation neuropsychology is proving that these so-called dead areas can be awakened. Rehabilitation neuropsychologists are using a technique called constrain-induced movement therapy, in which patients' functional limbs are restrained so they are forced to try to use their paralyzed side.

Constrain-induced movement therapy was the brainchild of Dr. Edward Taub at the University of Alabama, and it has completely changed the way medicine looks at stroke rehabilitation. It, too, is based on the relatively new science of neuroplasticity that shows that the brain is malleable and has the ability to change throughout life.

WHAT THE STUDIES SHOW

To think that a child with a behavioral problem needs only behavioral training or that a child with a reading problem needs only more help with reading is foolish and shows a complete lack of understanding of how the brain works.

When you look deeply enough, you can find that children with these disorders share a number of symptoms. These symptoms are not coincidental. They are all signs of FDS, and they differ only in terms of the side of the brain that's out of balance and the severity of that imbalance. Other than the anecdotal evidence of the thousands of children who have been through the Brain Balance Program, dozens of scientific studies support the validity of our theory.

In 2009, shortly after the publication of *Disconnected Kids*, we opened the nonprofit F. R. Carrick Research Institute and its subdivision, the Children's Autism Hope Project, which is dedicated to studying children with neurological disorders and publishing the outcomes from various programs and treatments, such as Brain Balance.

One of our most recent studies, published in the *International Journal of Adolescent Medicine and Health* in 2010, followed sixty randomly selected children who enrolled in the Brain Balance Program after being independently diagnosed with ADHD. Our own evaluation concurred with these findings. The children went through a three-month multimodal program focused on stimulating the right hemisphere of the brain. After three months on the program, we found the following:

■ 100 percent showed improvement in more than one area that was shown to be deficient.
■ 82 percent no longer met the criteria for ADHD based on a standardized behavioral assessment.
■ Approximately 85 percent showed statistically significant improvement in multiple areas of deficiency.
■ Approximately 60 percent showed a minimum of a two-grade-level increase in various standardized academic measures.
■ Approximately 35 percent showed a four-grade-level increase or better based on standardized academic achievement.
■ No children showed a decrease in any area tested.

Many old-school professionals still scoff at the idea that there is a relationship between poorly developing posture and gait and problems with behavioral and cognitive development. In 2010, we presented evidence at the Third International Congress on Gait and Mental Function in Washington, DC, showing a direct correlation between balance and posture and academic and behavioral scores. We showed that an improvement in one was mirrored by an identical increase in the others. "The evidence is clear that these problems can be corrected both functionally and physically and these changes can be permanent changes," the studies concluded.

A case study, published in the *International Journal of Neuroscience*, reported the effects of the twelve-week multimodal hemispheric-based program similar to the Brain Balance Program on a child with a severe form of autism and mental retardation that most people believed impossible to change. The program, which stimulated specific weaknesses in the right brain, showed "significant improvement" in objective measurements of academic, social, and behavioral skills.

In another study at the University of Connecticut, brain-imaging tests found that changes in the brains of children diagnosed with autism coincided with a decrease in the severity of their symptoms.

Kids with dyslexia, a left brain deficiency, are poor at processing detailed information (a left brain trait), but their ability to process the big picture (a right brain trait) is exceptional. In children with autism, a right brain deficiency, we see the exact opposite.

This was further documented in research I did with colleague Gerry Leisman, PhD, when we showed through electroencephalography (EEG) measurements that synchronized activity between two areas of the brain (called temporal coherence) was greater in the right brain of people with dyslexia than in the left. In another study of children with autism we found the opposite—improved coherence in the left hemisphere, decreased coherence in the right, and reduced sharing between the two hemispheres.

It is well documented that the brains in children with autism and dyslexia are underconnected and desynchronized. The area that is most underconnected is the bridge between the two halves of the brain, which supports our findings that these children are also lacking in more than one sensory and motor skill. We have also documented that the processing speeds between the two sides of the brain are out of balance, which explains the increased skill in certain processing and motor abilities as well as cognitive abilities that can exist with the deficits.

At Carnegie Mellon University, scientists Timothy Keller and Marcel Just uncovered the first evidence that intensive instruction to improve reading skills in young children causes the brain to physically rewire itself, creating new white matter and improving communication within the brain.

Reporting in the journal *Neuron*, they found that brain imaging of children between the ages of eight and ten showed that the quality of white matter—the brain tissue that carries signals between areas of gray matter where information is processed—improved substantially after the children received a hundred hours of remedial training. After the training, imaging indicated that the capability of the white matter to transmit signals efficiently had increased, and testing showed the children could read better.

"Showing that it's possible to rewire a brain's white matter has important implications for treating reading disabilities and other developmental disorders, including autism," said Just, D. O. Hebb Professor of Psychology and director of Carnegie Mellon's Center for Cognitive Brain Imaging.

Out of the seventy-two children in the study, forty-seven tested as poor readers and twenty-five were reading at a normal level. The good readers and a group of twelve poor readers did not receive remedial instruction, and their brain scans did not show any changes. "The lack of change in the control groups demonstrates that the change in the treated group cannot be attributed to naturally occurring maturation during the study," Keller said.

Keller and Just also found that the children who showed the most white matter change also showed the most improvement in reading ability, confirming the link between alterations in the brain tissue and progress in reading.

Other studies involving dyslexia include the following:

■ At the University of Freiburg in Germany, researchers found that adults with dyslexia made twice as many errors on visual attention and eye movement tasks as people without dyslexia—no surprise there. However, when researchers trained the brains of children with dyslexia through a series of eye exercises, the children made half as many mistakes after just three to six weeks of training.

■ Children with dyslexia also have auditory processing deficits, particularly with phonics. For example, they have difficulty distinguishing the initial sounds of *b* and *p*. This is believed to be, at least in part, why these children reverse or transpose letters. Researchers at the University of Wurzburg in Germany found that mental exercises directed at building awareness of speech sounds significantly improve reading and writing skills in children with dyslexia.

▪ A study involving 682 children with dyslexia and auditory processing disorders found that exercises addressing these weakness significantly improved reading skills and reduced errors in spelling by 40 percent.

These are all exciting discoveries. This kind of research is the proof we hope will draw attention to the fact that much more than genetics explains the increased frequency of mental disabilities in children.

It is obvious that children with reading problems need remedial reading tutoring, but if other problems associated with dyslexia—including poor fine motor or gross motor and sensory processing problems—are not addressed, the brain will not change, and the problem will not be remediated. It is the same for autism, Asperger's syndrome, ADHD, and other behavior and learning problems we are seeing today.

· 16 ·

What Parents Have to Say About Brain Balance

Anyone can give up. It's the easiest thing in the world to do.
But to hold it together when everyone else would understand
if you fell apart, that's true strength.

—UNKNOWN

In *Disconnected Kids*, we chronicled dozens of true-life stories of young children who overcame their mental disabilities by going through the Brain Balance Program. Autism, attention deficit/hyperactivity disorder (ADHD), dyslexia, Asperger's syndrome, or a combination of disorders profoundly affected these children. Combination disorders were not unusual, as comorbidity—meaning the likelihood of one mental problem bringing on another—is common in children with FDS.

Since our first center opened on Long Island in 1994 and *Disconnected Kids* was published in 2009, we have received thousands of letters and testimonials from grateful parents. The following stories and letters are just a small sample of the kind of feedback we receive about our program. They are being printed with permission, though we have changed names to protect family privacy. We hope these stories inspire you and show you what is possible when you have a clear vision, a powerful purpose, and take massive action. Never lose hope!

AN ADOPTIVE MOM'S STORY: ATTACHMENT DISORDER

When I first met Kim she was a ten-year-old emotionless child who had been adopted from China before the age of one. She had never attached to her adoptive mother and, obviously, had not experienced the parental bonding that is so important during the first six months of life.

I met her mother, Michele, when she came to a lecture I was giving at Loyola University in Chicago. Michele told me that Kim had been diagnosed with attachment disorder, sensory integration disorder, and Asperger's syndrome.

When we enrolled Kim in the Brain Balance Program, she clearly tested for a right hemisphere delay, which is associated with all of these disorders. Her primary problem, however, started with attachment disorder. The most telling symptom was that Kim had only recently started to recognize herself in a mirror and in pictures—something that should have occurred when she was a toddler. When she looked at family photos she could recognize everybody except herself!

Kim was very bright. Her IQ and left brain skills were off the charts, but she exhibited virtually no nonverbal communication—she could not show emotion and had no facial expression at all. She couldn't even respond to pain.

She was clumsy and walked awkwardly and looked very much like a robot. She wore heavy boots all the time just so she could feel in touch with her own body.

Her sense of smell was very poor and she was hypersensitive

to light touch. She hated people touching her and she wore loose clothing. She hated loud, high-pitched noises but could not hear emotional tones in a voice.

Psychiatrists and other attachment specialists told Michele that Kim was psychologically damaged due to her lack of attachment as a newborn, and it was too late to do anything about it now. Michele, obviously, was heartbroken and devastated.

I told Michele that I disagreed with the diagnosis and prognosis. Her problem was not psychological; it was neurological. I explained that Kim had never become embodied because she could not feel her body in space—she was a disconnected kid. She never attached to her mom because she couldn't attach to herself. Her severe symptoms were a sign that her brain was very immature in these areas—a good sign that Brain Balance could help. At the time of testing, certain areas in her right brain were on the level of a two-year-old.

In Brain Balance, we concentrated on stimulating only the areas of the brain that had lagged behind. Within three months, Kim showed a dramatic change: She stopped wearing her clunky boots, she developed a sense of smell, and for the first time she expressed an interest in food. She also responded to pain. When her mom saw Kim cry for the first time, Michele was in heaven!

Once Kim attached to her own body, she could attach to her mom's. I can report that today Michele and Kim have a wonderful mother–daughter relationship.

GIANT LEAPS FOR JOSH

When we first met Josh, he was a ten-year-old fourth-grader struggling academically. He was constantly making mistakes in school, was easily distracted, spoke out of turn, and was slow to begin and finish his homework. He had difficulty making friends. He was so fidgety that he had difficulty remaining seated at meals and doing his homework. His handwriting was extremely poor. He also had a lot of tics—cracking knuckles, blowing bubbles, and closing and opening his eyes and mouth constantly.

Josh's evaluation proved to be classic FDS with ADHD and some Asperger's syndrome—a right brain deficit. All his visual processing skills fell well below average. His core body stability—gait, balance, timing, rhythm, and proprioception (ability to feel himself in space)—put him in the developmental age of a five- or six-year-old.

After three months in the Brain Balance Program, Josh's proprioception, balance, and gait/aerobic ability increased to the developmental age of a twelve-year-old. Initially, he tested below average in five academic areas and was severely deficient in one area. After Brain Balance, he tested normal in all six areas.

His father wrote:

> My wife and I wanted to take a moment to send you a formal letter expressing how impressed we are with your program and our gratitude for your work with our son. We firmly believe that your program was instrumental in [Josh's] successful integration into a new school environment as well as his continued success academically.
>
> We have seen vast improvements in his overall interactions with his age peers and have seen marked improvement in his ability to interpret social cues. We have also noticed improvements in his general coordination and ability to participate at a higher level in recreational sports.

A MOTHER'S STORY: MELTDOWNS AND TANTRUMS

I remember pulling into the Brain Balance parking lot with a heart of desperation, hoping for some answers. My daughter,

Diana, was not eating and was having major meltdowns several times a day. She was in a constant state of anger and unwilling to transition from one task to the next. It made every minute of our day stressful.

We had driven more than 1,000 miles to get there, and we were desperate. We needed answers. All the doctors we had seen told us that she'd "just grow out of it," but we knew this was not normal behavior. Not only did we fear she wouldn't grow out of it—we couldn't wait any longer!

When we went into the Brain Balance center for an evaluation, little did I know that, just three months later, I would have a happy, loving little girl who was eating everything that was presented to her. The evaluation made so much sense! It gave us the answers that we had never received. We found out she wasn't smelling, that her gross motor and fine motor skills were delayed. The doctors explained to us about primitive reflexes and how they are supposed to go away, only Diana's hadn't been inhibited. We also found out that she still had the majority of primitive reflexes that inhibits brain development. That weekend, we drove the 1,000 miles back home and packed our bags. We were moving to be closer to the Brain Balance Center in Georgia!

On the drive back to Georgia, my husband and I were in two separate cars. Diana's meltdowns were so bad that we had to take turns driving her because it was so difficult having her in the car. She would scream, cry, throw things, kick the seat, and demand us to pull over every few minutes. But we finally made it to Georgia! And we couldn't wait for her to start Brain Balance.

What we didn't expect was how fast we would see an improvement. By her fourth session, we began to see drastic changes. She started to eat and say she was hungry! I couldn't believe it! Initially, her meltdowns became worse, but I was so excited because this is exactly what Brain Balance told us would happen. I knew that something was changing and she was meeting all the expectations of what Brain Balance prepared us for! First, her motor skills began to improve. She was willing to color and she was making bracelets. I couldn't believe it! For the very first time, she was doing activities independently. She even loved coming to Brain Balance! There was no coaxing and having to pull her out of the car, like we had to before.

After about eight weeks in the program, I began to see snapshots of a sweet little girl—the one I always knew was there but was hidden somewhere. Her meltdowns became less and less. When her dad would call, she would talk with him on the phone and even carry on a conversation! He would come and visit, and be able to play with her without meltdowns. We couldn't believe the changes, she was able to reason and communicate without crying, screaming, kicking, or throwing things. She was making friends for the first time in school!

We completed the program two months ago, and I must say the changes have stuck. She continues to do well. She is our happy little girl who we always wanted! I am now able to go out with her on Mommy/Diana dates and truly enjoy her. Moving to a different state, sacrificing my comfortable lifestyle is nothing compared to having my daughter back. It's priceless!

SAM: PDD, ADHD, AND ASPERGER'S

Sam was basically living in a bubble when his mother first brought the fourteen-year-old to a Brain Balance center. His diagnosis was a parental nightmare: ADHD, pervasive developmental disorder

(PDD), and Asperger's syndrome. He was functioning at a very low level, and we could tell he was feeling the frustration.

When speaking, for example, he would get stuck frequently and would make awkward gestures and noises to get his point across. He was unable to comprehend unwritten social cues and rules.

Before coming to the Brain Balance Program, his mother had tried the gamut of therapies—speech, occupational, cognitive, behavioral—but with little success. The gluten-free diet she tried had virtually no effect on his bigger issues.

"Sam has been awakened in ways I never imagined possible," his mother wrote, after going through the three-month program. "Sam is able to articulate in a much more mature fashion, especially what he is feeling. He is even using examples. In fact, he was able to articulate to his teacher that he no longer was going to let her make him 'feel humiliated' in the classroom anymore."

Sam was put through a motor-sensory program aimed at the deficient areas of the right brain. He was also put on a nutritional program to correct specific food deficiencies. The results were astounding. He became calmer, he was able to reason, and he learned to logically understand how to deal with his anger and frustration.

"He no longer has to eat one thing at a time or demands that none of the food on his plate touches each other," said his mother. "His handwriting has improved. It is actually legible! He actually listens now. He is much better able to articulate his position and how he feels."

A MOTHER'S STORY: AUTISM

Two years ago, my family moved from Kansas City to suburban Atlanta so our son Matthew, who has autism, could be enrolled in Dr. Melillo's Brain Balance Program. Matthew was age 7 at the time and had hit a plateau in terms of the gains he made in his current program. We were looking for a way to better help him.

When we learned about Brain Balance, we were encouraged by its philosophy to stimulate the brain to alleviate the imbalance in the brain and not just treat the symptoms of autism.

After about three months into the program, we were out for dinner. We could finally take Matthew along. Matthew looked over at my empty plate and asked, "What are YOU getting?" My younger son, Ethan, who was five at the time, gasped and pointed to Matthew. I nearly fell out of my chair. A *what* question! That was the first of many major breakthroughs we have had since starting in Brain Balance.

After six months in the program, Matthew started asking about our feelings and about characters in books. He started talking about smelling things like his stinky socks and kitchen scents. The number and types of foods he would eat were expanding.

We returned home from Georgia just flabbergasted with the changes in our son. I could not stop talking about Brain Balance to everyone I met. I knew our community in Kansas City needed a Brain Balance center, so I convinced the founder of Brain Balance, Dr. Robert Melillo, and president, Bill Fowler, that they needed to fly out to Kansas City to give a presentation. (Four hundred people showed up on February 17, 2009.) From there, we were able to generate enough interest to get an investment group together to open a center. In less than eight months from the time Dr. Melillo presented in Overland Park, Kansas, a center was built and open.

We felt like our son was drowning in autism, but Brain Balance has changed everything. The Brain Balance Program, with its dietary and nutritional interventions as well as motor, sensory, and academic stimulation, has propelled Matthew toward his true potential. Every day we are recognizing new gains with him and are eternally grateful we took a leap of faith toward helping our son through Dr. Melillo's program. Matthew's journey has helped change the lives of so many others in our community.

KATIE: A SOCIAL OUTCAST NO LONGER

Katie was seven years old when she started Brain Balance, but her parents started to notice her lack of social skills when she was three. She seemed fine and comfortable in the presence of her parents, but she never connected with her peers. In preschool, she did well, but would not sit with the class in circle time. She would always sit outside of the circle. If somebody sat too close or in her square on the rug, she would move away.

Even when she started kindergarten and first grade, she played by herself and thought nothing of it. She sat by herself at lunch. It didn't bother her that she was never invited to birthday parties. The only child she could call a friend was a little boy who was autistic and barely spoke.

When Katie came to the Brain Balance center, it was obvious that she herself was autistic, and it was no surprise when our evaluation proved this to be correct. We also found out that she was plagued with headaches and had food allergies.

Katie never made eye contact with anyone. She spoke with almost no expression and said exactly what was on her mind, regardless of how it would affect the other person. She had no idea how to start a conversation and did not know how to invite somebody else to play with her or how to just be part of another group of girls by just joining in.

"These behaviors were brought up at every parent-teacher conference for four years," her mother reported. "We assumed she was just shy. We tried to get her evaluated through the school district but could not get her any services at all.

"I heard about Brain Balance from my sister, who had two friends with kids who went through the program. I asked tons of questions and then tons more. It was a lot of money for us to spend, but we knew we had to do something."

Three months after Brain Balance began, Katie was a different person. "She is a social butterfly who has lots of friends," reported her mother. "She can be the leader and initiator in her group of friends. She speaks softly and lovingly toward her sister and her friends. She is concerned about the well-being of her friends when they miss school, and she is the first one to try and call them to make sure they are okay."

She looks people in the eye when she speaks to them and offers lots of hugs and kisses to her parents and grandparents—something she seldom did in the past.

She's now in Girl Scouts and is able to really feel proud of her accomplishments. "She has the ability to help out people in our community who are in need and she always knows just what to say and maybe even offer a funny joke to make them feel better.

"In general she is just a sweet girl," wrote her mother. "We have waited so long to see the person that God had created her to be."

A MOTHER'S STORY: PDD

My son was diagnosed with nonspecific PDD [pervasive developmental disorder] six months before he started preschool. I remember that time so well: getting him school clothes, his first backpack, his supplies. That first day, drop-off at school went smoothly. Though I had that typical motherly first-day-of-school weepiness, I was so excited for him. I was still excited when I picked him up at noon.

I drove up to the school, and I saw all the children coming out, running to their parents, carrying their backpacks and chatting about all the fun things they'd done that day. Grinning, I got in the car with Neil and asked, "How was your first day, buddy?"

No response.

He was fully awake and aware; he was not sick. I was still learning about autism and realizing the extent of his diagnosis based on his speech therapies. He wasn't very interactive or communicating. Even though he was very smart, he wasn't able to respond to direct questions.

Each day, I'd watch the children come out of the school, talking to their parents and teachers. And each day, I'd ask Neil how his day was at school. Each day I got no response. I wanted so badly for my baby to tell me about his day, what he liked, what he disliked, what he ate for lunch.

As he progressed in school, his speech and occupational therapy improved dramatically. He started playing with other children, was reading, developing math skills. But still, no answer when I asked about his day. Nevertheless, I continued to ask after each pickup.

Then I heard about Brain Balance and decided to enroll him. Neil was fascinated by the sensory exercises, the cognitive work. He was excited on Brain Balance days; he couldn't wait to go. We noticed very quickly that he was using much longer sentences. He started to develop opinions—about things, about people. He'd look at me and ask me questions.

We got his December report from school, and we were blown away. The report indicated that the number of correct math problems he could do in a minute had *tripled*. His sight reading had doubled. His reading comprehension had improved. And this after only a little over a *month* in Brain Balance.

But that was not the greatest miracle.

Recently, we moved and Neil changed schools. I admit I was concerned about how he would transition, even though his old and new school did a great job prepping him. The teachers said he fit right in. Two days ago, when I picked him up, I asked him what he did that day, like I always do.

The voice came from the back of the car. "I had an awesome day. I ate chicken nuggets for lunch." I almost ran the car up on the curb.

I was on a high all evening from those 11 words, and it only continued. At dinner he mentioned how a little girl he likes in his class wore sandals that warm day.

Thanks to Brain Balance, my son has his own thoughts, his own opinions. But most of all, I now know that my son had an awesome day.

MELANIE: ADHD

Melanie was a thirteen-year-old seventh-grader who was having trouble paying attention in school. Her teachers suspected ADHD, but her parents resisted taking her to a doctor who would put her on medication. They brought her to Brain Balance hoping she could find emotional stability and academic confidence.

Our evaluations confirmed her parents' concern. She scored only one year behind on reading comprehension and math operations, but her oral expression was on the level of a nine-year-old.

Melanie was physically very active and scored average on our motor-sensory assessment, revealing no primitive reflex issues. She showed few food sensitivities and digestive issues. However, she had significant visual and auditory processing problems. Her real problem was inattention, mostly because her processing issues were making her miss much of what her teacher was saying.

We found Melanie to be a dream to work with. She was always engaged and cooperative, and well liked by the staff. When we worked with her, she did not display any of the emotional or behavioral concerns that troubled her parents, who had scored her high on behavior and attention issues. After two months, that score dropped 100 points and her attention and hyperactivity issues went down 30 percent.

At the end of her three-month program, Melanie was performing even better than her parents and teachers had hoped. Her academic scores were up 1.5 grade levels for word reading, 4 grade levels in reading comprehension, 6 levels in pseudo-decoding, 2.5 levels in math reasoning, 5 levels in written expression, and 9 levels in oral expression. She went from being below grade level in half the categories to being above grade level in all but one.

Her visual processing went from slightly below average, to low, before moving up to slightly above average. Her auditory processing improved from five years lower than her age norm to one year above her age norm.

Melanie didn't really have ADHD in the classic sense, but her processing problem was frustrating her. Because she didn't know what was wrong, she was expressing her troubles through her behavior. It's the perfect illustration of how such an integral deficit—so easily correctable—can unnecessarily disrupt a young life and send a child on a wrong academic path.

BRADLEY: FOOD SENSITIVITIES

Eight-year-old Bradley came walking into our Brain Balance Achievement Center with his head hung low and shoulders slumped. He was having trouble reading in school and couldn't understand why. His mother said he would come home from school with blurred vision and headaches—even though the doctor said his eyes were fine—and cry from frustration.

We found Bradley was quite shy and avoided eye contact. Testing showed he was delayed in all his major motor abilities. He had the gait of a four-year-old. We also found he had a lot of food sensitivities. Gluten, diary, casein, egg, and mustard were the most severe.

In addition to the physical exercises, we immediately removed these foods from his diet. Within weeks he was reading without blurred vision and he no longer complained of headaches. Within three months, all his physical delays increased to his current age level, or higher.

"Everything, including penmanship, reading, math, drawing, motor skills, and his sense of smell has improved greatly," his parents later reported. "His self-esteem has improved so much over the last few months and, to us, this in itself is priceless."

The last time we saw Bradley, he was walking with his shoulders back and his head held high!

A MOTHER'S STORY: LANGUAGE TROUBLES

We knew David had a language delay but we knew he did not have autism. He received language therapy privately and went to an early childhood center for special needs children in addition to going to preschool for a half a day. Even with all of the therapy, David was making very little progress. He was steadily falling further and further behind his same-aged peers in communication, socialization, and academics.

We worked with David every day. We did language, reading, math, and basic academic skills. I am a certified teacher in elementary education and I have been trained to work with children who are language delayed. I used all the tricks of the trade and still saw little progress. I could see that he was getting frustrated. That's when I heard Dr. Melillo speak and decided to enroll him in Brain Balance.

David went to each session willingly. We did the home program faithfully. We eliminated dairy from his diet and gave him his vitamins and minerals—all to remedy dietary issues found their Brain Balance testing.

Gradually we started to see changes. First, he started asking questions. "What does that mean? Who is that person? What does he do?" We were getting bombarded with questions from the moment he woke up until he fell asleep at night. Then he started sharing information about his day at school. But more importantly he started to pick up language. He was learning new language and using it appropriately. Gradually, reading, math, and learning new concepts became easier, too. What used to be frustrating to him became easier.

We continue to work with him each day on listening comprehension, reading comprehension, word problems, etc. What was a heartbreaking, frustrating time in our day has become the most enjoyable part of my day. David now enjoys doing his work. He smiles with a confidence that he never had before. I love to hear him say, "That was easy, Mom."

We faithfully continue his home program that Brain Balance devised for him. We continue to see progress daily. David still has a language impairment, there is not a cure. But Brain Balance opened a door. David was shut off from us and from learning. The door is open to language, learning, socialization, and relationships with his family. Brain Balance gave David the ability to learn. What happens now is up to us and David."

STAY IN TOUCH

It is stories like these that make my job so rewarding and keep me motivated to continue our research and find answers to so many of the questions that are still baffling scientists concerning the mental health of our children.

I sincerely hope that you will find similar success with your children from using the program in *Reconnected Kids* and the Family Empowerment Program. It was inquisitive parents who convinced me that this book is needed, and I welcome your questions and feedback. They are important to the growth and success of Brain Balance and its ancillary programs.

Don't forget that you can find help and downloadable materials used in this book on our website (www.brainbalancecenters.com). You can contact me personally and get information about a Brain Balance center near you through the website.

Reconnected Kids and *Disconnected Kids* represent only the beginning of our work. Much more research needs to be done. If you wish to support this research, you can send your donation through the F. R. Carrick Research Institute website (www.frcarrickresearch .org), or you can mail a check directly to: F. R. Carrick Research Institute, 647 Franklin Avenue, Garden City, NY 11530.

APPENDIX

Family Empowerment Worksheets

What is it about my life that I absolutely hate? (Make a list.)

1. _____

2. _____

3. _____

4. _____

5. _____

How important is it to change this situation? (Write a sentence or two describing how you feel.)

_____

_____

_____

What am I willing to do to in order to change what I don't like about my life?

_____

_____

_____

What do I want? (This is my goal.)

_____

_____

_____

Why do I want it? (This is my purpose.)

_____

_____

_____

What do I have to do to get it? (These are my action steps.)

_____

_____

_____

My Personal Areas of Focus

1. _____

2. _____

3. _____

4. _____

5. _____

6. _____

7. _____

8. _____

9. _____

10. _____

AREA OF FOCUS BALANCE GRAPH

Enter your areas of focus in the spaces provided at the bottom of the graph. Place a dot next to the number that represents your level of satisfaction in each of the areas. Connect the dots to form a graph.

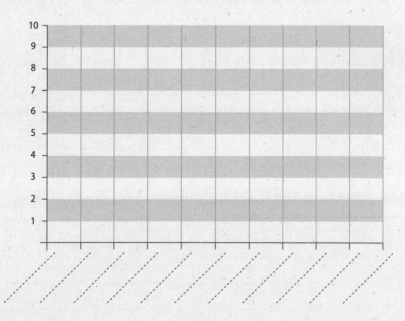

MY VISION AND PURPOSE

Create a vision for what you wish your life would be like in each of your areas of focus. Then state your purpose for wanting to attain your vision. For inspiration, reread the section on creating your vision on page 169. Then list your top three goals for each area of focus.

Area of Focus

_____

My Ultimate Vision

_____

_____

_____

My Purpose for Wanting This

_____

_____

_____

My goals for achieving this in _____ months are as follows:

1. _____

2. _____

3. _____

Area of Focus

_____

My Ultimate Vision

_____

_____

_____

My Purpose for Wanting This

_____

_____

_____

My goals for achieving this in _____ months are as follows:

1. _____

2. _____

3. _____

Area of Focus

_____

My Ultimate Vision

_____

_____

_____

My Purpose for Wanting This

_____

_____

_____

My goals for achieving this in _____ months are as follows:

1. _____

2. _____

3. _____

Area of Focus

_____

My Ultimate Vision

_____

_____

_____

My Purpose for Wanting This

_____

_____

_____

My goals for achieving this in _____ months are as follows:

1. _____

2. _____

3. _____

Area of Focus

_____

My Ultimate Vision

_____

_____

_____

My Purpose for Wanting This

_____

_____

_____

My goals for achieving this in _____ months are as follows:

1. _____

2. _____

3. _____

Area of Focus

_____

My Ultimate Vision

_____

_____

_____

My Purpose for Wanting This

_____

_____

_____

My goals for achieving this in _____ months are as follows:

1. _____

2. _____

3. _____

Area of Focus

_____

My Ultimate Vision

_____

_____

_____

My Purpose for Wanting This

_____

_____

_____

My goals for achieving this in _____ months are as follows:

1. _____

2. _____

3. _____

Area of Focus

_____

My Ultimate Vision

_____

_____

_____

My Purpose for Wanting This

_____

_____

_____

My goals for achieving this in _____ months are as follows:

1. _____

2. _____

3. _____

Area of Focus

_____

My Ultimate Vision

_____

_____

_____

My Purpose for Wanting This

_____

_____

_____

My goals for achieving this in _____ months are as follows:

1. _____

2. _____

3. _____

Area of Focus

_____

My Ultimate Vision

_____

_____

_____

My Purpose for Wanting This

_____

_____

_____

My goals for achieving this in _____ months are as follows:

1. _____

2. _____

3. _____

Area of Focus

_____

My Ultimate Vision

_____

_____

_____

My Purpose for Wanting This

_____

_____

_____

My goals for achieving this in _____ months are as follows:

1. _____

2. _____

3. _____

FAMILY EMPOWERMENT FEEDBACK FORMS

Copy these forms so you can keep track of your children's progress toward attaining their goals.

PARENTS GOAL CARD

Enter your child's areas of focus in the gray lines. List goals in the left-hand column. While filling out this form, please leave room for improvement by giving your child between a 1 and 10 to begin the evaluation process and allow room for growth.

Area of Evaluation	Quality Rating (Please circle the appropriate number)										TOTAL
AREA OF FOCUS											**TOTAL**
Goal 1	1	2	3	4	5	6	7	8	9	10	
	11	12	13	14	15	16	17	18	19	20	
	21	22	23	24	25	26	27	28	29	30	
	31	32	33	34	35	36	37	38	39	40	
	41	42	43	44	45	46	47	48	49	50	
Goal 2	1	2	3	4	5	6	7	8	9	10	
	11	12	13	14	15	16	17	18	19	20	
	21	22	23	24	25	26	27	28	29	30	
	31	32	33	34	35	36	37	38	39	40	
	41	42	43	44	45	46	47	48	49	50	
Goal 3	1	2	3	4	5	6	7	8	9	10	
	11	12	13	14	15	16	17	18	19	20	
	21	22	23	24	25	26	27	28	29	30	
	31	32	33	34	35	36	37	38	39	40	
	41	42	43	44	45	46	47	48	49	50	
AREA OF FOCUS											**TOTAL**
Goal 1	1	2	3	4	5	6	7	8	9	10	
	11	12	13	14	15	16	17	18	19	20	
	21	22	23	24	25	26	27	28	29	30	
	31	32	33	34	35	36	37	38	39	40	
	41	42	43	44	45	46	47	48	49	50	
Goal 2	1	2	3	4	5	6	7	8	9	10	
	11	12	13	14	15	16	17	18	19	20	
	21	22	23	24	25	26	27	28	29	30	
	31	32	33	34	35	36	37	38	39	40	
	41	42	43	44	45	46	47	48	49	50	
Goal 3	1	2	3	4	5	6	7	8	9	10	
	11	12	13	14	15	16	17	18	19	20	
	21	22	23	24	25	26	27	28	29	30	
	31	32	33	34	35	36	37	38	39	40	
	41	42	43	44	45	46	47	48	49	50	

Area of Evaluation	Quality Rating (Please circle the appropriate number)										
AREA OF FOCUS											TOTAL
Goal 1	1	2	3	4	5	6	7	8	9	10	
	11	12	13	14	15	16	17	18	19	20	
	21	22	23	24	25	26	27	28	29	30	
	31	32	33	34	35	36	37	38	39	40	
	41	42	43	44	45	46	47	48	49	50	
Goal 2	1	2	3	4	5	6	7	8	9	10	
	11	12	13	14	15	16	17	18	19	20	
	21	22	23	24	25	26	27	28	29	30	
	31	32	33	34	35	36	37	38	39	40	
	41	42	43	44	45	46	47	48	49	50	
Goal 3	1	2	3	4	5	6	7	8	9	10	
	11	12	13	14	15	16	17	18	19	20	
	21	22	23	24	25	26	27	28	29	30	
	31	32	33	34	35	36	37	38	39	40	
	41	42	43	44	45	46	47	48	49	50	
Goal 4	1	2	3	4	5	6	7	8	9	10	
	11	12	13	14	15	16	17	18	19	20	
	21	22	23	24	25	26	27	28	29	30	
	31	32	33	34	35	36	37	38	39	40	
	41	42	43	44	45	46	47	48	49	50	
Goal 5	1	2	3	4	5	6	7	8	9	10	
	11	12	13	14	15	16	17	18	19	20	
	21	22	23	24	25	26	27	28	29	30	
	31	32	33	34	35	36	37	38	39	40	
	41	42	43	44	45	46	47	48	49	50	
Goal 6	1	2	3	4	5	6	7	8	9	10	
	11	12	13	14	15	16	17	18	19	20	
	21	22	23	24	25	26	27	28	29	30	
	31	32	33	34	35	36	37	38	39	40	
	41	42	43	44	45	46	47	48	49	50	
Goal 7	1	2	3	4	5	6	7	8	9	10	
	11	12	13	14	15	16	17	18	19	20	
	21	22	23	24	25	26	27	28	29	30	
	31	32	33	34	35	36	37	38	39	40	
	41	42	43	44	45	46	47	48	49	50	
Goal 8	1	2	3	4	5	6	7	8	9	10	
	11	12	13	14	15	16	17	18	19	20	
	21	22	23	24	25	26	27	28	29	30	
	31	32	33	34	35	36	37	38	39	40	
	41	42	43	44	45	46	47	48	49	50	

Area of Evaluation	Quality Rating (Please circle the appropriate number)										
AREA OF FOCUS											TOTAL
Goal 1	1	2	3	4	5	6	7	8	9	10	
	11	12	13	14	15	16	17	18	19	20	
	21	22	23	24	25	26	27	28	29	30	
	31	32	33	34	35	36	37	38	39	40	
	41	42	43	44	45	46	47	48	49	50	
Goal 2	1	2	3	4	5	6	7	8	9	10	
	11	12	13	14	15	16	17	18	19	20	
	21	22	23	24	25	26	27	28	29	30	
	31	32	33	34	35	36	37	38	39	40	
	41	42	43	44	45	46	47	48	49	50	
AREA OF FOCUS											TOTAL
Goal 1	1	2	3	4	5	6	7	8	9	10	
	11	12	13	14	15	16	17	18	19	20	
	21	22	23	24	25	26	27	28	29	30	
	31	32	33	34	35	36	37	38	39	40	
	41	42	43	44	45	46	47	48	49	50	
Goal 2	1	2	3	4	5	6	7	8	9	10	
	11	12	13	14	15	16	17	18	19	20	
	21	22	23	24	25	26	27	28	29	30	
	31	32	33	34	35	36	37	38	39	40	
	41	42	43	44	45	46	47	48	49	50	
Goal 3	1	2	3	4	5	6	7	8	9	10	
	11	12	13	14	15	16	17	18	19	20	
	21	22	23	24	25	26	27	28	29	30	
	31	32	33	34	35	36	37	38	39	40	
	41	42	43	44	45	46	47	48	49	50	
AREA OF FOCUS											TOTAL
Goal 1	1	2	3	4	5	6	7	8	9	10	
	11	12	13	14	15	16	17	18	19	20	
	21	22	23	24	25	26	27	28	29	30	
	31	32	33	34	35	36	37	38	39	40	
	41	42	43	44	45	46	47	48	49	50	
Goal 2	1	2	3	4	5	6	7	8	9	10	
	11	12	13	14	15	16	17	18	19	20	
	21	22	23	24	25	26	27	28	29	30	
	31	32	33	34	35	36	37	38	39	40	
	41	42	43	44	45	46	47	48	49	50	

TEACHER GOAL CARD

Dear Teacher:
Thank you for your participation in helping our child achieve important goals. While filling out this form, please leave room for improvement by giving the student between a 1 and 5 to begin the evaluation process and allow room for growth.

Area of Evaluation	Quality Rating (Please circle the appropriate number)	TOTAL
AREA OF FOCUS		
Goal 1	1 2 3 4 5 6 7 8 9 10 11 12 13 14 15 16 17 18 19 20	
Goal 2	1 2 3 4 5 6 7 8 9 10 11 12 13 14 15 16 17 18 19 20	
AREA OF FOCUS		
Goal 1	1 2 3 4 5 6 7 8 9 10 11 12 13 14 15 16 17 18 19 20	
Goal 2	1 2 3 4 5 6 7 8 9 10 11 12 13 14 15 16 17 18 19 20	
Goal 3	1 2 3 4 5 6 7 8 9 10 11 12 13 14 15 16 17 18 19 20	
Goal 4	1 2 3 4 5 6 7 8 9 10 11 12 13 14 15 16 17 18 19 20	

Additional comments (optional):

Signature: _____   Date: _____

COACH/INSTRUCTOR GOAL CARD

Dear Coach/Instructor:

Thank you for your participation in helping our child achieve important goals. While filling out this form, please leave room for improvement by giving the student between a 1 and 5 to begin the evaluation process and allow room for growth.

Area of Evaluation	Quality Rating (Please circle the appropriate number)	
AREA OF FOCUS		TOTAL
Goal 1	1 2 3 4 5 6 7 8 9 10	
	11 12 13 14 15 16 17 18 19 20	
Goal 2	1 2 3 4 5 6 7 8 9 10	
	11 12 13 14 15 16 17 18 19 20	
AREA OF FOCUS		
Goal 1	1 2 3 4 5 6 7 8 9 10	
	11 12 13 14 15 16 17 18 19 20	
Goal 2	1 2 3 4 5 6 7 8 9 10	
	11 12 13 14 15 16 17 18 19 20	
Goal 3	1 2 3 4 5 6 7 8 9 10	
	11 12 13 14 15 16 17 18 19 20	
Goal 4	1 2 3 4 5 6 7 8 9 10	
	11 12 13 14 15 16 17 18 19 20	

Additional comments (optional):

Signature: _____   Date: _____

REINFORCEMENT PLAN WORKSHEET

AREA OF FOCUS				
Action Steps:				
Sunday				
Monday				
Tuesday				
Wednesday				
Thursday				
Friday				
Saturday				
Weekly Total				
Goals:	Baseline	Baseline	Baseline	Baseline

				Daily Total
Baseline	Baseline	Baseline	Baseline	

Brain Balance
Achievement Centers

As of publication of this book, Brain Balance Achievement Centers can be found in these locations:

CALIFORNIA

Brain Balance of Folsom
Opening in 2011

Brain Balance of Fresno
Opening in 2011

Brain Balance of Sacramento
Opening in 2011

Brain Balance of San Francisco
3380 Geary Boulevard
San Francisco, CA 94118

Brain Balance of Westlake Village
650 Hampshire Road, Suite 102
Westlake Village, CA 91361
805-371-8085

COLORADO

Brain Balance of Golden
1211 Avery Street
Golden, CO 80403
303-278-1780

Brain Balance of Highlands Ranch
Opening in 2011

CONNECTICUT

Brain Balance of Norwalk
15 Cross Street
Norwalk, CT 06581
203-847-3000

FLORIDA

Brain Balance of Miami
6836B Southwest 40th Street
Miami, FL 33155
305-665-9444

Brain Balance of Tampa
4022 Tampa Road, Suite 6
Oldsmar, FL 34677
813-475-6977

GEORGIA

Brain Balance of Atlanta
357 Highway 74 N, Suite 5
Peachtree City, GA 30269
770-631-3033

Brain Balance of North Fulton
30 East Crossville Road, Suite 150
Roswell, GA 30075
770-650-8010

Brain Balance of Suwanee
3525 Lawrenceville Suwanee Road,
Suite 101
Suwanee, GA 30024
770-614-4790

ILLINOIS

Brain Balance of Vernon Hills
1101 South Milwaukee Avenue,
Suite 105
Vernon Hills, IL 60061
770-614-4790

INDIANA

Brain Balance of Indianapolis
9510 North Meridian Street, Suite D
Indianapolis, IN 46260
317-843-9200

IOWA

Brain Balance of Johnston
Opening in 2011

KANSAS

Brain Balance of Overland Park
6406 College Boulevard
Overland Park, KS 66211
913-627-9400

MASSACHUSETTS

Brain Balance of Boston
156 Andover Street
Danvers, MA 01923
978-705-9499

Brain Balance of West Springfield
1472 Riverdale Street
West Springfield, MA 01089
413-737-5437

MICHIGAN

Brain Balance of Kingsford
818 Pyle Drive

Kingsford, MI 49802
906-828-1919

Brain Balance of Kalamazoo
6778 South Westnedge Avenue
Portage, MI 49024
269-532-1332

MINNESOTA

Brain Balance of Excelsior
386 Oak Street
Excelsior, MN 55331
952-474-4535

NEW JERSEY

Brain Balance of Millburn
Opening in 2011

Brain Balance of Ridgewood
Opening in 2011

NEW YORK

Brain Balance of Lake Success
444 Lakeville Road, Suite 103
Lake Success, NY 11042
516-208-9360

Brain Balance of Rockville Centre
220 Maple Avenue, Suite 202
Rockville Centre, NY 11570
516-763-2200

Brain Balance of Ronkonkoma
2805 Veterans Highway, Suite 10
Ronkonkoma, NY 11779
631-471-1900

NORTH CAROLINA

Brain Balance of Cary
8204 Tryon Woods Drive,
Suite 114
Cary, NC 27518
919-851-2333

Brain Balance of Charlotte
9101 Pineville-Matthews Road,
Suite 12
Pineville, NC 28134
704-540-6363

OHIO

Brain Balance of Cincinnati
12084 Montgomery Road
Cincinnati, OH 45249
513-257-0705

PENNSYLVANIA

Brain Balance of Springfield
Stoney Creek Center
451 Baltimore Pike
Springfield, PA 19064
(610) 880-0009

Brain Balance of Wayne
250 West Lancaster Avenue
Wayne, PA 19087
(610) 688-2206

Brain Balance of York
Opening in 2011

SOUTH CAROLINA

Brain Balance of Greenville
2531 Woodruff Road, Suite 113
Simpsonville, SC 29681
864-329-9933

TEXAS

Brain Balance of Austin
3267 Bee Caves Road, Suite 118
Austin, TX 78746
(512) 328-7771

Brain Balance of Plano
1501 Preston Road, Suite 550
Plano, TX 75093
972-248-9482

Brain Balance of San Antonio-
Stone Oak
Opening in 2011

Brain Balance of Southlake
Opening in 2011

WISCONSIN

Brain Balance of Mequon
11649 North Port Washington
Road, Suite 101
Mequon, WI 53092
(262) 240-9915

Please visit our website at www.brainbalancecenters.com for updated
center location information.

INDEX

Page numbers in **bold** indicate tables or graphs.